Building Data Streaming Applications with Apache Kafka

Designing and deploying enterprise messaging queues

Manish Kumar
Chanchal Singh

BIRMINGHAM - MUMBAI

Building Data Streaming Applications with Apache Kafka

First published: August 2017

Production reference: 1170817

Published by Packt Publishing Ltd.
Livery Place
35 Livery Street
Birmingham
B3 2PB, UK.

ISBN 978-1-78728-398-5

www.packtpub.com

Credits

Authors
Manish Kumar
Chanchal Singh

Copy Editor
Manisha Sinha

Reviewer
Anshul Joshi

Project Coordinator
Manthan Patel

Commissioning Editor
Amey Varangaonkar

Proofreader
Safis Editing

Acquisition Editor
Tushar Gupta

Indexer
Tejal Daruwale Soni

Content Development Editor
Tejas Limkar

Graphics
Tania Dutta

Technical Editor
Dinesh Chaudhary

Production Coordinator
Deepika Naik

About the Authors

Manish Kumar is a Technical Architect at DataMetica Solution Pvt. Ltd.. He has approximately 11 years, experience in data management, working as a Data Architect and Product Architect. He has extensive experience in building effective ETL pipelines, implementing security over Hadoop, and providing the best possible solutions to Data Science problems. Before joining the world of big data, he worked as an Tech Lead for Sears Holding, India. He is a regular speaker on big data concepts such as Hadoop and Hadoop Security in various events. Manish has a Bachelor's degree in Information Technology.

I would like to thank my parents, Dr. N.K. Singh and Mrs. Rambha Singh, for their support and blessings, my wife; Mrs. Swati Singh, for her successfully keeping me healthy and happy; and my adorable son, Master Lakshya Singh, for teaching me how to enjoy the small things in life. I would like to extend my gratitude to Mr. Prashant Jaiswal, whose mentorship and friendship will remain gems of my life, and Chanchal Singh, my esteemed friend, for standing by me in times of trouble and happiness. This note will be incomplete if I do not mention Mr. Anand Deshpande, Mr. Parashuram Bastawade, Mr. Niraj Kumar, Mr. Rajiv Gupta, and Dr. Phil Shelley for giving me exciting career opportunities and showing trust in me, no matter how adverse the situation was.

Chanchal Singh is a Software Engineer at DataMetica Solution Pvt. Ltd.. He has over three years' experience in product development and architect design, working as a Product Developer, Data Engineer, and Team Lead. He has a lot of experience with different technologies such as Hadoop, Spark, Storm, Kafka, Hive, Pig, Flume, Java, Spring, and many more. He believes in sharing knowledge and motivating others for innovation. He is the co-organizer of the Big Data Meetup - Pune Chapter.

He has been recognized for putting innovative ideas into organizations. He has a Bachelor's degree in Information Technology from the University of Mumbai and a Master's degree in Computer Application from Amity University. He was also part of the Entrepreneur Cell in IIT Mumbai.

I would like to thank my parents, Mr. Parasnath Singh and Mrs. Usha Singh, for showering their blessings on me and their loving support. I am eternally grateful to my love, Ms. Jyoti, for being with me in every situation and encouraging me. I would also like to express my gratitude to all the mentors I've had over the years. Special thanks to Mr Abhijeet Shingate who helped me as a mentor and guided me in the right direction during the initial phase of my career. I am highly indebted to Mr. Manish Kumar, without whom writing this book would have been challenging, for always enlightening me and sharing his knowledge with me. I would like to extend my sincere thanks by mentioning a few great personalities: Mr Rajiv Gupta, Mr. Niraj Kumar, Mr. Parashuram Bastawade, and Dr.Phil Shelley for giving me ample opportunities to explore solutions for real customer problems and believing in me.

About the Reviewer

Anshul Joshi is a Data Scientist with experience in recommendation systems, predictive modeling, neural networks, and high performance computing. His research interests are deep learning, artificial intelligence, computational physics, and biology.

Most of the time, he can be caught exploring GitHub or trying anything new that he can get his hands on. He blogs on `https://anshuljoshi.com/`.

www.PacktPub.com

For support files and downloads related to your book, please visit www.PacktPub.com.

Did you know that Packt offers eBook versions of every book published, with PDF and ePub files available? You can upgrade to the eBook version at; www.PacktPub.com and as a print book customer, you are entitled to a discount on the eBook copy. Get in touch with us at service@packtpub.com for more details.

At www.PacktPub.com, you can also read a collection of free technical articles, sign up for a range of free newsletters and receive exclusive discounts and offers on Packt books and eBooks.

https://www.packtpub.com/mapt

Get the most in-demand software skills with Mapt. Mapt gives you full access to all Packt books and video courses, as well as industry-leading tools to help you plan your personal development and advance your career.

Why subscribe?

- Fully searchable across every book published by Packt
- Copy and paste, print, and bookmark content
- On demand and accessible via a web browser

Customer Feedback

Thanks for purchasing this Packt book. At Packt, quality is at the heart of our editorial process. To help us improve, please leave us an honest review on this book's Amazon page at https://www.amazon.com/dp/1787283984.

If you'd like to join our team of regular reviewers, you can e-mail us at customerreviews@packtpub.com. We award our regular reviewers with free eBooks and videos in exchange for their valuable feedback. Help us be relentless in improving our products!

Table of Contents

Preface   1

Chapter 1: Introduction to Messaging Systems   7

  Understanding the principles of messaging systems   8
  Understanding messaging systems   9
  Peeking into a point-to-point messaging system   12
  Publish-subscribe messaging system   15
  Advance Queuing Messaging Protocol   18
  Using messaging systems in big data streaming applications 19
  Summary   23

Chapter 2: Introducing Kafka the Distributed Messaging Platform   25

  Kafka origins   26
  Kafka's architecture   27
  Message topics   29
  Message partitions   31
  Replication and replicated logs   34
  Message producers   37
  Message consumers   37
  Role of Zookeeper   38
  Summary   39

Chapter 3: Deep Dive into Kafka Producers   41

  Kafka producer internals   42
  Kafka Producer APIs   46
    Producer object and ProducerRecord object   48
    Custom partition   51
    Additional producer configuration   52
  Java Kafka producer example   54
  Common messaging publishing patterns   56
  Best practices   58
  Summary   59

Chapter 4: Deep Dive into Kafka Consumers   61

  Kafka consumer internals   62
    Understanding the responsibilities of Kafka consumers 62
  Kafka consumer APIs   65

Consumer configuration   65
Subscription and polling   67
Committing and polling   68
Additional configuration   70
Java Kafka consumer   71
Scala Kafka consumer   73
Rebalance listeners   74
Common message consuming patterns   75
Best practices   78
Summary   79

Chapter 5: Building Spark Streaming Applications with Kafka   81

Introduction to Spark   82
Spark architecture   82
Pillars of Spark   84
The Spark ecosystem   86
Spark Streaming   88
Receiver-based integration   88
Disadvantages of receiver-based approach   90
Java example for receiver-based integration   91
Scala example for receiver-based integration   92
Direct approach   93
Java example for direct approach   95
Scala example for direct approach   96
Use case log processing - fraud IP detection   97
Maven   97
Producer   101
Property reader   101
Producer code   102
Fraud IP lookup   104
Expose hive table   105
Streaming code   106
Summary   108

Chapter 6: Building Storm Applications with Kafka   109

Introduction to Apache Storm   110
Storm cluster architecture   110
The concept of a Storm application   112
Introduction to Apache Heron   114
Heron architecture   114
Heron topology architecture   115
Integrating Apache Kafka with Apache Storm - Java   117

Example	118
Integrating Apache Kafka with Apache Storm - Scala	122
Use case – log processing in Storm, Kafka, Hive	125
Producer	129
Producer code	130
Fraud IP lookup	132
Running the project	141
Summary	141

Chapter 7: Using Kafka with Confluent Platform — 143

Introduction to Confluent Platform	143
Deep driving into Confluent architecture	145
Understanding Kafka Connect and Kafka Stream	149
Kafka Streams	149
Playing with Avro using Schema Registry	150
Moving Kafka data to HDFS	151
Camus	152
Running Camus	153
Gobblin	154
Gobblin architecture	154
Kafka Connect	157
Flume	157
Summary	160

Chapter 8: Building ETL Pipelines Using Kafka — 161

Considerations for using Kafka in ETL pipelines	162
Introducing Kafka Connect	163
Deep dive into Kafka Connect	165
Introductory examples of using Kafka Connect	167
Kafka Connect common use cases	170
Summary	171

Chapter 9: Building Streaming Applications Using Kafka Streams — 173

Introduction to Kafka Streams	174
Using Kafka in Stream processing	174
Kafka Stream - lightweight Stream processing library	175
Kafka Stream architecture	177
Integrated framework advantages	180
Understanding tables and Streams together	180
Maven dependency	181
Kafka Stream word count	181

KTable	183
Use case example of Kafka Streams	184
Maven dependency of Kafka Streams	184
Property reader	185
IP record producer	186
IP lookup service	188
Fraud detection application	190
Summary	191

Chapter 10: Kafka Cluster Deployment — 193

Kafka cluster internals	194
Role of Zookeeper	194
Replication	195
Metadata request processing	197
Producer request processing	198
Consumer request processing	198
Capacity planning	199
Capacity planning goals	200
Replication factor	200
Memory	200
Hard drives	201
Network	202
CPU	202
Single cluster deployment	202
Multicluster deployment	203
Decommissioning brokers	205
Data migration	206
Summary	207

Chapter 11: Using Kafka in Big Data Applications — 209

Managing high volumes in Kafka	210
Appropriate hardware choices	210
Producer read and consumer write choices	212
Kafka message delivery semantics	213
At least once delivery	214
At most once delivery	217
Exactly once delivery	219
Big data and Kafka common usage patterns	220
Kafka and data governance	222
Alerting and monitoring	224

Useful Kafka matrices   224

    Producer matrices   225

    Broker matrices   226

    Consumer metrics   226

Summary   227

Chapter 12: Securing Kafka   229

An overview of securing Kafka   229

Wire encryption using SSL   230

    Steps to enable SSL in Kafka   231

        Configuring SSL for Kafka Broker   232

        Configuring SSL for Kafka clients   232

Kerberos SASL for authentication   233

    Steps to enable SASL/GSSAPI - in Kafka   235

        Configuring SASL for Kafka broker   236

        Configuring SASL for Kafka client - producer and consumer   237

Understanding ACL and authorization   238

    Common ACL operations   239

        List ACLs   240

Understanding Zookeeper authentication   241

Apache Ranger for authorization   242

    Adding Kafka Service to Ranger   242

    Adding policies   244

Best practices   246

Summary   247

Chapter 13: Streaming Application Design Considerations   249

Latency and throughput   250

Data and state persistence   251

Data sources   252

External data lookups   252

Data formats   253

Data serialization   254

Level of parallelism   254

Out-of-order events   255

Message processing semantics   255

Summary   256

Index   257

Preface

Apache Kafka is a popular distributed streaming platform that acts as a messaging queue or an enterprise messaging system. It lets you publish and subscribe to a stream of records and process them in a fault-tolerant way as they occur.

This book is a comprehensive guide to designing and architecting enterprise-grade streaming applications using Apache Kafka and other big data tools. It includes best practices for building such applications and tackles some common challenges such as how to use Kafka efficiently to handle high data volumes with ease. This book first takes you through understanding the type messaging system and then provides a thorough introduction to Apache Kafka and its internal details. The second part of the book takes you through designing streaming application using various frameworks and tools such as Apache Spark, Apache Storm, and more. Once you grasp the basics, we will take you through more advanced concepts in Apache Kafka such as capacity planning and security.

By the end of this book, you will have all the information you need to be comfortable with using Apache Kafka and to design efficient streaming data applications with it.

What this book covers

Chapter 1, *Introduction to Messaging System*, introduces concepts of messaging systems. It covers an overview of messaging systems and their enterprise needs. It further emphasizes the different ways of using messaging systems such as point to point or publish/subscribe. It introduces AMQP as well.

Chapter 2, *Introducing Kafka - The Distributed Messaging Platform*, introduces distributed messaging platforms such as Kafka. It covers the Kafka architecture and touches upon its internal component. It further explores the roles and importance of each Kafka components and how they contribute towards low latency, reliability, and the scalability of Kafka Message Systems.

Chapter 3, *Deep Dive into Kafka Producers*, is about how to publish messages to Kafka Systems. This further covers Kafka Producer APIs and their usage. It showcases examples of using Kafka Producer APIs with Java and Scala programming languages. It takes a deep dive into Producer message flows and some common patterns for producing messages to Kafka Topics. It walks through some performance optimization techniques for Kafka Producers.

Chapter 4, *Deep Dive into Kafka Consumers*, is about how to consume messages from Kafka Systems. This also covers Kafka Consumer APIs and their usage. It showcases examples of using Kafka Consumer APIs with the Java and Scala programming languages. It takes a deep dive into Consumer message flows and some common patterns for consuming messages from Kafka Topics. It walks through some performance optimization techniques for Kafka Consumers.

Chapter 5, *Building Spark Streaming Applications with Kafka*, is about how to integrate Kafka with the popular distributed processing engine, Apache Spark. This also provides a brief overview about Apache Kafka, the different approaches for integrating Kafka with Spark, and their advantages and disadvantages. It showcases examples in Java as well as in Scala with use cases.

Chapter 6, *Building Storm Applications with Kafka*, is about how to integrate Kafka with the popular real-time processing engine Apache Storm. This also covers a brief overview of Apache Storm and Apache Heron. It showcases examples of different approaches of event processing using Apache Storm and Kafka, including guaranteed event processing.

Chapter 7, *Using Kafka with Confluent Platform*, is about the emerging streaming platform Confluent that enables you to use Kafka effectively with many other added functionalities. It showcases many examples for the topics covered in the chapter.

Chapter 8, *Building ETL Pipelines Using Kafka*, introduces Kafka Connect, a common component, which for building ETL pipelines involving Kafka. It emphasizes how to use Kafka Connect in ETL pipelines and discusses some in-depth technical concepts surrounding it.

Chapter 9, *Building Streaming Applications Using Kafka Streams*, is about how to build streaming applications using Kafka Stream, which is an integral part of the Kafka 0.10 release. This also covers building fast, reliable streaming applications using Kafka Stream, with examples.

Chapter 10, *Kafka Cluster Deployment*, focuses on Kafka cluster deployment on enterprise-grade production systems. It covers in depth, Kafka clusters such as how to do capacity planning, how to manager single/multi cluster deployments, and so on. It also covers how to manage Kafka in multi-tenant environments. It further walks you through the various steps involved in Kafka data migrations.

Chapter 11, *Using Kafka in Big Data Applications*, walks through some of the aspects of using Kafka in big data applications. This covers how to manage high volumes in Kafka, how to ensure guaranteed message delivery, the best ways to handle failures without any data loss, and some governance principles that can be applied while using Kafka in big data pipelines.

`Chapter 12`, *Securing Kafka*, is about securing your Kafka cluster. It covers authentication and authorization mechanisms along with examples.

`Chapter 13`, *Streaming Applications Design Considerations*, is about different design considerations for building a streaming application. It walks you through aspects such as parallelism, memory tuning, and so on. It provides comprehensive coverage of the different paradigms for designing a streaming application.

What you need for this book

You will need the following software to work with the examples in this book:

Apache Kafka, big data, Apache Hadoop, publish and subscribe, enterprise messaging system, distributed Streaming, Producer API, Consumer API, Streams API, Connect API

Who this book is for

If you want to learn how to use Apache Kafka and the various tools in the Kafka ecosystem in the easiest possible manner, this book is for you. Some programming experience with Java is required to get the most out of this book.

Conventions

In this book, you will find a number of text styles that distinguish between different kinds of information. Here are some examples of these styles and an explanation of their meaning.

Code words in text, database table names, folder names, filenames, file extensions, pathnames, dummy URLs, user input, and Twitter handles are shown as follows: "The next lines of code read the link and assign it to the to the `BeautifulSoup` function."

A block of code is set as follows:

```
import org.apache.Kafka.clients.producer.KafkaProducer;
import org.apache.Kafka.clients.producer.ProducerRecord;
import org.apache.Kafka.clients.producer.RecordMetadata;
```

Any command-line input or output is written as follows:

```
sudo su - hdfs -c "hdfs dfs -chmod 777 /tmp/hive"
 sudo chmod 777 /tmp/hive
```

New terms and **important words** are shown in bold. Words that you see on the screen, for example, in menus or dialog boxes, appear in the text like this: "In order to download new modules, we will go to **Files** | **Settings** | **Project Name** | **Project Interpreter**."

 Warnings or important notes appear in a box like this.

 Tips and tricks appear like this.

Reader feedback

Feedback from our readers is always welcome. Let us know what you think about this book-what you liked or disliked. Reader feedback is important for us as it helps us develop titles that you will really get the most out of.

To send us general feedback, simply e-mail `feedback@packtpub.com`, and mention the book's title in the subject of your message.

If there is a topic that you have expertise in and you are interested in either writing or contributing to a book, see our author guide at `www.packtpub.com/authors`.

Customer support

Now that you are the proud owner of a Packt book, we have a number of things to help you to get the most from your purchase.

Downloading the example code

You can download the example code files for this book from your account at `http://www.packtpub.com`. If you purchased this book elsewhere, you can visit `http://www.packtpub.com/support` and register to have the files e-mailed directly to you.

You can download the code files by following these steps:

1. Log in or register to our website using your e-mail address and password.
2. Hover the mouse pointer on the **SUPPORT** tab at the top.
3. Click on **Code Downloads & Errata**.
4. Enter the name of the book in the **Search** box.
5. Select the book for which you're looking to download the code files.
6. Choose from the drop-down menu where you purchased this book from.
7. Click on **Code Download**.

Once the file is downloaded, please make sure that you unzip or extract the folder using the latest version of:

- WinRAR / 7-Zip for Windows
- Zipeg / iZip / UnRarX for Mac
- 7-Zip / PeaZip for Linux

The code bundle for the book is also hosted on GitHub at `https://github.com/PacktPublishing/Building-Data-Streaming-Applications-with-Apache-Kafka`. We also have other code bundles from our rich catalog of books and videos available at `https://github.com/PacktPublishing/`. Check them out!

Downloading the color images of this book

We also provide you with a PDF file that has color images of the screenshots/diagrams used in this book. The color images will help you better understand the changes in the output. You can download this file from `https://www.packtpub.com/sites/default/files/downloads/BuildingDataStreamingApplicationswithApacheKafka_ColorImages.pdf`.

Errata

Although we have taken every care to ensure the accuracy of our content, mistakes do happen. If you find a mistake in one of our books-maybe a mistake in the text or the code-we would be grateful if you could report this to us. By doing so, you can save other readers from frustration and help us improve subsequent versions of this book. If you find any errata, please report them by visiting http://www.packtpub.com/submit-errata, selecting your book, clicking on the **Errata Submission Form** link, and entering the details of your errata. Once your errata are verified, your submission will be accepted and the errata will be uploaded to our website or added to any list of existing errata under the Errata section of that title.

To view the previously submitted errata, go to https://www.packtpub.com/books/content/support and enter the name of the book in the search field. The required information will appear under the **Errata** section.

Piracy

Piracy of copyrighted material on the Internet is an ongoing problem across all media. At Packt, we take the protection of our copyright and licenses very seriously. If you come across any illegal copies of our works in any form on the Internet, please provide us with the location address or website name immediately so that we can pursue a remedy.

Please contact us at copyright@packtpub.com with a link to the suspected pirated material.

We appreciate your help in protecting our authors and our ability to bring you valuable content.

Questions

If you have a problem with any aspect of this book, you can contact us at questions@packtpub.com, and we will do our best to address the problem.

1
Introduction to Messaging Systems

People have different styles of learning. This chapter will give you the necessary context to help you achieve a better understanding of the book.

The goal of any Enterprise Integration is to establish unification between separate applications to achieve a consolidated set of functionalities.

These discrete applications are built using different programming languages and platforms. To achieve any unified functionality, these applications need to share information among themselves. This information exchange happens over a network in small packets using different protocols and utilities.

So let us say that you are adding a new campaign component to an existing e-commerce application that needs to interact with a different application to calculate loyalty points. In this case, you will be integrating your e-commerce application with a different application using enterprise integration strategies.

This chapter will help you understand messaging systems, one of the common ways of establishing enterprise integration. It will walk you through various types of messaging system and their uses. At the end of this chapter, you will be able to distinguish between different messaging models available today and understand different design considerations for enterprise application integration.

We will be covering the following topics in this chapter:

- Principles of designing a good messaging system
- How a messaging system works
- A point-to-point messaging system
- A publish-subscribe messaging system
- The AMQP messaging protocol
- Finally we will go through the messaging system needed in designing streaming applications

Understanding the principles of messaging systems

Continuing our focus on messaging systems, you may have seen applications where one application uses data that gets processed by other external applications or applications consuming data from one or more data sources. In such scenarios, messaging systems can be used as an integration channel for information exchange between different applications. If you haven't built such an application yet, then don't worry about it. We will build it in upcoming chapters.

In any **application integration system** design, there are a few important principles that should be kept in mind, such as **loose coupling**, **common interface definitions**, **latency**, and **reliability**. Let's look into some of these one by one:

- **Loose coupling** between applications ensures minimal dependencies on each other. This ensures that any changes in one application do not affect other applications. Tightly coupled applications are coded as per predefined specifications of other applications. Any change in specification would break or change the functionality of other dependent applications.
- **Common interface definitions** ensure a common agreed-upon data format for exchange between applications. This not only helps in establishing message exchange standards among applications but also ensures that some of the best practices of information exchange can be enforced easily. For example, you can choose to use the Avro data format to exchange messages. This can be defined as your common interface standard for information exchange. **Avro** is a good choice for message exchanges as it serializes data in a compact binary format and supports schema evolution.

- **Latency** is the time taken by messages to traverse between the sender and receiver. Most applications want to achieve low latency as a critical requirement. Even in an asynchronous mode of communication, high latency is not desirable as significant delay in receiving messages could cause significant loss to any organization.
- **Reliability** ensures that temporary unavailability of applications does not affect dependent applications that need to exchange information. In general, the when source application sends a message to the remote application, sometimes the remote application may be running slow or it may not be running due to some failure. Reliable, asynchronous message communication ensures that the source application continues its work and feels confident that the remote application will resume its task later.

Understanding messaging systems

As mentioned earlier, application integration is key for any enterprise to achieve a comprehensive set of functionalities spanning multiple discrete applications. To achieve this, applications need to share information in a timely manner. A messaging system is one of the most commonly used mechanisms for information exchange in applications.

The other mechanisms used to share information could be **remote procedure calls** (**RPC**), **file share**, **shared databases**, and **web service invocation**. While choosing your application integration mechanism, it is important that you keep in mind the guiding principles discussed earlier. For example, in the case of shared databases, changes done by one application could directly affect other applications that are using the same database tables. Both of the applications are tightly coupled. You may want to avoid that in cases where you have additional rules to be applied before accepting the changes in the other application. Likewise, you have to think about all such guiding principles before finalizing ways of integrating your applications.

As depicted in the following figure, message-based application integration involves discrete enterprise applications connecting to a common messaging system and either sending or receiving data to it. A messaging system acts as an integration component between multiple applications. Such an integration invokes different application behaviors based on application information exchanges. It also adheres to some of the design principles mentioned earlier.

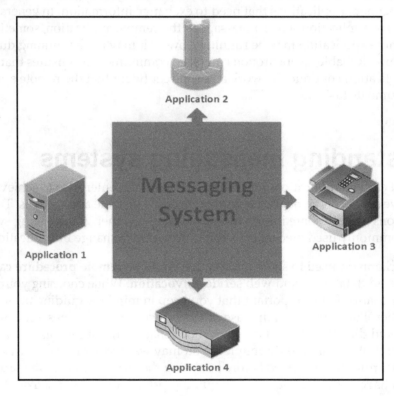

A graphical display of how messaging systems are linked to applications

Enterprises have started adopting micro service architecture and the main advantage of doing so is to make applications loosely coupled with each other. Applications communicate with each other asynchronously and it makes communication more reliable as both applications need not be running simultaneously. A messaging system helps in transferring data from one application to the other. It allows applications to think of what they need to share as data rather than how it needs to be shared. You can share small packets of data or data streams with other applications using messaging in a timely and real-time fashion. This fits the need of low latency real-time application integration.

For a start, you should understand some of the basic concepts of any messaging system. Understanding these concepts is beneficial to you as it will help you understand different messaging technologies such as Kafka. The following are some of the basic messaging concepts:

- **Message queues**: You will sometimes find *queues* referred as *channels* as well. In a simple way, they are connectors between sending and receiving applications. Their core function is to receive message packets from the source application and send it to the receiver application in a timely and reliable manner.

- **Messages (data packets)**: A message is an atomic data packet that gets transmitted over a network to a message queue. The sender application breaks data into smaller data packets and wraps it as a message with protocol and header information. It then sends it to the message queue. In a similar fashion, a receiver application receives a message and extracts the data from the message wrapper to further process it.

- **Sender (producer)**: Sender or producer applications are the sources of data that needs to be sent to a certain destination. They establish connections to message queue endpoints and send data in smaller message packets adhering to common interface standards. Depending on the type of messaging system in use, sender applications can decide to send data one by one or in a batch.

- **Receiver (consumer)**: Receiver or consumer applications are the receivers of messages sent by the sender application. They either pull data from message queues or they receive data from messages queues through a persistent connection. On receiving messages, they extract data from those message packets and use it for further processing.

- **Data transmission protocols**: Data transmission protocols determine rules to govern message exchanges between applications. Different queuing systems use different data transmission protocols. It depends on the technical implementation of the messaging endpoints. Kafka uses binary protocols over TCP. The client initiates a socket connection with Kafka queues and then writes messages along with reading back the acknowledgment message. Some examples of such data transmission protocols are **AMQP (Advance Message Queuing Protocol)**, **STOMP (Streaming Text Oriented Message Protocol)**, **MQTT (Message Queue Telemetry Protocol)**, and **HTTP (Hypertext Transfer Protocol)**.

- **Transfer mode**: The transfer mode in a messaging system can be understood as the manner in which data is transferred from the source application to the receiver application. Examples of transfer modes are synchronous, asynchronous, and batch modes.

Peeking into a point-to-point messaging system

This section focuses on the **point-to-point** (**PTP**) messaging model. In a PTP messaging model, message producers are called senders and consumers are called receivers. They exchange messages by means of a destination called a queue. Senders produce messages to a queue and receivers consume messages from this queue. What distinguishes point-to-point messaging is that a message can be consumed by only one consumer.

Point-to-point messaging is generally used when a single message will be received by only one message consumer. There may be multiple consumers listening on the queue for the same message but only one of the consumers will receive it. Note that there can be multiple producers as well. They will be sending messages to the queue but it will be received by only one receiver.

 A **PTP model** is based on the concept of sending a message to a named destination. This named destination is the message queue's endpoint that is listening to incoming messages over a port.

Typically, in the PTP model, a receiver requests a message that a sender sends to the queue, rather than subscribing to a channel and receiving all messages sent on a particular queue.

You can think of queues supporting PTP messaging models as FIFO queues. In such queues, messages are sorted in the order in which they were received, and as they are consumed, they are removed from the head of the queue. Queues such as Kafka maintain message offsets. Instead of deleting the messages, they increment the offsets for the receiver. Offset-based models provide better support for replaying messages.

The following figure shows an example model of PTP. Suppose there are two senders, S1 and S2, who send a message to a queue, Q1. On the other side, there are two receivers, R1 and R2, who receive a message from Q1. In this case, R1 will consume the message from S2 and R2 will consume the message from S1:

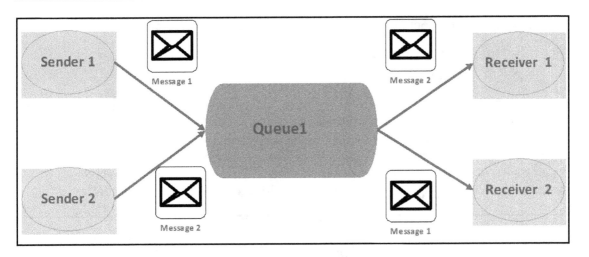

A graphical representation of how a point-to-point messaging model works

You can deduce the following important points about a PTP messaging system from the preceding figure:

- More than one sender can produce and send messages to a queue. Senders can share a connection or use different connections, but they can all access the same queue.
- More than one receiver can consume messages from a queue, but each message can be consumed by only one receiver. Thus, **Message 1**, **Message 2**, and **Message 3** are consumed by different receivers. (This is a message queue extension.)
- Receivers can share a connection or use different connections, but they can all access the same queue. (This is a message queue extension.)
- Senders and receivers have no timing dependencies; the receiver can consume a message whether or not it was running when the sender produced and sent the message.
- Messages are placed in a queue in the order they are produced, but the order in which they are consumed depends on factors such as message expiration date, message priority, whether a selector is used in consuming messages, and the relative message processing rate of the consumers.
- Senders and receivers can be added and deleted dynamically at runtime, thus allowing the messaging system to expand or contract as needed.

The PTP messaging model can be further categorized into two types:

- Fire-and-forget model
- Request/reply model

In **fire-and-forget processing**, the producer sends a message to a centralized queue and does not wait for any acknowledgment immediately. It can be used in a scenario where you want to trigger an action or send a signal to the receiver to trigger some action that does not require a response. For example, you may want to use this method to send a message to a logging system, to alert a system to generate a report, or trigger an action to some other system. The following figure represents a fire-and-forget PTP messaging model:

Fire-and-forget message model

With an asynchronous request/reply PTP model, the message sender sends a message on one queue and then does a blocking wait on a reply queue waiting for the response from the receiver. The request/reply model provides for a high degree of decoupling between the sender and receiver, allowing the message producer and consumer components to be heterogeneous languages or platforms. The following figure represents a request/reply PTP messaging model:

Request/reply message model

Before concluding this section, it is important for you to understand where you can use the PTP model of messaging. It is used when you want one receiver to process any given message once and only once. This is perhaps the most critical difference: only one consumer will process a given message.

Another use case for point-to-point messaging is when you need synchronous communication between components that are written in different technology platforms or programming languages. For example, you may have an application written in a language, say PHP, which may want to communicate with a Twitter application written in Java to process tweets for analysis. In this scenario, a point-to-point messaging system helps provide interoperability between these cross-platform applications.

Publish-subscribe messaging system

In this section, we will take a look at a different messaging model called the **publish/subscribe (Pub/Sub)** messaging model.

In this type of model, a subscriber registers its interest in a particular topic or event and is subsequently notified about the event asynchronously. Subscribers have the ability to express their interest in an event, or a pattern of events, and are subsequently notified of any event generated by a publisher that matches their registered interest. These events are generated by publishers. It is different from the PTP messaging model in a way that a topic can have multiple receivers and every receiver receives a copy of each message. In other words, a message is broadcast to all receivers without them having to poll the topic. In the PTP model, the receiver polls the queue for new messages.

A **Pub/Sub messaging model** is used when you need to broadcast an event or message to many message consumers. Unlike the PTP messaging model, all message consumers (called subscribers) listening on the topic will receive the message.

One of the important aspects of Pub/Sub messaging models is that the topic abstraction is easy to understand and enforces platform interoperability. Moreover, messages can be retained in the topic until they are delivered to the active subscribers.

There is an option to have durable subscriptions in the Pub/Sub model that allows the subscriber to disconnect, reconnect, and collect the messages that were delivered when it was not active. The Kafka messaging system incorporates some of these important design principles.

The following figure describes a basic model of publish/subscribe messaging. Such event services are generally called queues. This kind of interaction need a service that provides storage of the event, a notification service, a way of managing subscriptions and ensuring the efficient guaranteed delivery of the event to destination. Generally, we call this service a queue. Queues act as a neutral mediator between the event producer and event consumer. The producer can produce all the data to queue that they want to and all the consumers will subscribe to the queue that they are interested in. The consumer does not care about the source and the producer does not care about consumers. Consumers can unsubscribe to a queue whenever they want to:

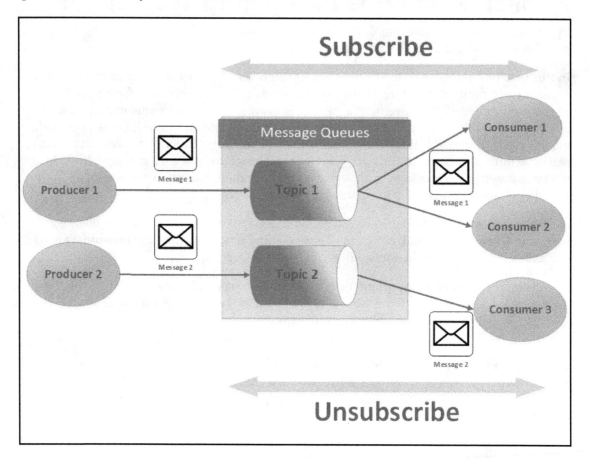

A graphical representation of a publish/subscribe message model

You can deduce the following important points about the Pub/Sub messaging system from the preceding figure:

- Messages are shared through a channel called a topic. A topic is a centralized place where producers can publish, and subscribers can consume, messages.
- Each message is delivered to one or more message consumers, called subscribers.
- The publisher generally does not know and is not aware of which subscribers are receiving the topic messages.
- Messages are pushed to consumers, which means that messages are delivered to consumers without their having to request them. Messages are exchanged through a virtual channel called a topic. Messages delivered to a topic are automatically pushed to all qualified consumers.
- There is no coupling of the producers to the consumers. Subscribers and publishers can be added dynamically at runtime, which allows the system to grow or shrink in complexity over time.
- Every client that subscribes to a topic receives its own copy of messages published to that topic. A single message produced by one publisher may be copied and distributed to hundreds, or even thousands, of subscribers.

You should use the Pub/Sub model when you want to broadcast a message or event to multiple message consumers. The important point here is that multiple consumers may consume the message.

By design, the Pub/Sub model will push copies of the message out to multiple subscribers. Some common examples are notifying exceptions or errors and change the notification of a particular data item in the database.

Any situation where you need to notify multiple consumers of an event is a good use of the Pub/Sub model. For example, you want to send out a notification to a topic whenever an exception occurs in your application or a system component. You may not know how that information will be used or what types of component will use it. Will the exception be e-mailed to various parties of interest? Will a notification be sent to a beeper or pager? This is the beauty of the Pub/Sub model. The publisher does not care or need to worry about how the information will be used. It simply publishes it to a topic.

Advance Queuing Messaging Protocol

As discussed in previous sections, there are different data transmission protocols using which messages can be transmitted among sender, receiver, and message queues. It is difficult to cover all such protocols in the scope of this book. However, it is important to understand how these data transmission protocols work and why it is an important design decision for your message-oriented application integration architecture. In the light of this, we will cover one example of such a protocol: **Advance Message Queuing Protocol** also known as **AQMP**.

AQMP is an open protocol for asynchronous message queuing that developed and matured over several years. AMQP provides richer sets of messaging functionalities that can be used to support very advanced messaging scenarios. As depicted in the following figure, there are three main components in any AQMP-based messaging system:

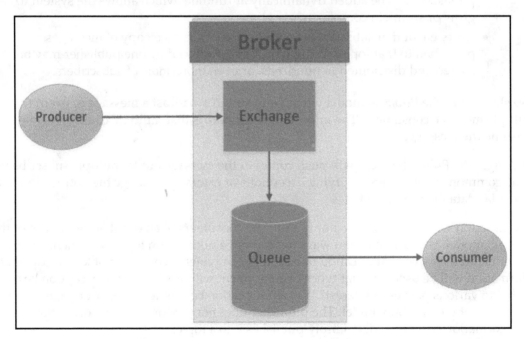

AQMP architecture

As the name suggests, producers sends messages to brokers that in turn deliver them to consumers. Every broker has a component called exchange that is responsible for routing the messages from producers to appropriate message queues.

An AQMP messaging system consists of three main components:

- Publisher(s)
- Consumer(s)
- Broker/server(s)

Each component can be multiple in number and situated on independent hosts. Publishers and consumers communicate with each other through message queues bound to exchanges within the brokers. AQMP provides reliable, guaranteed, in-order message delivery. Message exchanges in an AQMP model can follow various methods. Let's look at each one of them:

- **Direct exchange**: This is a key-based routing mechanism. In this, a message is delivered to the queue whose name is equal to the routing key of the message.
- **Fan-out exchange**: A fan-out exchange routes messages to all of the queues that are bound to it and the routing key is ignored. If N queues are bound to a fan-out exchange, when a new message is published to that exchange, a copy of the message is delivered to all N queues. Fan-out exchanges are ideal for the broadcast routing of messages. In other words, the message is cloned and sent to all queues connected to this exchange.
- **Topic exchange**: In topic exchange, the message can be routed to some of the connected queues using wildcards. The topic exchange type is often used to implement various publish/subscribe pattern variations. Topic exchanges are commonly used for the multicast routing of messages.

Using messaging systems in big data streaming applications

In this section, we will talk about how messaging systems play important role in a big data application.

Let's understand the different layers in a big data application:

- **Ingestion layer**: The input data required for the processing gets ingested in some storage system. There can be many sources of data for which the same or different processing needs to be done.

- **Processing layer**: This contains the business logic that processes the data received in the ingestion layer and applies some transformation to make it into a usable form. You can call it converting raw data to information. There can be multiple processing applications for the same or different data. Each application may have its different processing logic and capability.
- **Consumption layer**: This layer contains data processed by the processing layer. This processed data is a single point of truth and contains important information for business decision makers. There can be multiple consumers who can use the same data for different purposes or different data for the same purpose.

Streaming applications would probably fall into the second layer--the processing layer. The same data can be used by many applications simultaneously, and there can be different ways of serving this data to the application. So, applications can be either streaming, batch, or micro-batch. All these applications consume data in different ways: streaming applications may require data as a continuous stream and batch applications may require data as batches. However, we have already said that there can be multiple sources for this data.

We can see multiple producer and multiple consumer use cases here, so we have to go for a messaging system. The same message can be consumed by multiple consumers so we need to retain the message until all the consumers consume it. How about having a messaging system that can retain the data until we want it, provides a high degree of fault tolerance, and provides a different way of consuming data streams, batches, and micro-batches?

Streaming applications will simply consume the data from the messaging queue that they want and process it as needed. However, there is one problem. What if the message received by the streaming application fails, what if there are a lot of such messages? In such cases, we may want to have a system that will help us provide those messages based on the request and reprocess them.

We need a messaging system that immediately tells the streaming application that, *Something got published; please process it*. The following diagram helps you understand a messaging system use case with a streaming application:

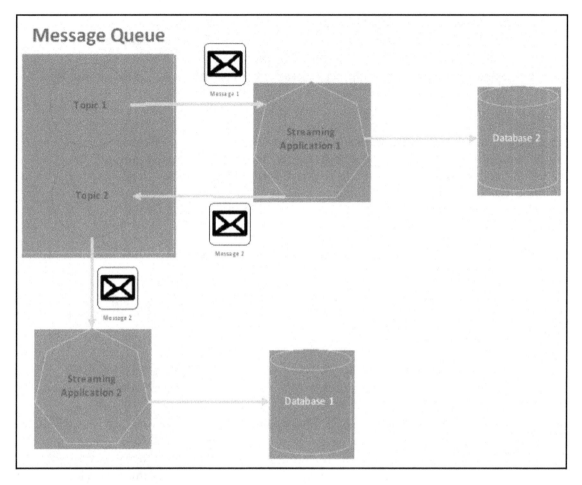

Real-time streaming with queues

The preceding figure explains the following points:

- Streaming application 1 has subscribed to Topic 1, which means any event published to topic 1 will be immediately available to Streaming Application 1.
- Streaming Application 1 processes the event and stores them into two destinations; one is a database and other is Topic 2 of the messaging system. Here, the the streaming application acts as the producer for Topic 2. Remember there can be other applications that may consume the event from Topic 1.

- Streaming application 2 has subscribed to Topic 2, which will immediately receive the event when it gets published to Topic 2. Remember that there can be other applications that can publish the event to either Topic 1 or Topic 2.
- Streaming Application 2 processes the event and stores it in the database.

In streaming application, each stream or message has its own importance; something will be triggered based on the type or nature of the message. There can be a scenario where one streaming application processes the event and passes it to another streaming application for further processing. In this case, they both need to have a medium of communication. Remember that the application should care about what it wants to do rather than how to send the data somewhere. This is the best use case for a publish/subscribe messaging system as it would ensure that a message published by the producer will reach to all the applications who have subscribed to it.

Concluding our discussion on messaging systems, these are the points that are important for any streaming application:

- **High consuming rate:** Streaming data sources can be click-stream data or social media data where the rate of message producing is too high. Stream applications may or may not be required to consume at a similar rate. We may want to have a messaging queue that can consume data at a higher rate.
- **Guaranteed delivery:** Some streaming applications cannot afford to lose messages; we need a system that guarantees the delivery of messages to the streaming application whenever needed.
- **Persisting capability:** There can be multiple applications consuming similar data at a different rate. We may want to have a messaging system that retains data for a period of time and serves the data to a different application asynchronously. This helps in decoupling all the applications and designing micro service architecture.
- **Security:** Some applications may want to have security over the data that they consume; you may not want to share some data with other applications consuming from the same messaging system. You want to have a system that ensures such security.
- **Fault tolerance:** Applications never want to have a system that does not deliver messages or data whenever they need. We want to have a system that guarantees fault tolerance and serves messages irrespective of the failure of the server serving the data before.

There are many other points that force us to go for a messaging system that has at least the capabilities mentioned earlier. We will discuss how Kafka is different from other messaging systems, and meets the requirement of a messaging system for a streaming application, in upcoming chapters.

Summary

In this chapter, we covered concepts of messaging systems. We learned the need for Messaging Systems in Enterprises. We further emphasized different ways of using messaging systems such as point to point or publish/subscribe. We introduced **Advance Message Queuing Protocol (AQMP)** as well.

In next chapter, we will learn about the Kafka architecture and its component in detail. We will also learn about implementation part of what we discuss in messaging system and its type.

2

Introducing Kafka the Distributed Messaging Platform

In this chapter, we will introduce **Kafka**, a widely adopted scalable, performant, and distributed messaging platform. We will touch-base on different Kafka components and how they work in coherence to achieve reliable message delivery. You should see this chapter as a foundation chapter on Kafka that will help you establish familiarity with the systems involved. This chapter will help you better grasp the next chapters, which cover various Kafka components in detail. At the end of this chapter, you will have a clear understanding of Kafka's architecture and fundamental components of the Kafka messaging system.

We will cover the following topics in this chapter:

- Kafka origins
- Kafka's architecture
- Message topics
- Message partitions
- Replication and replicated logs
- Message producers
- Message consumers
- Role of Zookeeper

Kafka origins

Most of you must have used the **LinkedIn** portal in your professional career. The Kafka system was first built by the LinkedIn technical team. LinkedIn constructed a software metrics collecting system using custom in-house components with some support from existing open source tools. The system was used to collect user activity data on their portal. They use this activity data to show relevant information to each respective user on their web portal. The system was originally built as a traditional XML-based logging service, which was later processed using different **Extract Transform Load** (ETL) tools. However, this arrangement did not work well for a long time. They started running into various problems. To solve these problems, they built a system called Kafka.

LinkedIn built Kafka as a distributed, fault-tolerant, publish/subscribe system. It records messages organized into topics. Applications can produce or consume messages from topics. All messages are stored as logs to persistent filesystems. Kafka is a **write-ahead logging** (WAL) system that writes all published messages to log files before making it available for consumer applications. Subscribers/consumers can read these written messages as required in an appropriate time-frame. Kafka was built with the following goals in mind:

- Loose coupling between message Producers and message Consumers
- Persistence of message data to support a variety of data consumption scenarios and failure handling
- Maximum end-to-end throughput with low latency components
- Managing diverse data formats and types using binary data formats
- Scaling servers linearly without affecting the existing cluster setup

While we will introduce Kafka in more detail in up coming sections, you should understand that one of the common uses of Kafka is in its stream processing architecture. With its reliable message delivery semantics, it helps in consuming high rates of events. Moreover, it provides message replaying capabilities along with support for different types of consumer.

This further helps in making streaming architecture fault-tolerant and supports a variety of alerting and notification services.

Kafka's architecture

This section introduces you to Kafka architecture. By the end of this section, you will have a clear understanding of both the logical and physical architecture of Kafka. Let's see how Kafka components are organized logically.

Every message in **Kafka topics** is a collection of bytes. This collection is represented as an **array**. **Producers** are the applications that store information in **Kafka queues**. They send messages to Kafka topics that can store all types of messages. Every topic is further differentiated into **partitions**. Each partition stores messages in the sequence in which they arrive. There are two major operations that producers/consumers can perform in Kafka. Producers append to the end of the write-ahead log files. **Consumers** fetch messages from these log files belonging to a given topic partition. Physically, each topic is spread over different Kafka brokers, which host one or two partitions of each topic.

Ideally, Kafka pipelines should have a uniform number of partitions per broker and all topics on each machine. Consumers are applications or processes that subscribe to a topic or receive messages from these topics.

The following diagram shows you the conceptual layout of a Kafka cluster:

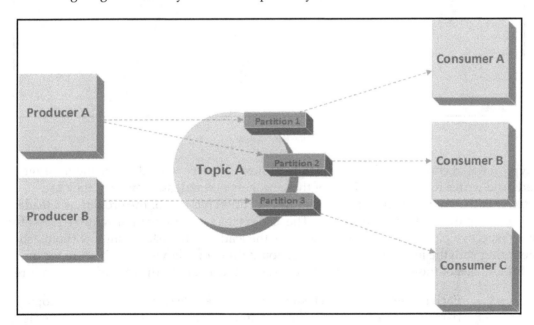

Kafka's logical architecture

The preceding paragraphs explain the logical architecture of Kafka and how different logical components coherently work together. While it is important to understand how Kafka architecture is divided logically, you also need to understand what Kafka's physical architecture looks like. This will help you in later chapters as well. A Kafka cluster is basically composed of one or more servers (nodes). The following diagram depicts how a multi-node Kafka cluster looks:

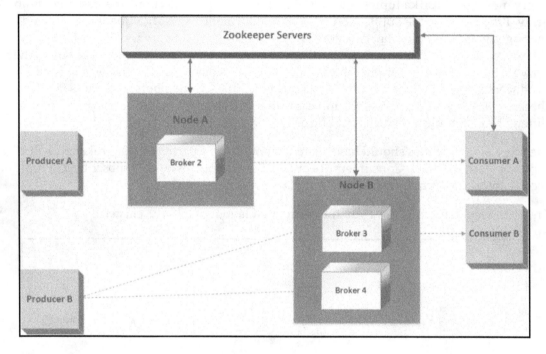

Kafka's physical architecture

A typical Kafka cluster consists of **multiple brokers**. It helps in load-balancing message reads and writes to the cluster. Each of these brokers is **stateless**. However, they use Zookeeper to maintain their states. Each topic partition has one of the brokers as a **leader** and zero or more brokers as **followers**. The leaders manage any read or write requests for their respective partitions. Followers replicate the leader in the background without actively interfering with the leader's working. You should think of followers as a backup for the leader and one of those followers will be chosen as the leader in the case of leader failure.

 Each server in a Kafka cluster will either be a leader for some of the topic's partitions or a follower for others. In this way, the load on every server is equally balanced. Kafka broker leader election is done with the help of Zookeeper.

Zookeeper is an important component of a Kafka cluster. It manages and coordinates Kafka brokers and consumers. Zookeeper keeps track of any new broker additions or any existing broker failures in the Kafka cluster. Accordingly, it will notify the producer or consumers of Kafka queues about the cluster state. This helps both producers and consumers in coordinating work with active brokers. Zookeeper also records which broker is the leader for which topic partition and passes on this information to the producer or consumer to read and write the messages.

At this juncture, you must be familiar with producer and consumer applications with respect to the Kafka cluster. However, it is beneficial to touch on these briefly so that you can verify your understanding. Producers push data to brokers. At the time of publishing data, producers search for the elected leader (broker) of the respective topic partition and automatically send a message to that leader broker server. Similarly, the consumer reads messages from brokers.

The consumer records its state with the help of Zookeeper as Kafka brokers are stateless. This design helps in scaling Kafka well. The consumer offset value is maintained by Zookeeper. The consumer records how many messages have been consumed by it using partition offset. It ultimately acknowledges that message offset to Zookeeper. It means that the consumer has consumed all prior messages.

 This brings us to an end of our section on Kafka architecture. Hopefully, by this time, you are well versed with Kafka architecture and understand all logical and physical components. The next sections cover each of these components in detail. However, it is imperative that you understand the overall Kafka architecture before delving into each of the components.

Message topics

If you are into software development and services, I am sure you will have heard terms such as database, tables, records, and so on. In a database, we have multiple tables; let's say, Items, Price, Sales, Inventory, Purchase, and many more. Each table contains data of a specific category. There will be two parts in the application: one will be inserting records into these tables and the other will be reading records from these tables. Here, tables are the topics in Kafka, applications that are inserting data into tables are producers, and applications that are reading data are consumers.

In a messaging system, messages need to be stored somewhere. In Kafka, we store messages into topics. Each topic belongs to a category, which means that you may have one topic storing item information and another may store sales information. A producer who wants to send a message may send it to its own category of topics. A consumer who wants to read these messages will simply subscribe to the category of topics that he is interested in and will consume it. Here are a few terms that we need to know:

- **Retention Period**: The messages in the topic need to be stored for a defined period of time to save space irrespective of throughput. We can configure the retention period, which is by default seven days, to whatever number of days we choose. Kafka keeps messages up to the defined period of time and then ultimately deletes them.

- **Space Retention Policy**: We can also configure Kafka topics to clear messages when the size reaches the threshold mentioned in the configuration. However, this scenario may occur if you haven't done enough capacity planning before deploying Kafka into your organization.

- **Offset**: Each message in Kafka is assigned with a number called as an offset. Topics consist of many partitions. Each partition stores messages in the sequence in which they arrive. Consumers acknowledge messages with an offset, which means that all the messages before that message offset are received by the consumer.

- **Partition**: Each Kafka topic consists of a fixed number of partitions. During topic creation in Kafka, you need to configure the number of partitions. Partitions are distributed and help in achieving high throughput.

- **Compaction**: Topic compaction was introduced in Kafka 0.8. There is no way to change previous messages in Kafka; messages only get deleted when the retention period is over. Sometimes, you may get new Kafka messages with the same key that includes a few changes, and on the consumer side, you only want to process the latest data. Compaction helps you achieve this goal by compacting all messages with the same key and creating a map offset for key: *offset*. It helps in removing duplicates from a large number of messages.

- **Leader**: Partitions are replicated across the Kafka cluster based on the replication factor specified. Each partition has a leader broker and followers and all the read write requests to the partition will go through the leader only. If the leader fails, another leader will get elected and the process will resume.

- **Buffering**: Kafka buffers messages both at the producer and consumer side to increase throughput and reduce **Input/Output (IO)**. We will talk about it in detail later.

Message partitions

Suppose that we have in our possession a purchase table and we want to read records for an item from the purchase table that belongs to a certain category, say, electronics. In the normal course of events, we will simply filter out other records, but what if we partition our table in such a way that we will be able to read the records of our choice quickly?

This is exactly what happens when topics are broken into partitions known as **units of parallelism** in Kafka. This means that the greater the number of partitions, the more throughput. This does not mean that we should choose a huge number of partitions. We will talk about the pros and cons of increasing the number of partitions further.

While creating topics, you can always mention the number of partitions that you require for a topic. Each of the messages will be appended to partitions and each message is then assigned with a number called an offset. Kafka makes sure that messages with similar keys always go to the same partition; it calculates the hash of the message key and appends the message to the partition. Time ordering of messages is not guaranteed in topics but within a partition, it's always guaranteed. This means that messages that come later will always be appended to the end of the partition.

 Partitions are fault-tolerant; they are replicated across the Kafka brokers. Each partition has its leader that serves messages to the consumer that wants to read the message from the partition. If the leader fails a new leader is elected and continues to serve messages to the consumers. This helps in achieving high throughput and latency.

Let's understand the pros and cons of a large number of partitions:

- **High throughput**: Partitions are a way to achieve parallelism in Kafka. Write operations on different partitions happen in parallel. All time-consuming operations will happen in parallel as well; this operation will utilize hardware resources at the maximum. On the consumer side, one partition will be assigned to one consumer within a consumer group, which means that different consumers available in different groups can read from the same partition, but different consumers from the same consumer group will not be allowed to read from the same partition.

So, the degree of parallelism in a single consumer group depends on the number of partitions it is reading from. A large number of partitions results in high throughput.

Choosing the number of partitions depends on how much throughput you want to achieve. We will talk about it in detail later. Throughput on the producer side also depends on many other factors such as batch size, compression type, number of replications, types of acknowledgement, and some other configurations, which we will see in detail in Chapter 3, *Deep Dive into Kafka Producers*.

However, we should be very careful about modifying the number of partitions--the mapping of messages to partitions completely depends on the hash code generated based on the message key that guarantees that messages with the same key will be written to the same partition. This guarantees the consumer about the delivery of messages in the order which they were stored in the partition. If we change the number of partitions, the distribution of messages will change and this order will no longer be guaranteed for consumers who were looking for the previous order subscribed. Throughput for the producer and consumer can be increased or decreased based on different configurations that we will discuss in detail in upcoming chapters.

- **Increases producer memory**: You must be wondering how increasing the number of partitions will force us to increase producer memory. A producer does some internal stuff before flushing data to the broker and asking them to store it in the partition. The producer buffers incoming messages per partition. Once the upper bound or the time set is reached, the producer sends his messages to the broker and removes it from the buffer.

  If we increase the number of partitions, the memory allocated for the buffering may exceed in a very short interval of time, and the producer will block producing messages until it sends buffered data to the broker. This may result in lower throughput. To overcome this, we need to configure more memory on the producer side, which will result in allocating extra memory to the producer.

- **High availability issue**: Kafka is known as high-availability, high-throughput, and distributed messaging system. Brokers in Kafka store thousands of partitions of different topics. Reading and writing to partitions happens through the leader of that partition. Generally, if the leader fails, electing a new leader takes only a few milliseconds. Observation of failure is done through controllers. **Controllers** are just one of the brokers. Now, the new leader will serve the request from the producer and consumer. Before serving the request, it reads metadata of the partition from Zookeeper. However, for normal and expected failure, the window is very small and takes only a few milliseconds. In the case of unexpected failure, such as killing a broker unintentionally, it may result in a delay of a few seconds based on the number of partitions. The general formula is:

  *Delay Time = (Number of Partition/replication * Time to read metadata for single partition)*

The other possibility could be that the failed broker is a controller, the controller replacement time depends on the number of partitions, the new controller reads the metadata of each partition, and the time to start the controller will increase with an increase in the number of partitions.

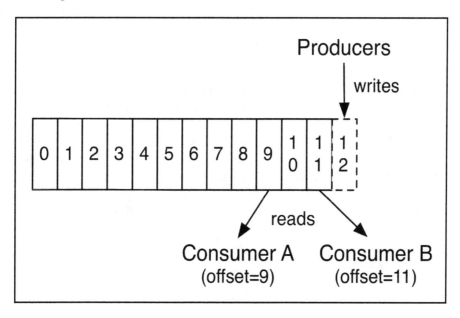

Kafka partitions (Ref: https://kafka.apache.org/documentation/)

We should take care while choosing the number of partitions and we will talk about this in upcoming chapters and how we can make the best use of Kafka's capability.

Replication and replicated logs

Replication is one of the most important factors in achieving reliability for Kafka systems. Replicas of message logs for each topic partition are maintained across different servers in a Kafka cluster. This can be configured for each topic separately. What it essentially means is that for one topic, you can have the replication factor as 3 and for another, you can use 5. All the reads and writes happen through the leader; if the leader fails, one of the followers will be elected as leader.

Generally, followers keep a copy of the leader's log, which means that the leader does not make the message as committed until it receives acknowledgment from all the followers. There are different ways that the log replication algorithm has been implemented; it should ensure that, if leader tells the producer that the message is committed, it must be available for the consumer to read it.

To maintain such replica consistency, there are two approaches. In both approaches, there will be a leader through which all the read and write requests will be processed. There is a slight difference in replica management and leader election:

- **Quorum-based approach**: In this approach, the leader will mark messages committed only when the majority of replicas have an acknowledged receiving the message. If the leader fails, the election of the new a leader will only happen with coordination between followers. There are many algorithms that exist for electing leader and going to depth of those algorithm is beyond the scope of this book. Zookeeper follows a quorum-based approach for leader election.
- **Primary backup approach**: Kafka follows a different approach to maintaining replicas; the leader in Kafka waits for an acknowledgement from all the followers before marking the message as committed. If the leader fails, any of the followers can take over as leader.

This approach can cost you more in terms of latency and throughput but this will guarantee better consistency for messages or data. Each leader records an in-sync replica set abbreviated to **in sync replica** (**ISR**). This means that for each partition, we will have a leader and ISR stored in Zookeeper. Now the writes and reads will happen as follows:

- **Write**: All the leaders and followers have their own local log where they maintain the log end offset that represents the tail of the log. The last committed message offset is called the High Watermark. When a client requests to write a message to partition, it first picks the leader of the partition from Zookeeper and creates a write request. The leader writes a message to the log and subsequently waits for the followers in ISR to return an acknowledgement. Once acknowledgement is received, it simply increases the pointer to High Watermark and sends an acknowledgment to the client. If any followers present in ISR fail, the leader simply drops them from ISR and continues its operation with other followers. Once failed followers come back, they catch up with a leader by making the logs sync. Now, the leader adds this follower to ISR again.
- **Read**: All the reads happen through the leader only. The message that is acknowledged successfully by the leader will be available for the client to read.

Here is the diagram that will clear the Kafka Log Implementation:

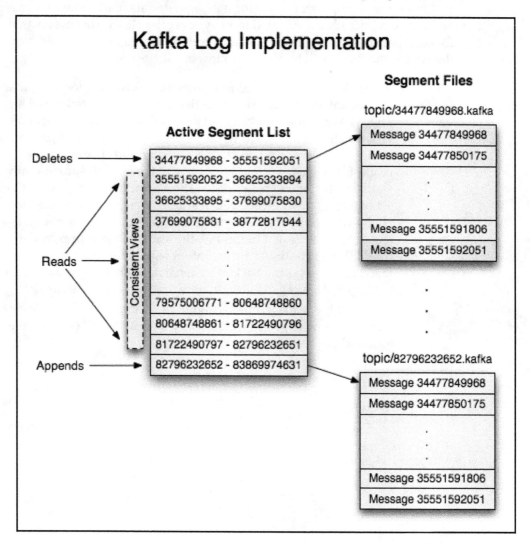

Kafka log implementation (Ref: https://kafka.apache.org/documentation/#log)

Message producers

In Kafka, the producer is responsible for sending data to the partition of the topic for which it is producing data.

 The producer generally does not write data to partitions, it creates write requests for messages and sends them to the leader broker. Partitioner calculates the hash value of the message, which helps the producer to choose which partition should be selected.

The hash value is generally calculated by the message key that we provide when writing the message to a Kafka topic. The message with a null key will be distributed in a round-robin fashion across partitions to ensure even distribution of messages. In Kafka, each partition has a leader and each read write request goes through the leader only. So a request to write messages to a partition of a topic will go through the leader broker. The producer waits for an acknowledgement of messages depending on the setting. Generally, it waits until the replication for a particular message is successfully acknowledged.

 Remember that until and unless all replicas have been acknowledged to commit the message, it will not be available to read. This setting is the default and ensures that a message cannot be lost if a leader broker fails.

However, you can set the configuration for acknowledgement to 1, which assumes that if a message is committed by the leader, it will be available to read and the Kafka producer can produce the next messages. This setting is dangerous because, if brokers fail before other replicas commit the message, the message will be lost. This leads to less durability but high throughput.

However, it's better to compromise on throughput if your consumer system does not want to lose a single message as part of the application. We will talk in detail about the producer in the next chapter.

Message consumers

The consumer is any one who subscribes for topics in Kafka. Each consumer belongs to a consumer group and some consumer groups contains multiple consumers. Consumers are an interesting part of Kafka and we will cover them in detail.

Two consumers from the same group cannot consume message from a similar partition because it will lead to the message being consumed out of order. However, consumers from the same group can consume message from a different partition of the same topic simultaneously. Similarly, consumers from a different group can consume messages from the same partition in parallel without affecting the order of consumption.

So, it's clear that groups play an important role; in Kafka's initial version, Zookeeper was used for group management, but in the latest version, Kafka has its own group protocol built in. One of the brokers will act as a group coordinator and will be responsible for assigning and managing partitions for groups. We will talk about Zookeeper and its own protocol in later chapters specific to the consumer.

Remember that we talked about assigning an offset to a message in a partition; each consumer reads the offset and commits the offset to the group coordinator or Zookeeper. So if consumers fail for any reason, it will start from the next message of the **committed offset**.

Offset helps guarantee the processing of messages by consumers, which is important for most applications that cannot afford losing any message as part of their processing.

Role of Zookeeper

We have already talked a lot about Zookeeper in the previous sections. Zookeeper plays a very important role in Kafka architecture and it is very important for you to understand how it records the Kafka cluster state. Therefore, we are dedicating a separate section to the role of Zookeeper in the Kafka cluster. Kafka cannot work without Zookeeper. Kafka uses Zookeeper for the following functions:

- **Choosing a controller**: The controller is one of the brokers responsible for partition management with respect to leader election, topic creation, partition creation, and replica management. When a node or server shuts down, Kafka controllers elect partition leaders from followers. Kafka uses Zookeeper's metadata information to elect a controller. Zookeeper ensures that a new controller is elected in case the current controller crashes.

- **Brokers metadata:** Zookeeper records the state of each of the brokers that are part of the Kafka cluster. It records all relevant metadata about each broker in a cluster. The producer/consumer interacts with Zookeeper to get the broker's state.
- **Topic metadata:** Zookeeper also records topic metadata such as the number of partitions, specific configuration parameters, and so on.
- **Client quota information:** With newer versions of Kafka, quota features have been introduced. Quotas enforce byte-rate thresholds on clients to read and write messages to a Kafka topic. All the information and states are maintained by Zookeeper.
- **Kafka topic ACLs:** Kafka has an in-built authorization module that is defined as **Access Control Lists** (**ACLs**). These ACLs determine user roles and what kind of read and write permissions each of these roles has on respective topics. Kafka uses Zookeeper to store all ACLs.

The preceding points summarize how Zookeeper is used in the Kafka cluster and why a Kafka cluster cannot run without Zookeeper. In upcoming chapters, you will understand Zookeeper concepts in more technical depth.

Summary

We have come to the end of this chapter, and by now you should have a basic understanding of the Kafka messaging system. An important aspect of mastering any system is that you should understand the system end to end at a high level first. This will put you in a better position when you understand individual components of the system in detail. You can always establish the logical connection with end-to-end system understanding and understand why individual components are designed in a particular way. In this chapter, our goal was the same.

We started by discovering why Kafka was built in the first place. We have put forward problems in LinkedIn systems that led to the creation of Kafka. That section will give you a very clear understanding of the types of problem that Kafka can solve.

We further covered Kafka's logical and system architecture. Putting Kafka architecture in two viewpoints will help you with both a functional and technical understanding of Kafka. The logical viewpoint is more from the perspective of establishing data flows and seeing how different components depend on each other. The technical viewpoint will help you in technically designing producer/consumer applications and understanding the Kafka physical design. The physical viewpoint is more a system-wise view of the logical structure. The physical architecture covers producer Applications, consumer Applications, Kafka brokers (nodes), and Zookeeper.

In this chapter, we have touched on all components that we have illustrated in the Kafka architecture. We will cover all these components in depth in upcoming chapters. However, the important goal for you should be to understand the roles and responsibilities of each Kafka component. Every component in Kafka has some specific role to play, and, even if one of these is missing overall Kafka functionality cannot be achieved. The other key takeaways from this chapter should be understanding how the unit of parallelism and partitioning system works in Kafka. This is one of the key aspects in designing low'- latency systems with Kafka.

In the next chapter, we will delve into Kafka producers and how you should design a producer application. We will cover different producer APIs and some of the best practices associated with Kafka producers.

3
Deep Dive into Kafka Producers

In previous chapters, you have learned about messaging systems and Kafka architecture. While it is a good start, we will now take a deeper look into Kafka producers. Kafka can be used as a message queue, message bus, or data storage system. Irrespective of how Kafka is used in your enterprise, you will need an application system that can write data to the Kafka cluster. Such a system is called a **producer**. As the name suggests, they are the source or producers of messages for Kafka topics. Kafka producers publish messages as per Kafka protocols defined by the makers of Kafka. This chapter is all about producers, their internal working, examples of writing producers using Java or Scala APIs, and some of the best practices of writing Kafka APIs. We will cover the following topics in this chapter:

- Internals of a Kafka producer
- The Kafka Producer API and its uses
- Partitions and their uses
- Additional configuration for producers
- Some common producer patterns
- An example of a producer
- Best practices to be followed for a Kafka producer

Kafka producer internals

In this section, we will walk through different Kafka producer components, and at a higher level, cover how messages get transferred from a Kafka producer application to Kafka queues. While writing producer applications, you generally use Producer APIs, which expose methods at a very abstract level. Before sending any data, a lot of steps are performed by these APIs. So it is very important to understand these internal steps in order to gain complete knowledge about Kafka producers. We will cover these in this section. First, we need to understand the responsibilities of Kafka producers apart from publishing messages. Let's look at them one by one:

- **Bootstrapping Kafka broker URLs**: The Producer connects to at least one broker to fetch metadata about the Kafka cluster. It may happen that the first broker to which the producer wants to connect may be down. To ensure a failover, the producer implementation takes a list of more than one broker URL to bootstrap from. Producer iterates through a list of Kafka broker addresses until it finds the one to connect to fetch cluster metadata.

- **Data serialization:** Kafka uses a binary protocol to send and receive data over TCP. This means that while writing data to Kafka, producers need to send the ordered byte sequence to the defined Kafka broker's network port. Subsequently, it will read the response byte sequence from the Kafka broker in the same ordered fashion. Kafka producer serializes every message data object into **ByteArrays** before sending any record to the respective broker over the wire. Similarly, it converts any byte sequence received from the broker as a response to the message object.

- **Determining topic partition:** It is the responsibility of the Kafka producer to determine which topic partition data needs to be sent. If the partition is specified by the caller program, then Producer APIs do not determine topic partition and send data directly to it. However, if no partition is specified, then producer will choose a partition for the message. This is generally based on the key of the message data object. You can also code for your custom partitioner in case you want data to be partitioned as per specific business logic for your enterprise.

- **Determining the leader of the partition**: Producers send data to the leader of the partition directly. It is the producer's responsibility to determine the leader of the partition to which it will write messages. To do so, producers ask for metadata from any of the Kafka brokers. Brokers answer the request for metadata about active servers and leaders of the topic's partitions at that point of time.

- **Failure handling/retry ability:** Handling failure responses or number of retries is something that needs to be controlled through the producer application. You can configure the number of retries through Producer API configuration, and this has to be decided as per your enterprise standards. Exception handling should be done through the producer application component. Depending on the type of exception, you can determine different data flows.

- **Batching:** For efficient message transfers, batching is a very useful mechanism. Through Producer API configurations, you can control whether you need to use the producer in **asynchronous** mode or not. Batching ensures reduced I/O and optimum utilization of producer memory. While deciding on the number of messages in a batch, you have to keep in mind the end-to-end latency. End-to-end latency increases with the number of messages in a batch.

Hopefully, the preceding paragraphs have given you an idea about the prime responsibilities of Kafka producers. Now, we will discuss Kafka producer data flows. This will give you a clear understanding about the steps involved in producing Kafka messages.

Internal implementation or the sequence of steps in Producer APIs may differ for respective programming languages. Some of the steps can be done in parallel using threads or callbacks.

The following image shows the high-level steps involved in producing messages to the Kafka cluster:

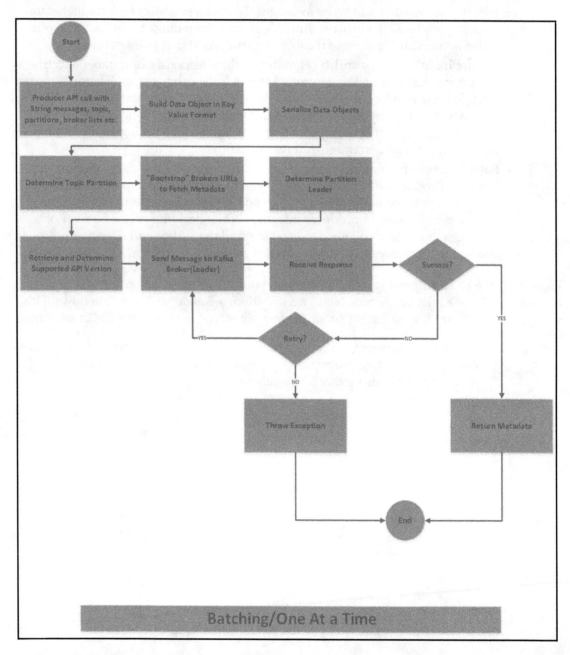

Kafka producer high-level flow

Publishing messages to a Kafka topic starts with calling Producer APIs with appropriate details such as messages in string format, topic, partitions (optional), and other configuration details such as broker URLs and so on. The Producer API uses the passed on information to form a data object in a form of nested key-value pair. Once the data object is formed, the producer serializes it into byte arrays. You can either use an inbuilt serializer or you can develop your custom serializer. **Avro** is one of the commonly used data serializers.

 Serialization ensures compliance to the Kafka binary protocol and efficient network transfer.

Next, the partition to which data needs to be sent is determined. If partition information is passed in API calls, then producer would use that partition directly. However, in case partition information is not passed, then producer determines the partition to which data should be sent. Generally, this is decided by the keys defined in data objects. Once the record partition is decided, producer determines which broker to connect to in order to send messages. This is generally done by the bootstrap process of selecting the producers and then, based on the fetched metadata, determining the leader broker.

Producers also need to determine supported API versions of a Kafka broker. This is accomplished by using API versions exposed by the Kafka cluster. The goal is that producer will support different versions of Producer APIs. While communicating with the respective leader broker, they should use the highest API version supported by both the producers and brokers.

Producers send the used API version in their write requests. Brokers can reject the write request if a compatible API version is not reflected in the write request. This kind of setup ensures incremental API evolution while supporting older versions of APIs.

Once a serialized data object is sent to the selected Broker, producer receives a response from those brokers. If they receive metadata about the respective partition along with new message offsets, then the response is considered successful. However, if error codes are received in the response, then producer can either throw the exception or retry as per the received configuration.

As we move further in the chapter, we will dive deeply into the technical side of Kafka Producer APIs and write them using Java and Scala programs.

Kafka Producer APIs

Kafka has provided you with a rich set of APIs to create applications to interact with it. We will go through Producer API details and understand its uses.

Creating a Kafka producer involves the following steps:

1. Required configuration.
2. Creating a producer object.
3. Setting up a producer record.
4. Creating a custom partition if required.
5. Additional configuration.

Required configuration: In most applications, we first start with creating the initial configuration without which we cannot run the application. The following are three mandatory configuration parameters:

- `bootstrap.servers`: This contains a list of Kafka brokers addresses. The address is specified in terms of `hostname:port`. We can specify one or more broker detail, but we recommend that you provide at least two so that if one broker goes down, producer can use the other one.

     It is not necessary to specify all brokers as the Kafka producer queries this configured broker for information about other brokers. In older versions of Kafka, this property was `metadata.broker.list`, where we used to specify a list of brokers `host:port`.

- `key.serializer`: The message is sent to Kafka brokers in the form of a key-value pair. Brokers expect this key-value to be in byte arrays. So we need to tell producer which serializer class is to be used to convert this key-value object to a byte array. This property is set to tell the producer which class to use to serialize the key of the message.

    Kafka provides us with three inbuilt serializer classes: `ByteArraySerializer`, `StringSerializer`, and `IntegerSerializer`. All these classes are present in the `org.apache.kafka.common.serialization` package and implement the serializer interface.

- `value.serializer`: This is similar to the `key.serializer` property, but this property tells the producer which class to use in order to serialize the value. You can implement your own serialize class and assign to this property.

Let's see how we do it in a programming context.

Here is how Java works for Producer APIs:

```
Properties producerProps = new Properties();
producerProps.put("bootstrap.servers", "broker1:port,broker2:port");
producerProps.put("key.serializer",
    "org.apache.kafka.common.serialization.StringSerializer");
    producerProps.put("value.serializer",
      "org.apache.kafka.common.serialization.StringSerializer");
KafkaProducer<String, String> producer = new
KafkaProducer<String,String>(producerProps);
```

The Producer API in Scala:

```
val producerProps = new Properties()
producerProps.put("bootstrap.servers", "broker1:port,broker2:port");

    producerProps.put("key.serializer",
"org.apache.kafka.common.serialization.StringSerializer")
    producerProps.put("value.serializer",
"org.apache.kafka.common.serialization.StringSerializer")

val producer = new KafkaProducer[String, String](producerProps)
```

The preceding code contains three specific points:

- **Properties object**: We start with creating a property object; this object contains the `put` method that is used to put the configuration key-value pair in place
- **Serializer class**: We will use `StringSerializer` for both key and value as our key and value will be of the string type
- **Producer object**: We create a producer object by passing the configuration object to it, which provides the producer with specific information about broker servers, serializer classes, and other configurations that we will see later

Producer object and ProducerRecord object

Producer accepts the `ProducerRecord` object to send records to the `.ProducerRecord` topic. It contains a topic name, partition number, `timestamp`, key, and value. Partition number, `timestamp`, and key are optional parameters, but the topic to which data will be sent and value that contains the data is mandatory.

- If the partition number is specified, then the specified partition will be used when sending the record
- If the partition is not specified but a key is specified, a partition will be chosen using a hash of the key
- If both key and partition are not specified, a partition will be assigned in a round-robin fashion

Here is the `producerRecord` in Java:

```
ProducerRecord producerRecord = new ProducerRecord<String,
String>(topicName, data);
Future<RecordMetadata> recordMetadata = producer.send(producerRecord);
```

Here is an example of `producerRecord` in Scala:

```
val producerRecord = new ProducerRecord<String, String>(topicName, data);
val recordMetadata = producer.send(producerRecord);
```

We have different constructors available for `ProducerRecord`:

- Here is the first constructor for `producerRecord`:

  ```
  ProducerRecord(String topicName, Integer numberOfpartition, K key,
  V value)
  ```

- The second constructor goes something like this:

  ```
  ProducerRecord(String topicName, Integer numberOfpartition, Long
  timestamp, K key, V value)
  ```

- The third constructor is as follows:

  ```
  ProducerRecord(String topicName, K key, V value)
  ```

- The final constructor of our discussion is as follows:

  ```
  ProducerRecord(String topicName, V value)
  ```

Each record also has a `timestamp` associated with it. If we do not mention a `timestamp`, the producer will stamp the record with its current time. The `timestamp` eventually used by Kafka depends on the `timestamp` type configured for the particular topic:

- **CreateTime**: The `timestamp` of `ProducerRecord` will be used to append a `timestamp` to the data
- **LogAppendTime**: The Kafka broker will overwrite the `timestamp` of `ProducerRecord` to the message and add a new `timestamp` when the message is appended to the log

Once data is sent using the `send()` method, the broker persists that message to the partition log and returns `RecordMetadata`, which contains metadata of the server response for the record, which includes `offset`, `checksum`, `timestamp`, `topic`, `serializedKeySize`, and so on. We previously discussed common messaging publishing patterns. The sending of messages can be either synchronous or asynchronous.

Synchronous messaging: Producer sends a message and waits for brokers to reply. The Kafka broker either sends an error or `RecordMetdata`. We can deal with errors depending on their type. This kind of messaging will reduce throughput and latency as the producer will wait for the response to send the next message.

Generally, Kafka retries sending the message in case certain connection errors occur. However, errors related to serialization, message, and so on have to be handled by the application, and in such cases, Kafka does not try to resend the message and throws an exception immediately.

Java:

```
ProducerRecord producerRecord = new ProducerRecord<String,
String>(topicName, data);

Object recordMetadata = producer.send(producerRecord).get();
```

Scala:

```
val producerRecord = new ProducerRecord<String, String>(topicName, data);

val recordMetadata = producer.send(producerRecord);
```

Asynchronous messaging: Sometimes, we have a scenario where we do not want to deal with responses immediately or we do not care about losing a few messages and we want to deal with it after some time.

Kafka provides us with the callback interface that helps in dealing with message reply, irrespective of error or successful. `send()` can accept an object that implements the callback interface.

```
send(ProducerRecord<K,V> record,Callback callback)
```

The callback interface contains the `onCompletion` method, which we need to override. Let's look at the following example:

Here is the example in Java:

```java
public class ProducerCallback implements Callback {
    public void onCompletion(RecordMetadata recordMetadata, Exception ex) {
        if(ex!=null){
            //deal with exception here
        }
        else{
            //deal with RecordMetadata here
        }
    }
}
```

Scala:

```scala
class ProducerCallback extends Callback {
  override def onCompletion(recordMetadata: RecordMetadata, ex: Exception):
Unit = {
    if (ex != null) {
      //deal with exception here
    }
    else {
      //deal with RecordMetadata here
    }
  }
}
```

Once we have the `Callback` class implemented, we can simply use it in the `send` method as follows:

```scala
val callBackObject = producer.send(producerRecord,new ProducerCallback());
```

If Kafka has thrown an exception for the message, we will not have a null exception object. We can also deal with successful and error messages accordingly in `onCompletion()`.

Custom partition

Remember that we talked about key serializer and value serializer as well as partitions used in Kafka producer. As of now, we have just used the default partitioner and inbuilt serializer. Let's see how we can create a custom partitioner.

Kafka generally selects a partition based on the hash value of the key specified in messages. If the key is not specified/null, it will distribute the message in a round-robin fashion. However, sometimes you may want to have your own partition logic so that records with the same partition key go to the same partition on the broker. We will see some best practices for partitions later in this chapter. Kafka provides you with an API to implement your own partition.

In most cases, a hash-based default partition may suffice, but for some scenarios where a percentage of data for one key is very large, we may be required to allocate a separate partition for that key. This means that if key K has 30 percent of total data, it will be allocated to partition N so that no other key will be assigned to partition N and we will not run out of space or slow down. There can be other use cases as well where you may want to write Custom Partition. Kafka provides the partitioner interface, which helps us create our own partition.

Here is an example in Java:

```java
public class CustomePartition implements Partitioner {
    public int partition(String topicName, Object key, byte[] keyBytes,
Object value, byte[] valueByte, Cluster cluster) {
        List<PartitionInfo> partitions =
cluster.partitionsForTopic(topicName);

        int numPartitions = partitions.size();
        //Todo: Partition logic here
        return 0;
    }

    public void close() {

    }

    public void configure(Map<String, ?> map) {

    }
}
```

Scala:

```scala
class CustomPartition extends Partitioner {
  override def close(): Unit = {}

  override def partition(topicName: String, key: scala.Any, keyBytes:
Array[Byte], value: scala.Any, valueBytes: Array[Byte], cluster: Cluster):
Int = {

    val partitions: util.List[PartitionInfo] =
cluster.partitionsForTopic(topicName)

    val numPartitions: Int = partitions.size

    //TODO : your partition logic here
    0
  }

  override def configure(map: util.Map[String, _]): Unit = {}
}
```

Additional producer configuration

There are other optional configuration properties available for Kafka producer that can play an important role in performance, memory, reliability, and so on:

- `buffer.memory`: This is the amount of memory that producer can use to buffer a message that is waiting to be sent to the Kafka server. In simple terms, it is the total memory that is available to the Java producer to collect unsent messages. When this limit is reached, the producer will block the messages for `max.block.ms` before raising an exception. If your batch size is more, allocate more memory to the producer buffer.

  Additionally, to avoid keeping records queued indefinitely, you can set a timeout using `request.timeout.ms`. If this timeout expires before a message can be successfully sent, then it will be removed from the queue and an exception will be thrown.

- `acks`: This configuration helps in configuring when producer will receive acknowledgment from the leader before considering that the message is committed successfully:

- `acks=0`: Producer will not wait for any acknowledgment from the server. Producer will not know if the message is lost at any point in time and is not committed by the leader broker. Note that no retry will happen in this case and the message will be completely lost. This can be used when you want to achieve very high throughput and when you don't care about potential message loss.
- `acks=1`: Producer will receive an acknowledgment as soon as the leader has written the message to its local log. If the leader fails to write the message to its log, producer will retry sending the data according to the retry policy set and avoid potential loss of messages. However, we can still have message loss in a scenario where the leader acknowledges to producer but does not replicate the message to the other broker before it goes down.
- `acks=all`: Producer will only receive acknowledgment when the leader has received acknowledgment for all the replicas successfully. This is a safe setting where we cannot lose data if the replica number is sufficient to avoid such failures. Remember, throughput will be lesser then the first two settings.

- `batch.size`: This setting allows the producer to batch the messages based on the partition up to the configured amount of size. When the batch reaches the limit, all messages in the batch will be sent. However, it's not necessary that producer wait for the batch to be full. It sends the batch after a specific time interval without worrying about the number of messages in the batch.
- `linger.ms`: This represents an amount of time that a producer should wait for additional messages before sending a current batch to the broker. Kafka producer waits for the batch to be full or the configured `linger.ms` time; if any condition is met, it will send the batch to brokers. Producer will wait till the configured amount of time in milliseconds for any additional messages to get added to the current batch.
- `compression.type`: By default, producer sends uncompressed messages to brokers. When sending a single message, it will not make that much sense, but when we use batches, it's good to use compression to avoid network overhead and increase throughput. The available compressions are GZIP, Snappy, or LZ4. Remember that more batching would lead to better compression.
- `retires`: If message sending fails, this represents the number of times producer will retry sending messages before it throws an exception. It is irrespective of reseeding a message after receiving an exception.

- `max.in.flight.requests.per.connection`: This is the number of messages producer can send to brokers without waiting for a response. If you do not care about the order of the messages, then setting its value to more than 1 will increase throughput. However, ordering may change if you set it to more than 1 with retry enabled.
- `partitioner.class`: If you want to use a custom partitioner for your producer, then this configuration allows you to set the partitioner class, which implements the partitioner interface.
- `timeout.ms`: This is the amount of time a leader will wait for its followers to acknowledge the message before sending an error to producer. This setting will only help when `acks` is set to all.

Java Kafka producer example

We have covered different configurations and APIs in previous sections. Let's start coding one simple Java producer, which will help you create your own Kafka producer.

Prerequisite

- IDE: We recommend that you use a Scala-supported IDE such as IDEA, NetBeans, or Eclipse. We have used JetBrains IDEA: https://www.jetbrains.com/idea/download/.
- Build tool: Maven, Gradle, or others. We have used Maven to build our project.
- `Pom.xml`: Add Kafka dependency to the `pom` file:

```
<dependency>
    <groupId>org.apache.kafka</groupId>
    <artifactId>kafka_2.11</artifactId>
    <version>0.10.0.0</version>
</dependency>
```

Java:

```
import java.util.Properties;
import java.util.concurrent.Future;
import org.apache.kafka.clients.producer.KafkaProducer;
import org.apache.kafka.clients.producer.ProducerRecord;
import org.apache.kafka.clients.producer.RecordMetadata;

public class DemoProducer {

    public static void main(final String[] args) {
```

```java
        Properties producerProps = new Properties();
        producerProps.put("bootstrap.servers", "localhost:9092");
        producerProps.put("key.serializer",
"org.apache.kafka.common.serialization.StringSerializer");
        producerProps.put("value.serializer",
"org.apache.kafka.common.serialization.StringSerializer");
        producerProps.put("acks", "all");
        producerProps.put("retries", 1);
        producerProps.put("batch.size", 20000);
        producerProps.put("linger.ms", 1);
        producerProps.put("buffer.memory", 24568545);
        KafkaProducer<String, String> producer = new KafkaProducer<String,
String>(producerProps);

        for (int i = 0; i < 2000; i++) {
            ProducerRecord data = new ProducerRecord<String,
String>("test1", "Hello this is record " + i);
            Future<RecordMetadata> recordMetadata = producer.send(data);
        }
    producer.close();
    }
}
```

Scala:

```scala
import java.util.Properties
import org.apache.kafka.clients.producer._

object DemoProducer extends App {
  override def main(args: Array[String]): Unit = {

    val producerProps = new Properties()
    producerProps.put("bootstrap.servers", "localhost:9092")
    producerProps.put("key.serializer",
"org.apache.kafka.common.serialization.StringSerializer")
    producerProps.put("value.serializer",
"org.apache.kafka.common.serialization.StringSerializer")
    producerProps.put("client.id", "SampleProducer")
    producerProps.put("acks", "all")
    producerProps.put("retries", new Integer(1))
    producerProps.put("batch.size", new Integer(16384))
    producerProps.put("linger.ms", new Integer(1))
    producerProps.put("buffer.memory", new Integer(133554432))

    val producer = new KafkaProducer[String, String](producerProps)

    for (a <- 1 to 2000) {
      val record: ProducerRecord[String, String] = new
```

```
ProducerRecord("test1", "Hello this is record"+a)
    producer.send(record);
    }

    producer.close()
    }

}
```

The preceding example is a simple Java producer where we are producing string data without a key. We have also hardcoded the topic name, which probably can be read through configuration file or as an command line input. To understand producer, we have kept it simple. However, we will see good examples in upcoming chapters where we will follow good coding practice.

Common messaging publishing patterns

Applications may have different requirements of producer--a producer that does not care about acknowledgement for the message they have sent or a producer that cares about acknowledgement but the order of messages does not matter. We have different producer patterns that can be used for application requirement. Let's discuss them one by one:

- **Fire-and-forget**: In this pattern, producers only care about sending messages to Kafka queues. They really do not wait for any success or failure response from Kafka. Kafka is a highly available system and most of the time, messages would be delivered successfully. However, there is some risk of message loss in this pattern. This kind of pattern is useful when latency has to be minimized to the lowest level possible and one or two lost messages does not affect the overall system functionality. To use the fire and forget model with Kafka, you have to set producer `acks` config to `0`. The following image represents the Kafka-based fire and forget model:

Kafka producer fire and forget model

- **One message transfers**: In this pattern, producer sends one message at a time. It can do so in synchronous or asynchronous mode. In synchronous mode, producer sends the message and waits for a success or failure response before retrying the message or throwing the exception. In asynchronous mode, producer sends the message and receives the success or failure response as a callback function. The following image indicates this model. This kind of pattern is used for highly reliable systems where guaranteed delivery is the requirement. In this model, producer thread waits for response from Kafka. However, this does not mean that you cannot send multiple messages at a time. You can achieve that using multithreaded producer applications.

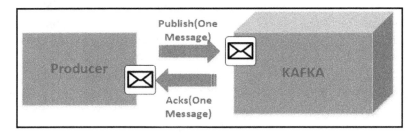

Kafka producer one message transfer model

- **Batching**: In this pattern, producers send multiple records to the same partition in a batch. The amount of memory required by a batch and wait time before sending the batch to Kafka is controlled by producer configuration parameters. Batching improves performance with bigger network packets and disk operations of larger datasets in a sequential manner. Batching negates the efficiency issues with respect to random reads and writes on disks. All the data in one batch would be written in one sequential fashion on hard drives. The following image indicates the batching message model:

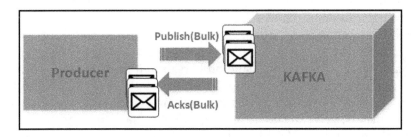

Kafka producer batching message model

Best practices

Hopefully, at this juncture, you are very well aware of Kafka Producer APIs, their internal working, and common patterns of publishing messages to different Kafka topics. This section covers some of the best practices associated with Kafka producers. These best practices will help you in making some of the design decisions for the producer component.

Let's go through some of the most common best practices to design a good producer application:

- **Data validation**: One of the aspects that is usually forgotten while writing a producer system is to perform basic data validation tests on data that is to be written on the Kafka cluster. Some such examples could be conformity to schema, not null values for Key fields, and so on. By not doing data validation, you are risking breaking downstream consumer applications and affecting the load balancing of brokers as data may not be partitioned appropriately.

- **Exception handling**: It is the sole responsibility of producer programs to decide on program flows with respect to exceptions. While writing a producer application, you should define different exception classes and as per your business requirements, decide on the actions that need to be taken. Clearly defining exceptions not only helps you in debugging but also in proper risk mitigation. For example, if you are using Kafka for critical applications such as fraud detection, then you should capture relevant exceptions to send e-mail alerts to the OPS team for immediate resolution.

- **Number of retries**: In general, there are two types of errors that you get in your producer application. The first type are errors that producer can retry, such as network timeouts and leader not available. The second type are errors that need to be handled by producer programs as mentioned in the preceding section. Configuring the number of retries will help you in mitigating risks related to message losses due to Kafka cluster errors or network errors.

- **Number of bootstrap URLs**: You should always have more than one broker listed in your bootstrap broker configuration of your producer program. This helps producers to adjust to failures because if one of the brokers is not available, producers try to use all the listed brokers until it finds the one it can connect to. An ideal scenario is that you should list all your brokers in the Kafka cluster to accommodate maximum broker connection failures. However, in case of very large clusters, you can choose a lesser number that can significantly represent your cluster brokers. You should be aware that the number of retries can affect your end-to-end latency and cause duplicate messages in your Kafka queues.

- **Avoid poor partitioning mechanism**: Partitions are a unit of parallelism in Kafka. You should always choose an appropriate partitioning strategy to ensure that messages are distributed uniformly across all topic partitions. Poor partitioning strategy may lead to non-uniform message distribution and you would not be able to achieve the optimum parallelism out of your Kafka cluster. This is important in cases where you have chosen to use keys in your messages. In case you do not define keys, then producer will use the default round-robin mechanism to distribute your messages to partitions. If keys are available, then Kafka will hash the keys and based on the calculated hash code, it will assign the partitions. In a nutshell, you should choose your keys in a way that your message set uses all available partitions.
- **Temporary persistence of messages**: For highly reliable systems, you should persist messages that are passing through your producer applications. Persistence could be on disk or in some kind of database. Persistence helps you replay messages in case of application failure or in case the Kafka cluster is unavailable due to some maintenance. This again, should be decided based on enterprise application requirements. You can have message purging techniques built in your producer applications for messages that are written to the Kafka cluster. This is generally used in conjunction with the acknowledgement feature that is available with Kafka Producer APIs. You should purge messages only when Kafka sends a success acknowledgement for a message set.
- **Avoid adding new partitions to existing topics**: You should avoid adding partitions to existing topics when you are using key-based partitioning for message distribution. Adding new partitions would change the calculated hash code for each key as it takes the number of partitions as one of the inputs. You would end up having different partitions for the same key.

Summary

This concludes our section on Kafka producers. This chapter addresses one of the key functionalities of Kafka message flows. The major emphasis in this chapter was for you to understand how Kafka producers work at the logical level and how messages are passed from Kafka producers to Kafka queues. This was covered in the *Kafka Internals* section. This is an important section for you to understand before you learn how to code with Kafka APIs. Unless you understand the logical working of Kafka producers, you will not be able to do justice to producer application technical designing.

We discussed Kafka Producer APIs and different components around it such as custom practitioners. We gave both Java and Scala examples as both languages are heavily used in enterprise applications. We would suggest you try all those examples on your consoles and get a better grasp of how Kafka producers work. Another important design consideration for Kafka producer is data flows. We covered some commonly used patterns in this chapter. You should have a thorough understanding of these patterns. We covered some of the common configuration parameters and performance tuning steps. These will definitely help you in case you are writing Kafka producer code for the first time.

In the end, we wanted to bring in some of the best practices of using Kafka producers. These best practices will help you in scalable designs and in avoiding some common pitfalls. Hopefully, by the end of this chapter, you have mastered the art of designing and coding Kafka producers.

In the next chapter, we will cover the internals of Kafka consumers, consumer APIs, and common usage patterns. The next chapter will give us a good understanding of how messages produced by producer are being consumed by different consumers irrespective of knowing their producer.

4

Deep Dive into Kafka Consumers

Every messaging system has two types of data flows. One flow pushes the data to the Kafka queues and the other flow reads the data from those queues. In the previous chapter, our focus was on the data flows that are pushing the data to Kafka queues using producer APIs. After reading the previous chapter, you should have sufficient knowledge about publishing data to Kafka queues using producer APIs in your application. In this chapter, our focus is on the second type of data flow--reading the data from Kafka queues.

Before we start with a deep dive into Kafka consumers, you should have a clear understanding of the fact that reading data from Kafka queues involves understanding many different concepts and they may differ from reading data from traditional queuing systems.

 With Kafka, every consumer has a unique identity and they are in full control of how they want to read data from each Kafka topic partition. Every consumer has its own consumer offset that is maintained in Zookeeper and they set it to the next location when they read data from a Kafka topic.

In this chapter, we will cover different concepts of Kafka consumers. Overall, this chapter covers how to consume messages from Kafka systems along with Kafka consumer APIs and their usage. It will walk you through some examples of using Kafka consumer APIs with Java and Scala programming languages and take a deep dive with you into consumer message flows along with some of the common patterns of consuming messages from Kafka topics.

We will cover the following topics in this chapter:

- Kafka consumer internals
- Kafka consumer APIs
- Java Kafka consumer example
- Scala Kafka consumer example
- Common message consuming patterns
- Best practices

Kafka consumer internals

In this section of the chapter, we will cover different Kafka consumer concepts and various data flows involved in consuming messages from Kafka queues. As already mentioned, consuming messages from Kafka is a bit different from other messaging systems. However, when you are writing consumer applications using consumer APIs, most of the details are abstracted. Most of the internal work is done by Kafka consumer libraries used by your application.

Irrespective of the fact that you do not have to code for most of the consumer internal work, you should understand these internal workings thoroughly. These concepts will definitely help you in debugging consumer applications and also in making the right application decision choices.

Understanding the responsibilities of Kafka consumers

On the same lines of the previous chapter on Kafka producers, we will start by understanding the responsibilities of Kafka consumers apart from consuming messages from Kafka queues.

Let's look at them one by one:

- **Subscribing to a topic**: Consumer operations start with subscribing to a topic. If consumer is part of a consumer group, it will be assigned a subset of partitions from that topic. Consumer process would eventually read data from those assigned partitions. You can think of topic subscription as a registration process to read data from topic partitions.

- **Consumer offset position**: Kafka, unlike any other queues, does not maintain message offsets. Every consumer is responsible for maintaining its own consumer offset. Consumer offsets are maintained by consumer APIs and you do not have to do any additional coding for this. However, in some use cases where you may want to have more control over offsets, you can write custom logic for offset commits. We will cover such scenarios in this chapter.

- **Replay / rewind / skip messages**: Kafka consumer has full control over starting offsets to read messages from a topic partition. Using consumer APIs, any consumer application can pass the starting offsets to read messages from topic partitions. They can choose to read messages from the beginning or from some specific integer offset value irrespective of what the current offset value of a partition is. In this way, consumers have the capability of replaying or skipping messages as per specific business scenarios.

- **Heartbeats**: It is the consumer's responsibility to ensure that it sends regular heartbeat signals to the Kafka broker (consumer group leader) to confirm their membership and ownership of designated partitions. If heartbeats are not received by the group leader in a certain time interval, then the partition's ownership would be reassigned to some other consumer in the consumer group.

- **Offset commits**: Kafka does not track positions or offsets of the messages that are read from consumer applications. It is the responsibility of the consumer application to track their partition offset and commit it. This has two advantages--this improves broker performance as they do not have to track each consumer offset and this gives flexibility to consumer applications in managing their offsets as per their specific scenarios. They can commit offsets after they finish processing a batch or they can commit offsets in the middle of very large batch processing to reduce side-effects of rebalancing.

- **Deserialization**: Kafka producers serialize objects into byte arrays before they are sent to Kafka. Similarly, Kafka consumers deserialize these Java objects into byte arrays. Kafka consumer uses the deserializers that are the same as serializers used in the producer application.

Now that you have a fair idea of the responsibilities of a consumer, we can talk about consumer data flows.

The following image depicts how data is fetched from Kafka consumers:

Consumer flows

The first step toward consuming any messages from Kafka is topic subscription. Consumer applications first subscribe to one or more topics. After that, consumer applications poll Kafka servers to fetch records. In general terms, this is called **poll loop**. This loop takes care of server co-ordinations, record retrievals, partition rebalances, and keeps alive the heartbeats of consumers.

 For new consumers that are reading data for the first time, poll loop first registers the consumer with the respective consumer group and eventually receives partition metadata. The partition metadata mostly contains partition and leader information of each topic.

Consumers, on receiving metadata, would start polling respective brokers for partitions assigned to them. If new records are found, they are retrieved and deserialized. They are finally processed and after performing some basic validations, they are stored in some external storage systems.

In very few cases, they are processed at runtime and passed to some external applications. Finally, consumers commit offsets of messages that are successfully processed. The poll loop also sends periodic keep-alive heartbeats to Kafka servers to ensure that they receive messages without interruption.

Kafka consumer APIs

Like Kafka producer, Kafka also provides a rich set of APIs to develop a consumer application. In previous sections of this chapter, you have learned about internal concepts of consumer, working of consumer within a consumer group, and partition rebalance. We will see how this concept helps in building a good consumer application.

- Consumer configuration
- KafkaConsumer object
- Subscription and polling
- Commit and offset
- Additional configuration

Consumer configuration

Creating Kafka consumer also requires a few mandatory properties to be set. There are basically four properties:

- `bootstrap.servers`: This property is similar to what we defined in Chapter 3, *Deep Dive into Kafka Producers*, for producer configuration. It takes a list of Kafka brokers' IPs.
- `key.deserializer`: This is similar to what we specified in producer. The difference is that in producer, we specified the class that can serialize the key of the message. Serialize means converting a key to a ByteArray. In consumer, we specify the class that can deserialize the ByteArray to a specific key type. Remember that the serializer used in producer should match with the equivalent deserializer class here; otherwise, you may get a serialization exception.

- `value.deserializer`: This property is used to deserialize the message. We should make sure that the deserializer class should match with the serializer class used to produce the data; for example, if we have used `StringSerializer` to serialize the message in producer, we should use `StringDeserializer` to deserialize the message.
- `group.id`: This property is not mandatory for the creation of a property but recommended to use while creating. You have learned in the previous section about consumer groups and their importance in performance. Defining a consumer group while creating an application always helps in managing consumers and increasing performance if needed.

Let's see how we set and create this in the real programming world.

Java:

```
Properties consumerProperties = new Properties();
consumerProperties.put("bootstrap.servers", "10.200.99.197:6667");
consumerProperties.put("group.id", "Demo");
consumerProperties.put("key.deserializer",
"org.apache.kafka.common.serialization.StringDeserializer");
consumerProperties.put("value.deserializer",
"org.apache.kafka.common.serialization.StringDeserializer");
KafkaConsumer<String, String> consumer = new KafkaConsumer<String,
String>(consumerProperties);
```

Scala:

```
val consumerProperties: Properties = new Properties();
consumerProperties.put("bootstrap.servers", "10.200.99.197:6667")
consumerProperties.put("group.id", "consumerGroup1")
consumerProperties.put("key.deserializer",
"org.apache.kafka.common.serialization.StringDeserializer")
consumerProperties.put("value.deserializer",
"org.apache.kafka.common.serialization.StringDeserializer")
val consumer: KafkaConsumer[String, String] = new KafkaConsumer[String,
String](consumerProperties)
```

The preceding code contains three specific things:

- `Properties` object: This object is used to initialize consumer properties. Mandatory properties discussed earlier can be set as a key-value pair, where the key would be the property name and value would be the value for the key.

- `Deserializer`: This is also a mandatory property that tells which deserializer class is to be used to convert ByteArray to the required object. Class can be different for key and value, but it should align with the serializer class used in producer while publishing data to the topic. Any mismatch will lead to a serialization exception.

- `KafkaConsumer`: Once properties are set, we can create a consumer object by passing this property to the class. Properties tell the consumer object about brokers IP to connect, the group name that the consumer should be part of, the deserialization class to use, and offset strategy to be used for the commit.

Subscription and polling

Consumer has to subscribe to some topic to receive data. The `KafkaConsumer` object has `subscribe()`, which takes a list of topics that the consumer wants to subscribe to. There are different forms of the subscribe method.

Let's talk about the subscribe method in detail with its different signatures:

- `public void subscribe(Collection<String> topics)`: This signature takes a list of topic names to which the consumer wants to subscribe. It uses the default rebalancer, which may affect data processing of the message.

- `public void subscribe(Pattern pattern, ConsumerRebalanceListener listener)`: This signature takes regex to match topics that exist in Kafka. This process is dynamic; any addition of a new topic matching the regex or deletion of a topic matching the regex will trigger the rebalancer. The second parameter, `ConsumerRebalanceListener`, will take your own class that implements this interface. We will talk about this in detail.

- `public void subscribe(Collection<String> topics, ConsumerRebalanceListener listener)`: This takes a list of topics and your implementation of `ConsumerRebalanceListner`.

Committing and polling

Polling is fetching data from the Kafka topic. Kafka returns the messages that have not yet been read by consumer. How does Kafka know that consumer hasn't read the messages yet?

Consumer needs to tell Kafka that it needs data from a particular offset and therefore, consumer needs to store the latest read message somewhere so that in case of consumer failure, consumer can start reading from the next offset.

Kafka commits the offset of messages that it reads successfully. There are different ways in which commit can happen and each way has its own pros and cons. Let's start looking at the different ways available:

- **Auto commit**: This is the default configuration of consumer. Consumer auto-commits the offset of the latest read messages at the configured interval of time. If we make `enable.auto.commit = true` and set `auto.commit.interval.ms=1000`, then consumer will commit the offset every second. There are certain risks associated with this option. For example, you set the interval to 10 seconds and consumer starts consuming the data. At the seventh second, your consumer fails, what will happen? Consumer hasn't committed the read offset yet so when it starts again, it will start reading from the start of the last committed offset and this will lead to duplicates.
- **Current offset commit**: Most of the time, we may want to have control over committing an offset when required. Kafka provides you with an API to enable this feature. We first need to do `enable.auto.commit = false` and then use the `commitSync()` method to call a commit offset from the consumer thread. This will commit the latest offset returned by polling. It would be better to use this method call after we process all instances of `ConsumerRecord`, otherwise there is a risk of losing records if consumer fails in between.

Java:

```
while (true) {
    ConsumerRecords<String, String> records = consumer.poll(2);
    for (ConsumerRecord<String, String> record : records)
        System.out.printf("offset = %d, key = %s, value = %sn",
                record.offset(), record.key(), record.value());
    try {
        consumer.commitSync();
    } catch (CommitFailedException ex) {
        //Logger or code to handle failed commit
    }
}
```

Scala:

```
while (true) {
  val records: ConsumerRecords[String, String] = consumer.poll(2)
  import scala.collection.JavaConversions._
  for (record <- records) println("offset = %d, key = %s, value = %sn",
record.offset, record.key, record.value)

  try
    consumer.commitSync()

  catch {
    case ex: CommitFailedException => {
      //Logger or code to handle failed commit
    }
  }
}
```

- **Asynchronous commit**: The problem with synchronous commit is that unless we receive an acknowledgment for a commit offset request from the Kafka server, consumer will be blocked. This will cost low throughput. It can be done by making commit happen asynchronously. However, there is a problem in asynchronous commit--it may lead to duplicate message processing in a few cases where the order of the commit offset changes. For example, offset of message 10 got committed before offset of message 5. In this case, Kafka will again serve message 5-10 to consumer as the latest offset 10 is overridden by 5.

Java:

```
while (true) {
    ConsumerRecords<String, String> records = consumer.poll(2);
    for (ConsumerRecord<String, String> record : records)
        System.out.printf("offset = %d, key = %s, value = %sn",
                record.offset(), record.key(), record.value());
    consumer.commitAsync(new OffsetCommitCallback() {
        public void onComplete(Map<TopicPartition, OffsetAndMetadata> map,
Exception e) {

        }
    });

}
```

Scala:

```
while (true) {
  val records: ConsumerRecords[String, String] = consumer.poll(2)
```

```
    for (record <- records) println("offset = %d, key = %s, value = %sn",
record.offset, record.key, record.value)

    consumer.commitAsync(new OffsetCommitCallback {
        override def onComplete(map: util.Map[TopicPartition,
OffsetAndMetadata], ex: Exception): Unit = {
        }
    })
}
```

You have learned about synchronous and asynchronous calls. However, the best practice is to use a combination of both. Asynchronous should be used after every poll call and synchronous should be used for behaviors such as the triggering of the rebalancer, closing consumer due to some condition, and so on.

Kafka also provides you with an API to commit a specific offset.

Additional configuration

You have learned a few mandatory parameters in the beginning. Kafka consumer has lots of properties and in most cases, some of them do not require any modification. There are a few parameters that can help you increase performance and availability of consumers:

- `enable.auto.commit`: If this is configured to true, then consumer will automatically commit the message offset after the configured interval of time. You can define the interval by setting `auto.commit.interval.ms`. However, the best idea is to set it to false in order to have control over when you want to commit the offset. This will help you avoid duplicates and miss any data to process.
- `fetch.min.bytes`: This is the minimum amount of data in bytes that the Kafka server needs to return for a fetch request. In case the data is less than the configured number of bytes, the server will wait for enough data to accumulate and then send it to consumer. Setting the value greater than the default, that is, one byte, will increase server throughput but will reduce latency of the consumer application.
- `request.timeout.ms`: This is the maximum amount of time that consumer will wait for a response to the request made before resending the request or failing when the maximum number of retries is reached.

- `auto.offset.reset`: This property is used when consumer doesn't have a valid offset for the partition from which it is reading the value.
  - **latest**: This value, if set to latest, means that the consumer will start reading from the latest message from the partition available at that time when consumer started.
  - **earliest**: This value, if set to earliest, means that the consumer will start reading data from the beginning of the partition, which means that it will read all the data from the partition.
  - **none**: This value, if set to none, means that an exception will be thrown to the consumer.
- `session.timeout.ms`: Consumer sends a heartbeat to the consumer group coordinator to tell it that it is alive and restrict triggering the rebalancer. The consumer has to send heartbeats within the configured period of time. For example, if timeout is set for 10 seconds, consumer can wait up to 10 seconds before sending a heartbeat to the group coordinator; if it fails to do so, the group coordinator will treat it as dead and trigger the rebalancer.
- `max.partition.fetch.bytes`: This represents the maximum amount of data that the server will return per partition. Memory required by consumer for the `ConsumerRecord` object must be bigger then *numberOfParition*valueSet*. This means that if we have 10 partitions and 1 consumer, and `max.partition.fetch.bytes` is set to 2 MB, then consumer will need *10*2 =20* MB for consumer record.

Remember that before setting this, we must know how much time consumer takes to process the data; otherwise, consumer will not be able to send heartbeats to the consumer group and the rebalance trigger will occur. The solution could be to increase session timeout or decrease partition fetch size to low so that consumer can process it as fast as it can.

Java Kafka consumer

The following program is a simple Java consumer which consumes data from topic test. Please make sure data is already available in the mentioned topic otherwise no record will be consumed.

```
import org.apache.kafka.clients.consumer.*;
import org.apache.kafka.common.TopicPartition;
import org.apache.log4j.Logger;

import java.util.*;
```

```java
public class DemoConsumer {
    private static final Logger log = Logger.getLogger(DemoConsumer.class);

    public static void main(String[] args) throws Exception {

        String topic = "test1";
        List<String> topicList = new ArrayList<>();
        topicList.add(topic);
        Properties consumerProperties = new Properties();
        consumerProperties.put("bootstrap.servers", "localhost:9092");
        consumerProperties.put("group.id", "Demo_Group");
        consumerProperties.put("key.deserializer",
"org.apache.kafka.common.serialization.StringDeserializer");
        consumerProperties.put("value.deserializer",
"org.apache.kafka.common.serialization.StringDeserializer");

        consumerProperties.put("enable.auto.commit", "true");
        consumerProperties.put("auto.commit.interval.ms", "1000");
        consumerProperties.put("session.timeout.ms", "30000");

        KafkaConsumer<String, String> demoKafkaConsumer = new
KafkaConsumer<String, String>(consumerProperties);

        demoKafkaConsumer.subscribe(topicList);
        log.info("Subscribed to topic " + topic);
        int i = 0;
        try {
            while (true) {
                ConsumerRecords<String, String> records =
demoKafkaConsumer.poll(500);
                for (ConsumerRecord<String, String> record : records)
                    log.info("offset = " + record.offset() + "key =" +
record.key() + "value =" + record.value());

                //TODO : Do processing for data here
                demoKafkaConsumer.commitAsync(new OffsetCommitCallback() {
                    public void onComplete(Map<TopicPartition,
OffsetAndMetadata> map, Exception e) {

                    }
                });

            }
        } catch (Exception ex) {
            //TODO : Log Exception Here
        } finally {
            try {
                demoKafkaConsumer.commitSync();
```

```
        } finally {
            demoKafkaConsumer.close();
        }
    }
  }
}
```

Scala Kafka consumer

This is the Scala version of the previous program and will work the same as the previous snippet. Kafka allows you to write consumer in many languages including Scala.

```scala
import org.apache.kafka.clients.consumer._
import org.apache.kafka.common.TopicPartition
import org.apache.log4j.Logger
import java.util._


object DemoConsumer {
  private val log: Logger = Logger.getLogger(classOf[DemoConsumer])

  @throws[Exception]
  def main(args: Array[String]) {
    val topic: String = "test1"
    val topicList: List[String] = new ArrayList[String]
    topicList.add(topic)
    val consumerProperties: Properties = new Properties
    consumerProperties.put("bootstrap.servers", "10.200.99.197:6667")
    consumerProperties.put("group.id", "Demo_Group")
    consumerProperties.put("key.deserializer",
"org.apache.kafka.common.serialization.StringDeserializer")
consumerProperties.put("value.deserializer","org.apache.kafka.common.serial
ization.StringDeserializer")
    consumerProperties.put("enable.auto.commit", "true")
    consumerProperties.put("auto.commit.interval.ms", "1000")
    consumerProperties.put("session.timeout.ms", "30000")
    val demoKafkaConsumer: KafkaConsumer[String, String] = new
KafkaConsumer[String, String](consumerProperties)
    demoKafkaConsumer.subscribe(topicList)
    log.info("Subscribed to topic " + topic)
    val i: Int = 0
    try
        while (true) {
          val records: ConsumerRecords[String, String] =
demoKafkaConsumer.poll(2)
          import scala.collection.JavaConversions._
```

```
            for (record <- records) {
              log.info("offset = " + record.offset + "key =" + record.key +
"value =" + record.value)
              System.out.print(record.value)
            }
            //TODO : Do processing for data here
            demoKafkaConsumer.commitAsync(new OffsetCommitCallback() {
              def onComplete(map: Map[TopicPartition, OffsetAndMetadata], e:
Exception) {
                }
            })
          }

      catch {
        case ex: Exception => {
          //TODO : Log Exception Here
        }
      } finally try
        demoKafkaConsumer.commitSync()
      finally demoKafkaConsumer.close()
    }
  }
```

Rebalance listeners

We discussed earlier that in case of addition or removal of consumer to the consumer group, Kafka triggers the rebalancer and consumer loses the ownership of the current partition. This may lead to duplicate processing when the partition is reassigned to consumer. There are some other operations such as database connection operation, file operation, or caching operations that may be part of consumer; you may want to deal with this before ownership of the partition is lost.

Kafka provides you with an API to handle such scenarios. It provides the `ConsumerRebalanceListener` interface that contains the `onPartitionsRevoked()` and `onPartitionsAssigned()` methods. We can implement these two methods and pass an object while subscribing to the topic using the `subscribe` method discussed earlier:

```
import org.apache.kafka.clients.consumer.ConsumerRebalanceListener;
import org.apache.kafka.common.TopicPartition;

import java.util.Collection;

public class DemoRebalancer implements ConsumerRebalanceListener {
    @Override
    public void onPartitionsRevoked(Collection<TopicPartition> collection)
```

```
{
        //TODO: Things to Do before your partition got revoked
    }

    @Override
    public void onPartitionsAssigned(Collection<TopicPartition> collection)
{
        //TODO : Things to do when  new partition get assigned
    }
}
```

Common message consuming patterns

Here are a few of the common message consuming patterns:

- **Consumer group - continuous data processing**: In this pattern, once consumer is created and subscribes to a topic, it starts receiving messages from the current offset. The consumer commits the latest offsets based on the count of messages received in a batch at a regular, configured interval. The consumer checks whether it's time to commit, and if it is, it will commit the offsets. Offset commit can happen synchronously or asynchronously. It uses the auto-commit feature of the consumer API.

  The key point to understand in this pattern is that consumer is not controlling the message flows. It is driven by the current offset of the partition in a consumer group. It receives messages from that current offset and commits the offsets as and when messages are received by it after regular intervals. The main advantage of this pattern is that you have a complete consumer application running with far less code, and as this kind of pattern mostly depends on the existing consumer APIs, it is less buggy.

The following image represents the continuous data processing pattern:

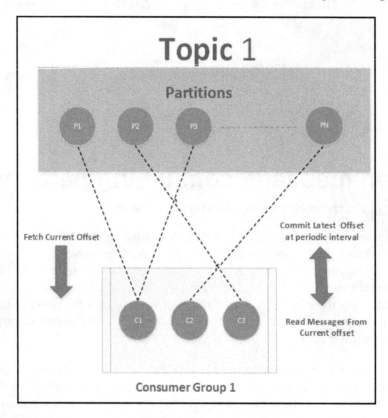

Consumer group - continuous data processing

- **Consumer group - discrete data processing**: Sometimes you want more control over consuming messages from Kafka. You want to read specific offsets of messages that may or may not be the latest current offset of the particular partition. Subsequently, you may want to commit specific offsets and not the regular latest offsets. This pattern outlines such a type of discrete data processing. In this, consumers fetch data based on the offset provided by them and they commit specific offsets that are as per their specific application requirements.

  Commit can happen synchronously or asynchronously. The consumer API allows you to call `commitSync()` and `commitAsync()` and pass a map of partitions and offsets that you wish to commit.

This pattern can be used in a variety of ways. For example, to go back a few messages or skip ahead a few messages (perhaps a time-sensitive application that is falling behind will want to skip ahead to more relevant messages), but the most exciting use case for this ability is when offsets are stored in a system other than Kafka.

Think about this common scenario - your application is reading events from Kafka (perhaps a clickstream of users in a website), processes the data (perhaps clean up clicks by robots and add session information), and then stores the results in a database, NoSQL store, or Hadoop. Suppose that we really don't want to lose any data nor do we want to store the same results in the database twice. The following image shows the discrete data processing pattern:

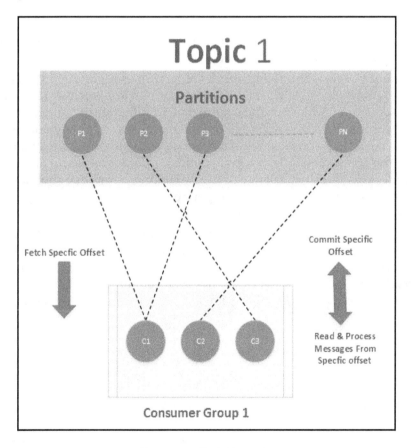

Consumer group - discrete data processing

Best practices

After going through the chapter, it is important to note a few of the best practices. They are listed as follows:

- **Exception handling**: Just like producers, it is the sole responsibility of consumer programs to decide on program flows with respect to exceptions. A consumer application should define different exception classes and, as per your business requirements, decide on the actions that need to be taken.

- **Handling rebalances**: Whenever any new consumer joins consumer groups or any old consumer shuts down, a partition rebalance is triggered. Whenever a consumer is losing its partition ownership, it is imperative that they should commit the offsets of the last event that they have received from Kafka. For example, they should process and commit any in-memory buffered datasets before losing the ownership of a partition. Similarly, they should close any open file handles and database connection objects.

- **Commit offsets at the right time**: If you are choosing to commit offset for messages, you need to do it at the right time. An application processing a batch of messages from Kafka may take more time to complete the processing of an entire batch; this is not a rule of thumb but if the processing time is more than a minute, try to commit the offset at regular intervals to avoid duplicate data processing in case the application fails. For more critical applications where processing duplicate data can cause huge costs, the commit offset time should be as short as possible if throughput is not an important factor.

- **Automatic offset commits:** Choosing an auto-commit is also an option to go with where we do not care about processing duplicate records or want consumer to take care of the offset commit automatically. For example, the auto-commit interval is 10 seconds and at the seventh second, consumer fails. In this case, the offset for those seven seconds has not been committed and the next time the consumer recovers from failure, it will again process those seven seconds records.

Keeping the auto-commit interval low will always result in avoiding less processing of duplicate messages.

- In the *Committing and polling* section, a call to the poll function will always commit the last offset of the previous poll. In such cases, you must ensure that all the messages from the previous poll have been successfully processed, otherwise you may lose records if the consumer application fails after a new previous poll last offset commit and before all the messages from the previous poll call are processed. So always make sure that the new call to polling only happens when all the data from the previous poll call is finished.

Summary

This concludes our section on Kafka consumers. This chapter addresses one of the key functionalities of Kafka message flows. The major focus was on understanding consumer internal working and how the number of consumers in the same group and number of topic partitions can be utilized to increase throughput and latency. We have also covered how to create consumers using consumer APIs and how to handle message offsets in case consumer fails.

We started with Kafka consumer APIs and also covered synchronous and asynchronous consumers and their advantages and disadvantages. We explained how to increase the throughput of a consumer application. We then went through the consumer rebalancer concept and when it gets triggered and how we can create our own rebalancer. We also focused on different consumer patterns that are used in different consumer applications. We focused on when to use it and how to use it.

In the end, we wanted to bring in some of the best practices of using Kafka consumers. These best practices will help you in scalable designs and in avoiding some common pitfalls. Hopefully, by the end of this chapter, you have mastered the art of designing and coding Kafka consumers.

In the next chapter, we will go through an introduction to Spark and Spark streaming, and then we will look at how Kafka can be used with Spark for a real-time use case and the different ways to integrate Spark with Kafka.

5
Building Spark Streaming Applications with Kafka

We have gone through all the components of Apache Kafka and different APIs that can be used to develop an application which can use Kafka. In the previous chapter, we learned about Kafka producer, brokers, and Kafka consumers, and different concepts related to best practices for using Kafka as a messaging system.

In this chapter, we will cover Apache Spark, which is distributed in memory processing engines and then we will walk through Spark Streaming concepts and how we can integrate Apache Kafka with Spark.

In short, we will cover the following topics:

- Introduction to Spark
- Internals of Spark such as RDD
- Spark Streaming
- Receiver-based approach (Spark-Kafka integration)
- Direct approach (Spark-Kafka integration)
- Use case (Log processing)

Introduction to Spark

Apache Spark is distributed in-memory data processing system. It provides rich set of API in Java, Scala, and Python. Spark API can be used to develop applications which can do batch and real-time data processing and analytics, machine learning, and graph processing of huge volumes of data on a single clustering platform.

 Spark development was started in 2009 by a team at Berkeley's AMPLab for improving the performance of MapReduce framework.

MapReduce is another distributed batch processing framework developed by Yahoo in context to Google research paper.

What they found was that an application which involves an iterative approach to solving certain problems can be improvised by reducing disk I/O. Spark allows us to cache a large set of data in memory and applications which uses iterative approach of transformation can use benefit of caching to improve performance. However, the iterative approach is just a small example of what Spark provides; there are a lot of features in the current version which can help you solve complex problems easily.

Spark architecture

Like Hadoop, Spark also follows the master/slave architecture, master daemons called **Spark drivers**, and multiple slave daemons called **executors**. Spark runs on a cluster and uses cluster resource managers such as YARN, Mesos, or Spark Standalone cluster manager.

Let's walk through each component:

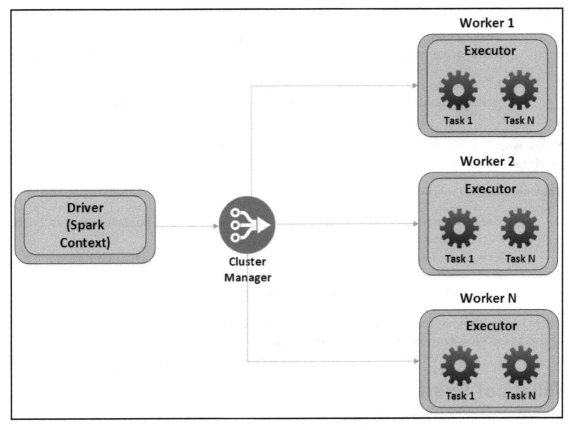

Spark architecture

Spark driver is master in the Spark architecture. It is the entry point of Spark application.

Spark driver is responsible for the following tasks:

- **Spark Context**: Spark Context is created in Spark driver. The Context object is also responsible for initializing application configuration.

- **DAG creation**: Spark driver is also responsible for creating lineage based on RDD operations and submitting that to DAG scheduler. Lineage is **direct acyclic graph (DAG)**. This graph is now submitted to DAG scheduler.

- **Stage Creation**: DAG Scheduler in a driver is responsible for creating stages of tasks based on a lineage graph.

- **Task Schedule and Execution**: Once the stage of tasks is created, task scheduler in the driver schedule this task using cluster manager and control its execution.

- **RDD metadata**: Driver maintains metadata of RDD and their partition. In case of partition failure, Spark can easily recompute the partition or RDD.

Spark workers: Spark workers are responsible for managing executors running on its own machine and making communication with master node.

They are listed as follows:

- **Backend process**: Each worker node contains one or more backend process. Each backend process is responsible for launching the executor.
- **Executors**: Each executor consists of a thread pool where each thread is responsible for executing tasks in parallel. Executors are responsible for reading, processing, and writing data to a target location or file.

There is a lot more to the internals of the Spark architecture but they are beyond the scope of this book. However, we are going to give a basic overview of Spark.

Pillars of Spark

The following are the important pillars of Spark:

Resilient Distributed Dataset (**RDD**): RDD is the backbone of Spark. RDD is an immutable, distributed, fault tolerant collection of objects. RDDs are divided into logical partitions which are computed on different worker machines.

In short, if you read any file in Spark, the data of that file will together form a single, large RDD. Any filtering operation on this RDD will produce a new RDD. Remember, RDD is immutable. This means that every time we modify the RDD, we have a new RDD. This RDD is divided into logical chunks known as partitions, which is a unit of parallelism in Spark. Each chunk or partition is processed on a separate distributed machine.

The following diagram will give you a better idea about partitioning:

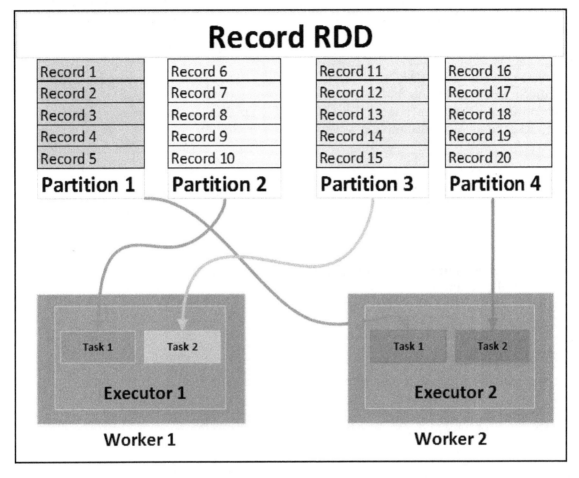

RDD partitions

There are two types of operations performed on RDD:

- **Transformation**: Transformation on RDD produces another RDD. Transformation means applying some filtering or modifying the existing RDD. This produces another RDD.

- **Action**: An action operation is responsible for the execution trigger to Spark. Spark lazily evaluates RDD, which means unless Spark encounters an action, it does not start execution. Action refers to storing the result in a file, dumping the result to the console, and so on.

Directed acyclic graph (DAG): As discussed earlier, RDD can be transformed and this results in a new RDD, and this process can go too deep until we execute some action on it. Whenever an action is encountered, Spark creates a DAG and then submits it to Scheduler. Let's take the following example of a word count in Spark:

```
val conf = new SparkConf().setAppName("wordCount")
val sc = new SparkContext(conf)
val input = sc.textFile(inputFile)
val words = input.flatMap(line => line.split(" "))
val word_counts = words.map(word => (word, 1)).reduceByKey{case (x, y) => x
+ y}
word_counts.saveAsTextFile(outputFile)
```

Once DAG is submitted, DAG scheduler creates stages of tasks based on operators. Task scheduler then launches this task with the help of cluster manager and worker nodes execute it.

The Spark ecosystem

As discussed previously, Spark can be used for various purposes, such as real-time processing, machine learning, graph processing, and so on. Spark consists of different independent components which can be used depending on use cases. The following figures give a brief idea about Spark's ecosystem:

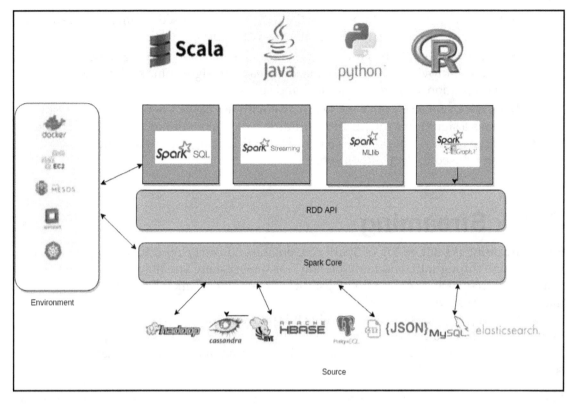

Spark ecosystem

- **Spark core**: Spark core is the base and generalized layer in Spark ecosystem. It contains basic and common functionality which can be used by all the layers preceding it. This means that any performance improvement on the core is automatically applied to all the components preceding it. RDD, which is main abstraction of Spark, is also part of core layer. It also contains API which can be used to manipulate RDDs.

    Other common functional components such as task scheduler, memory management, fault tolerance, and the storage interaction layer are also part of Spark core.

- **Spark Streaming**: Spark Streaming can be used for processing the real-time streaming data. We will be using this while discussing integration of Spark with Kafka. Spark Streaming is not real-time but its near real-time as it processes data in micro batches.

- **Spark SQL**: Spark SQL provides the API that can be used to run SQL like queries on a structured RDD, like JSONRDD and CSVRDD.
- **Spark MLlib**: MLlib is used to create scalable machine learning solutions over Spark. It provides a rich set of machine learning algorithms such as regressing, classification, clustering, filtering, and so on.
- **Spark GraphX**: GraphX is used to deal with use cases where graph processing plays a significant role, such as building a recommendation engine for complex social networks. It provides a rich set of efficient algorithms and their API which can be used to deal with graphs.

Spark Streaming

Spark Streaming is built on top of Spark core engine and can be used to develop a fast, scalable, high throughput, and fault tolerant real-time system. Streaming data can come from any source, such as production logs, click-stream data, Kafka, Kinesis, Flume, and many other data serving systems.

Spark streaming provides an API to receive this data and apply complex algorithms on top of it to get business value out of this data. Finally, the processed data can be put into any storage system. We will talk more about Spark Streaming integration with Kafka in this section.

Basically, we have two approaches to integrate Kafka with Spark and we will go into detail on each:

- Receiver-based approach
- Direct approach

The receiver-based approach is the older way of doing integration. Direct API integration provides lots of advantages over the receiver-based approach.

Receiver-based integration

Spark uses Kafka high level consumer API to implement receiver. This is an old approach and data received from Kafka topic partitions are stored in Spark executors and processes by streaming jobs. However, Spark receiver replicates the message across all the executors, so that if one executor fails, another executor should be able to provide replicated data for processing. In this way, Spark receiver provides fault tolerance for data.

The following diagram will give you a good idea about the receiver-based integration:

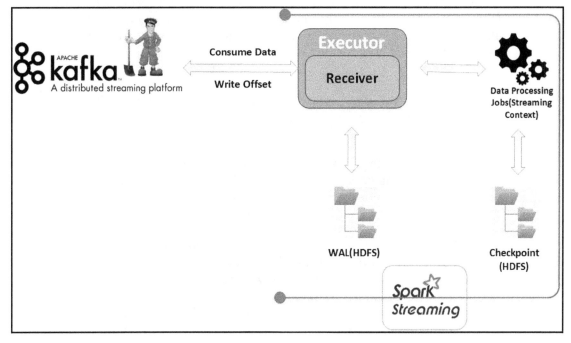

Spark receiver based approach

Spark receivers only acknowledge to broker when message is successfully replicated into executors otherwise it will not commit offset of messages to Zookeeper and message will be treated as unread. This seems to handle guaranteed processing but there are still some cases where it won't.

What would happen if Spark driver fails? When Spark driver fails, it also kills all the executors, which causes data to be lost which was available on executor. What if Spark receiver has already sent acknowledgment for those messages and has successfully committed offset to Zookeeper? You lose those records because you don't know how many of them have been processed and how many of them have not.

To avoid such problems, we can use a few techniques. Let's discuss them:

- **Write-ahead Log (WAL)**: We have discussed data loss scenarios when a driver fails. To avoid data loss, Spark introduced write-ahead logs in version 1.2, which allows you to save buffered data into a storage system, such as HDFS or S3. Once driver is recovered and executors are up, it can simply read data from WAL and process it.

  However, we need to explicitly enable the write-ahead log while executing the Spark streaming application and write the logic for processing the data available in WAL.

- **Exactly one Processing**: WAL may guarantee you no data loss but there can be duplicate processing of data by Spark jobs. WAL does not guarantee exactly one processing; in other words, it does not ensure avoiding duplicate processing of data.

  Let's take a scenario. Spark reads data from Kafka stores into executor buffer, replicates it to another executor for fault tolerance. Once the replication is done, it writes the same message to a write-ahead log and before sending acknowledgment back to Kafka driver it fails. Now when the driver recovers from failure, it will first process the data available in WAL and then will start consuming the messages from Kafka which will also replay all the messages which have not been acknowledged by Spark receiver but have been written to WAL and it leads to duplicate processing of message.

- **Checkpoint**: Spark also provides a way to put checkpoints in a streaming application. Checkpoint stores the information about what has been executed, what is still in the queue to be executed, configuration of application, and so on.

 Enabling checkpoints helps in providing an application's important metadata information which can be useful when driver recovers from failure to know what it has to process and what it has to with processed data. Checkpoint data is again stored into persistent systems, such as HDFS.

Disadvantages of receiver-based approach

The following are a few disadvantages of the receiver-based approach:

- **Throughput**: Enabling write-ahead log and checkpoint may cause you less throughput because time may be consumed in writing data to HDFS. It's obvious to have low throughput when there is lot of disk I/O involved.
- **Storage**: We store one set of data in Spark executor buffer and another set of the same data in write-ahead log HDFS. We are using two stores to store the same data and storage needs may vary, based on application requirements.
- **Data Loss**: If a write-ahead log is not enabled, there is a huge possibility of losing data and it may be very critical for some important applications.

Java example for receiver-based integration

Let us take an example to be sure:

```java
import org.apache.Spark.SparkConf;
import org.apache.Spark.api.java.function.FlatMapFunction;
import org.apache.Spark.api.java.function.Function;
import org.apache.Spark.api.java.function.Function2;
import org.apache.Spark.api.java.function.PairFunction;
import org.apache.Spark.streaming.Duration;
import org.apache.Spark.streaming.api.java.JavaDStream;
import org.apache.Spark.streaming.api.java.JavaPairDStream;
import org.apache.Spark.streaming.api.java.JavaPairReceiverInputDStream;
import org.apache.Spark.streaming.api.java.JavaStreamingContext;
import org.apache.Spark.streaming.kafka.KafkaUtils;
import scala.Tuple2;

import java.util.Arrays;
import java.util.HashMap;
import java.util.Iterator;
import java.util.Map;
import java.util.regex.Pattern;


public class KafkaWordCountJava {
    private static final Pattern WORD_DELIMETER = Pattern.compile(" ");
    public static void main(String[] args) throws Exception {
        String zkQuorum = "localhost:2181";
        String groupName = "stream";
        int numThreads = 3;
        String topicsName = "test";
        SparkConf SparkConf = new
SparkConf().setAppName("WordCountKafkaStream");

        JavaStreamingContext javaStreamingContext = new
JavaStreamingContext(SparkConf, new Duration(5000));
```

```
        Map<String, Integer> topicToBeUsedBySpark = new HashMap<>();
        String[] topics = topicsName.split(",");
        for (String topic : topics) {
            topicToBeUsedBySpark.put(topic, numThreads);
        }

        JavaPairReceiverInputDStream<String, String> streamMessages =
                KafkaUtils.createStream(javaStreamingContext, zkQuorum,
groupName, topicToBeUsedBySpark);

        JavaDStream<String> lines = streamMessages.map(new
Function<Tuple2<String, String>, String>() {
            @Override
            public String call(Tuple2<String, String> tuple2) {
                return tuple2._2();
            }
        });

        JavaDStream<String> words = lines.flatMap(new
FlatMapFunction<String, String>() {
            @Override
            public Iterator<String> call(String x) {
                return Arrays.asList(WORD_DELIMETER.split(x)).iterator();
            }
        });

        JavaPairDStream<String, Integer> wordCounts = words.mapToPair(
                new PairFunction<String, String, Integer>() {
                    @Override
                    public Tuple2<String, Integer> call(String s) {
                        return new Tuple2<>(s, 1);
                    }
                }).reduceByKey(new Function2<Integer, Integer, Integer>() {
            @Override
            public Integer call(Integer i1, Integer i2) {
                return i1 + i2;
            }
        });

        wordCounts.print();
        javaStreamingContext.start();
        javaStreamingContext.awaitTermination();
    }
}
```

Scala example for receiver-based integration

Here is an example on Scala:

```scala
import org.apache.Spark.SparkConf
import org.apache.Spark.streaming.{Minutes, Seconds, StreamingContext}
import org.apache.Spark.streaming.kafka._

object KafkaWordCount {
  def main(args: Array[String]) {
    val zkQuorum:String="localhost:2181"
    val group:String="stream"
    val numThreads:String="3"
    val topics:String="test"

    val SparkConf = new SparkConf().setAppName("KafkaWordCount")
    val ssc = new StreamingContext(SparkConf, Seconds(2))
    ssc.checkpoint("WALCheckpoint")
    val topicMap = topics.split(",").map((_, numThreads.toInt)).toMap
    val lines = KafkaUtils.createStream(ssc, zkQuorum, group,
topicMap).map(_._2)
    val words = lines.flatMap(_.split(" "))
    val wordCounts = words.map(x => (x, 1L))
      .reduceByKeyAndWindow(_ + _, _ - _, Minutes(10), Seconds(2), 2)
    wordCounts.print()

    ssc.start()
    ssc.awaitTermination()
  }
}
```

Direct approach

In receiver-based approach, we saw issues of data loss, costing less throughput using write-ahead logs and difficulty in achieving exactly one semantic of data processing. To overcome all these problems, Spark introduced the direct stream approach of integrating Spark with Kafka.

Spark periodically queries messages from Kafka with a range of offsets, which in short we call **batch**. Spark uses a low level consumer API and fetches messages directly from Kafka with a defined range of offsets. Parallelism is defined by a partition in Kafka and the Spark direct approach takes advantage of partitions.

The following illustration gives a little detail about parallelism:

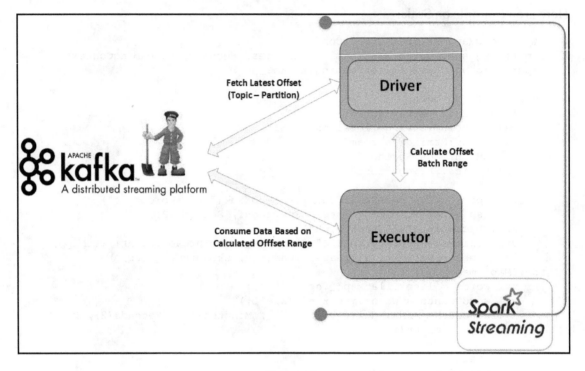

Direct approach

Let's look at a few features of the direct approach:

- **Parallelism and throughput**: The number of partitions in RDD is defined by the number of partitions in a Kafka topic. These RDD partitions read messages from Kafka topic partitions in parallel. In short, Spark Streaming creates RDD partition equal to the number of Kafka partitions available to consume data in parallel which increases throughput.
- **No write-ahead log**: Direct approach does not use write-ahead log to avoid data loss. Write-ahead log was causing extra storage and possibility of leading to duplicate data processing in few cases. Direct approach, instead, reads data directly from Kafka and commits the offset of processed messages to checkpoint. In case of failure, Spark knows where to start.

- **No Zookeeper**: By default, direct approach does not use Zookeeper for committing offset consumed by Spark. Spark uses a checkpoint mechanism to deal with data loss and to start execution from the last execution point in case of failure. However, Zookeeper based offset commit can be done using Curator Client.
- **Exactly one processing**: Direct approach provides opportunity to achieve exactly one processing, which means that no data is processed twice and no data is lost. This is done using checkpoint maintained by Spark Streaming application which tells Spark Streaming application about where to start in case of failure.

Java example for direct approach

Again, let us take a Java example:

```
import java.util.HashMap;
import java.util.HashSet;
import java.util.Arrays;
import java.util.Map;
import java.util.Set;
import java.util.regex.Pattern;

import scala.Tuple2;

import kafka.serializer.StringDecoder;

import org.apache.Spark.SparkConf;
import org.apache.Spark.streaming.api.java.*;
import org.apache.Spark.streaming.kafka.KafkaUtils;
import org.apache.Spark.streaming.Durations;

public class JavaDirectKafkaWordCount {
    private static final Pattern SPACE = Pattern.compile(" ");

    public static void main(String[] args) throws Exception {

        String brokers = "localhost:9092";
        String topics = "test";

        SparkConf SparkConf = new
SparkConf().setAppName("DirectKafkaWordCount");
        JavaStreamingContext javaStreamingContext = new
JavaStreamingContext(SparkConf, Durations.seconds(2));

        Set<String> topicsSet = new
HashSet<>(Arrays.asList(topics.split(",")));
```

```
        Map<String, String> kafkaConfiguration = new HashMap<>();
        kafkaConfiguration.put("metadata.broker.list", brokers);

        JavaPairInputDStream<String, String> messages =
KafkaUtils.createDirectStream(
                javaStreamingContext,
                String.class,
                String.class,
                StringDecoder.class,
                StringDecoder.class,
                kafkaConfiguration,
                topicsSet
        );

        JavaDStream<String> lines = messages.map(Tuple2::_2);

        JavaDStream<String> words = lines.flatMap(x ->
Arrays.asList(SPACE.split(x)).iterator());

        JavaPairDStream<String, Integer> wordCounts = words.mapToPair(s ->
new Tuple2<>(s, 1))
                .reduceByKey((i1, i2) -> i1 + i2);

        wordCounts.print();

        javaStreamingContext.start();
        javaStreamingContext.awaitTermination();
    }
}
```

Scala example for direct approach

Here is the Scala example for direct approach:

```
import kafka.serializer.StringDecoder
import org.apache.Spark.SparkConf
import org.apache.Spark.streaming.kafka.KafkaUtils
import org.apache.Spark.streaming.{Seconds, StreamingContext}

object DirectKafkaWordCount {
  def main(args: Array[String]) {

    val brokers: String = "localhost:2181"
    val topics: String = "test"

    val SparkConf = new SparkConf().setAppName("DirectKafkaWordCount")
```

```
    val ssc = new StreamingContext(SparkConf, Seconds(2))
    val topicsSet = topics.split(",").toSet
    val kafkaParams = Map[String, String]("metadata.broker.list" ->
brokers)
    val messages = KafkaUtils.createDirectStream[String, String,
StringDecoder, StringDecoder](
      ssc, kafkaParams, topicsSet)

    val lines = messages.map(_._2)
    val words = lines.flatMap(_.split(" "))
    val wordCounts = words.map(x => (x, 1L)).reduceByKey(_ + _)
    wordCounts.print()

    ssc.start()
    ssc.awaitTermination()
  }
}
```

Use case log processing - fraud IP detection

This section will cover a small use case which uses Kafka and Spark Streaming to detect a fraud IP, and the number of times the IP tried to hit the server. We will cover the use case in the following:

- **Producer**: We will use Kafka Producer API, which will read a log file and publish records to Kafka topic. However, in a real case, we may use Flume or producer application, which directly takes a log record on a real-time basis and publish to Kafka topic.
- **Fraud IPs list**: We will maintain a list of predefined fraud IP range which can be used to identify fraud IPs. For this application we are using in memory IP list which can be replaced by fast key based lookup, such as HBase.
- **Spark Streaming**: Spark Streaming application will read records from Kafka topic and will detect IPs and domains which are suspicious.

Maven

Maven is a build and project management tool and we will be building this project using Maven. I recommend using Eclipse or IntelliJ for creating projects. Add the following dependencies and plugins to your pom.xml:

```
<?xml version="1.0" encoding="UTF-8"?>
<project xmlns="http://Maven.apache.org/POM/4.0.0"
```

```
          xmlns:xsi="http://www.w3.org/2001/XMLSchema-instance"
          xsi:schemaLocation="http://Maven.apache.org/POM/4.0.0
http://Maven.apache.org/xsd/Maven-4.0.0.xsd">
     <modelVersion>4.0.0</modelVersion>

     <groupId>com.packt</groupId>
     <artifactId>ip-fraud-detetion</artifactId>
     <version>1.0-SNAPSHOT</version>
     <packaging>jar</packaging>

     <name>kafka-producer</name>

     <properties>
         <project.build.sourceEncoding>UTF-8</project.build.sourceEncoding>
     </properties>


     <dependencies>
         <!--
https://mvnrepository.com/artifact/org.apache.Spark/Spark-streaming-kafka_2
.10 -->
         <dependency>
             <groupId>org.apache.Spark</groupId>
             <artifactId>Spark-streaming-kafka_2.10</artifactId>
             <version>1.6.3</version>
         </dependency>


         <!--
https://mvnrepository.com/artifact/org.apache.hadoop/hadoop-common -->
         <dependency>
             <groupId>org.apache.hadoop</groupId>
             <artifactId>hadoop-common</artifactId>
             <version>2.7.2</version>
         </dependency>

         <!--
https://mvnrepository.com/artifact/org.apache.Spark/Spark-core_2.10 -->
         <dependency>
             <groupId>org.apache.Spark</groupId>
             <artifactId>Spark-core_2.10</artifactId>
             <version>2.0.0</version>
             <scope>provided</scope>

         </dependency>
         <!--
https://mvnrepository.com/artifact/org.apache.Spark/Spark-streaming_2.10 -
-->
```

```xml
        <dependency>
            <groupId>org.apache.Spark</groupId>
            <artifactId>Spark-streaming_2.10</artifactId>
            <version>2.0.0</version>
            <scope>provided</scope>

        </dependency>


        <dependency>
            <groupId>org.apache.kafka</groupId>
            <artifactId>kafka_2.11</artifactId>
            <version>0.10.0.0</version>
        </dependency>
    </dependencies>

    <build>
        <plugins>
            <plugin>
                <groupId>org.apache.Maven.plugins</groupId>
                <artifactId>Maven-shade-plugin</artifactId>
                <version>2.4.2</version>
                <executions>
                    <execution>
                        <phase>package</phase>
                        <goals>
                            <goal>shade</goal>
                        </goals>
                        <configuration>
                            <filters>
                                <filter>
                                    <artifact>junit:junit</artifact>
                                    <includes>
<include>junit/framework/**</include>
                                        <include>org/junit/**</include>
                                    </includes>
                                    <excludes>
<exclude>org/junit/experimental/**</exclude>
<exclude>org/junit/runners/**</exclude>
                                    </excludes>
                                </filter>
                                <filter>
                                    <artifact>*:*</artifact>
                                    <excludes>
                                        <exclude>META-INF/*.SF</exclude>
                                        <exclude>META-INF/*.DSA</exclude>
                                        <exclude>META-INF/*.RSA</exclude>
                                    </excludes>
```

```xml
                        </filter>
                    </filters>
                    <transformers>
                        <transformer
implementation="org.apache.Maven.plugins.shade.resource.ServicesResourceTra
nsformer"/>

                        <transformer
implementation="org.apache.Maven.plugins.shade.resource.ManifestResourceTra
nsformer">
<mainClass>com.packt.streaming.FraudDetectionApp</mainClass>
                        </transformer>
                    </transformers>
                </configuration>
            </execution>
        </executions>
    </plugin>
    <plugin>
        <groupId>org.codehaus.mojo</groupId>
        <artifactId>exec-Maven-plugin</artifactId>
        <version>1.2.1</version>
        <executions>
            <execution>
                <goals>
                    <goal>exec</goal>
                </goals>
            </execution>
        </executions>
        <configuration>
<includeProjectDependencies>true</includeProjectDependencies>
<includePluginDependencies>false</includePluginDependencies>
                <executable>java</executable>
                <classpathScope>compile</classpathScope>
<mainClass>com.packt.streaming.FraudDetectionApp</mainClass>
        </configuration>
    </plugin>


    <plugin>
        <groupId>org.apache.Maven.plugins</groupId>
        <artifactId>Maven-compiler-plugin</artifactId>
        <configuration>
            <source>1.8</source>
            <target>1.8</target>
        </configuration>
    </plugin>
</plugins>
</build>
```

```
</project>
```

Producer

You can use IntelliJ or Eclipse to build a producer application. This producer reads a log file taken from an Apache project which contains detailed records like:

```
64.242.88.10 - - [08/Mar/2004:07:54:30 -0800] "GET
/twiki/bin/edit/Main/Unknown_local_recipient_reject_code?topicparent=Main.C
onfigurationVariables HTTP/1.1" 401 12846
```

You can have just one record in the test file and the producer will produce records by generating random IPs and replace it with existing. So, we will have millions of distinct records with unique IP addresses.

Record columns are separated by space delimiters, which we change to commas in producer. The first column represents the IP address or the domain name which will be used to detect whether the request was from a fraud client. The following is the Java Kafka producer which remembers logs.

Property reader

We preferred to use a property file for some important values such as topic, Kafka broker URL, and so on. If you want to read more values from the property file, then feel free to change it in the code.
`streaming.properties` file:

```
topic=ipTest2
broker.list=10.200.99.197:6667
appname=IpFraud
group.id=Stream
```

The following is an example of the property reader:

```
import java.io.FileNotFoundException;
import java.io.IOException;
import java.io.InputStream;
import java.util.Properties;

public class PropertyReader {

    private Properties prop = null;
```

```
    public PropertyReader() {

        InputStream is = null;
        try {
            this.prop = new Properties();
            is =
this.getClass().getResourceAsStream("/streaming.properties");
            prop.load(is);
        } catch (FileNotFoundException e) {
            e.printStackTrace();
        } catch (IOException e) {
            e.printStackTrace();
        }
    }

    public String getPropertyValue(String key) {
        return this.prop.getProperty(key);
    }
}
```

Producer code

A producer application is designed to be like a real-time log producer where the producer runs every three seconds and produces a new record with random IP addresses. You can add a few records in the IP_LOG.log file and then the producer will take care of producing millions of unique records from those three records.

We have also enabled auto creation of topics so you need not create topic before running your producer application. You can change the topic name in the streaming.properties file mentioned before:

```
import com.packt.reader.PropertyReader;
import org.apache.kafka.clients.producer.KafkaProducer;
import org.apache.kafka.clients.producer.ProducerRecord;
import org.apache.kafka.clients.producer.RecordMetadata;

import java.io.BufferedReader;
import java.io.File;
import java.io.IOException;
import java.io.InputStreamReader;
import java.util.*;
import java.util.concurrent.Future;


public class IPLogProducer extends TimerTask {
    static String path = "";
```

```
    public BufferedReader readFile() {
        BufferedReader BufferedReader = new BufferedReader(new
InputStreamReader(
                this.getClass().getResourceAsStream("/IP_LOG.log")));
        return BufferedReader;


    }

    public static void main(final String[] args) {
        Timer timer = new Timer();
        timer.schedule(new IPLogProducer(), 3000, 3000);
    }

    private String getNewRecordWithRandomIP(String line) {
        Random r = new Random();
        String ip = r.nextInt(256) + "." + r.nextInt(256) + "." +
r.nextInt(256) + "." + r.nextInt(256);
        String[] columns = line.split(" ");
        columns[0] = ip;
        return Arrays.toString(columns);
    }

    @Override
    public void run() {
        PropertyReader propertyReader = new PropertyReader();

        Properties producerProps = new Properties();
        producerProps.put("bootstrap.servers",
propertyReader.getPropertyValue("broker.list"));
        producerProps.put("key.serializer",
"org.apache.kafka.common.serialization.StringSerializer");
        producerProps.put("value.serializer",
"org.apache.kafka.common.serialization.StringSerializer");
        producerProps.put("auto.create.topics.enable", "true");

        KafkaProducer<String, String> ipProducer = new
KafkaProducer<String, String>(producerProps);

        BufferedReader br = readFile();
        String oldLine = "";
        try {
            while ((oldLine = br.readLine()) != null) {
                String line =
getNewRecordWithRandomIP(oldLine).replace("[", "").replace("]", "");
                ProducerRecord ipData = new ProducerRecord<String,
String>(propertyReader.getPropertyValue("topic"), line);
                Future<RecordMetadata> recordMetadata =
ipProducer.send(ipData);
```

```
        }
    } catch (IOException e) {
        e.printStackTrace();
    }
    ipProducer.close();
    }
}
```

Fraud IP lookup

The following classes will help us as a lookup service which will help us to identify if request is coming from a fraud IP. We have used interface before implementing the class so that we can add more NoSQL databases or any fast lookup service. You can implement this service and add a lookup service by using HBase or any other fast key lookup service. We are using in-memory lookup and just added the fraud IP range in the cache. Add the following code to your project:

```
public interface IIPScanner {

    boolean isFraudIP(String ipAddresses);

}
```

CacheIPLookup is the implementation for the IIPSCanner interface which does in memory lookup:

```
import java.io.Serializable;
import java.util.HashSet;
import java.util.Set;


public class CacheIPLookup implements IIPScanner, Serializable {

    private Set<String> fraudIPList = new HashSet<>();

    public CacheIPLookup() {
        fraudIPList.add("212");
        fraudIPList.add("163");
        fraudIPList.add("15");
        fraudIPList.add("224");
        fraudIPList.add("126");
        fraudIPList.add("92");
        fraudIPList.add("91");
        fraudIPList.add("10");
        fraudIPList.add("112");
        fraudIPList.add("194");
```

```
            fraudIPList.add("198");
            fraudIPList.add("11");
            fraudIPList.add("12");
            fraudIPList.add("13");
            fraudIPList.add("14");
            fraudIPList.add("15");
            fraudIPList.add("16");
    }


    @Override
    public boolean isFraudIP(String ipAddresses) {

        return fraudIPList.contains(ipAddresses);
    }
}
```

Expose hive table

We will create hive table over base directory where a streaming record is getting pushed on HDFS. This will help us track the number of fraud records being generated over time:

```
hive> create database packt;

hive> create external table packt.teststream (iprecords STRING) LOCATION
'/user/packt/streaming/fraudips';
```

You can also expose hive tables on top of the incoming data which is being pushed to Kafka topic in order to track the percentage of IPs being detected as fraud from an overall record. Create one more table and add the following line to your streaming application explained later:

```
ipRecords.dstream().saveAsTextFiles("hdfs://localhost:8020/user/packt/strea
ming/iprecords", "");
```

Also, create the following table in hive:

```
create external table packt.iprecords(iprecords STRING) LOCATION
'/user/packt/streaming/iprecords';
```

Remember, we can also use SqlContext to push data to hive, but for this use case we made it very simple.

Streaming code

We haven't focused much on modularization in our code. The IP fraud detection application scans each record and filters those records which qualify as a the fraud record based on fraud IP lookup service. The lookup service can be changed to use any fast lookup database. We are using in memory lookup service for this application:

```java
import com.packt.reader.PropertyReader;
import org.apache.Spark.SparkConf;
import org.apache.Spark.api.java.function.Function;
import org.apache.Spark.streaming.api.java.JavaStreamingContext;
import java.util.Set;
import java.util.regex.Pattern;
import java.util.HashMap;
import java.util.HashSet;
import java.util.Arrays;
import java.util.Map;
import scala.Tuple2;
import kafka.serializer.StringDecoder;
import org.apache.Spark.streaming.api.java.*;
import org.apache.Spark.streaming.kafka.KafkaUtils;
import org.apache.Spark.streaming.Durations;

public class FraudDetectionApp {
    private static final Pattern SPACE = Pattern.compile(" ");

    private static void main(String[] args) throws Exception {
        PropertyReader propertyReader = new PropertyReader();
        CacheIPLookup cacheIPLookup = new CacheIPLookup();
        SparkConf SparkConf = new SparkConf().setAppName("IP_FRAUD");
        JavaStreamingContext javaStreamingContext = new
JavaStreamingContext(SparkConf, Durations.seconds(3));

        Set<String> topicsSet = new
HashSet<>(Arrays.asList(propertyReader.getPropertyValue("topic").split(",")
));
        Map<String, String> kafkaConfiguration = new HashMap<>();
        kafkaConfiguration.put("metadata.broker.list",
propertyReader.getPropertyValue("broker.list"));
        kafkaConfiguration.put("group.id",
propertyReader.getPropertyValue("group.id"));

        JavaPairInputDStream<String, String> messages =
KafkaUtils.createDirectStream(
                javaStreamingContext,
                String.class,
                String.class,
                StringDecoder.class,
```

```
                StringDecoder.class,
                kafkaConfiguration,
                topicsSet
        );
        JavaDStream<String> ipRecords = messages.map(Tuple2::_2);

        JavaDStream<String> fraudIPs = ipRecords.filter(new
Function<String, Boolean>() {
            @Override
            public Boolean call(String s) throws Exception {
                String IP = s.split(",")[0];
                String[] ranges = IP.split("\\.");
                String range = null;
                try {
                    range = ranges[0];
                } catch (ArrayIndexOutOfBoundsException ex) {

                }
                return cacheIPLookup.isFraudIP(range);

            }
        });

    fraudIPs.dstream().saveAsTextFiles("hdfs://localhost:8020/user/packt/stream
    ing/fraudips", "");

        javaStreamingContext.start();
        javaStreamingContext.awaitTermination();
    }
}
```

Run the application using the following command:

```
Spark-submit --class com.packt.streaming.FraudDetectionApp --master yarn
ip-fraud-detetion-1.0-SNAPSHOT-shaded.jar
```

Once the Spark Streaming application starts, run Kafka producer and check the records in respective hive tables.

Summary

In this chapter, we learned about Apache Spark, its architecture, and Spark ecosystem in brief. Our focus was on covering different ways we can integrate Kafka with Spark and their advantages and disadvantages. We also covered APIs for the receiver-based approach and direct approach. Finally, we covered a small use case about IP fraud detection through the log file and lookup service. You can now create your own Spark streaming application. In the next chapter, we will cover another real-time streaming application, Apache Heron (successor of Apache Storm). We will cover how Apache Heron is different from Apache Spark and when to use which one.

6

Building Storm Applications with Kafka

In the previous chapter, we learned about Apache Spark, a near real-time processing engine which can process data in micro batches. But when it comes to very low latency applications, where seconds of delay may cause big trouble, Spark may not be a good fit for you. You would need a framework which can handle millions of records per second and you would want to process record by record, instead of processing in batches, for lower latency. In this chapter, we will learn about the real-time processing engine, Apache Storm. Storm was first designed and developed by Twitter, which later became an open source Apache project.

In this chapter, we will learn about:

- Introduction to Apache Storm
- Apache Storm architecture
- Brief overview of Apache Heron
- Integrating Apache Storm with Apache Kafka (Java/Scala example)
- Use case (log processing)

Introduction to Apache Storm

Apache Storm is used to handle very sensitive applications where even a delay of 1 second can mean huge losses. There are many companies using Storm for fraud detection, building recommendation engines, triggering suspicious activity, and so on. Storm is stateless; it uses Zookeeper for coordinating purposes, where it maintains important metadata information.

 Apache Storm is a distributed real-time processing framework which has the ability to process a single event at a time with millions of records being processed per second per node. The streaming data can be bounded or unbounded; in both situations Storm has the capability to reliably process it.

Storm cluster architecture

Storm also follows the master-slave architecture pattern, where Nimbus is the master and Supervisors are the slaves:

- **Nimbus**: The master node of Storm cluster. All other nodes in the cluster are called worker nodes. Nimbus distributes data among the worker nodes and also assigns task to worker nodes. Nimbus also monitors for worker failure and if a worker fails, it reassigns a task to some other worker.
- **Supervisors**: Supervisors are responsible for completing tasks assigned by Nimbus and sending available resource information. Each worker node has exactly one supervisor and each worker node has one or more worker process and each supervisor manages multiple worker processes.

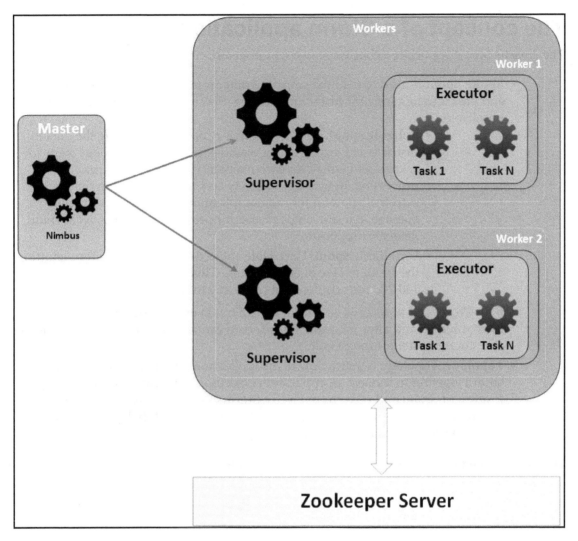

Storm architecture

Remember we said that Storm is stateless; both Nimbus and Supervisor save its state on Zookeeper. Whenever Nimbus receives a Storm application execution request, it asks for available resources from Zookeeper and then schedules the task on available supervisors. It also saves progress metadata to Zookeeper, so in case of failure, if Nimbus restarts, it knows where to start again.

The concept of a Storm application

The Apache Storm application consists of two components:

- **Spout**: Spout is used to read the stream of data from an external source system and pass it to topology for further processing. Spout can be either reliable or unreliable.

    - **Reliable spout**: Reliable spout is capable of replaying the data in case it failed during the processing. In such a case, spout waits for acknowledgement for each event it has emitted for further processing. Remember this may cost more processing time but is extremely helpful for those applications for which we cannot manage to lose a single record for processing, such as ATM fraud detection applications.

    - **Unreliable spout**: Unreliable spout does not care about re-emitting the spout in case of event failure. This can be useful where losing 100-200 records does not cause any loss.

- **Bolt**: Processing of records is done in bolts. Stream emitted by spout is received by Storm bolt, and after processing, the record can be stored in a database, file, or any storage system through bolt.

- **Topology:** Topology is entire flow of an application where spout and bolt are bound together to achieve an application objective. We create a Storm topology inside a program and then submit it to a Storm cluster. Unlike any batch job, Storm topology runs forever. If you want to stop a Storm topology, you need to handle it separately or kill it forcefully.

Here is a detailed image to help you better understand the different types of spouts:

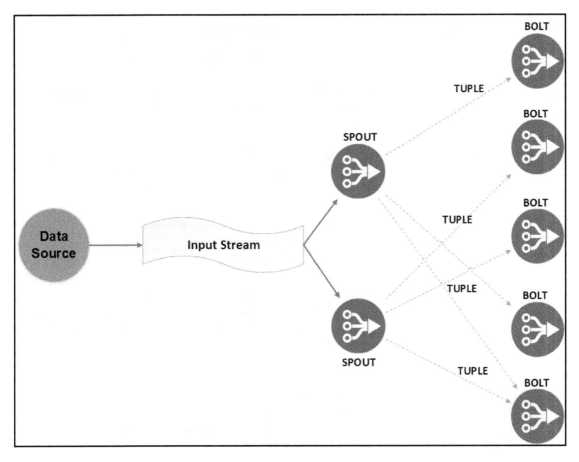

Storm topology architecture

One spout can emit data to multiple bolts at a time and can track for an acknowledgement for all bolts.

 Detailed explanation of the internals of Storm are beyond the scope of this book. You may refer to Apache Storm documentation at `http://Storm.apache.org`. Our focus will be on how we can leverage Apache Kafka with Apache Storm to build real-time processing application.

Introduction to Apache Heron

Apache Heron is the successor to Apache Storm with backward compatibility. Apache Heron
provides more power in terms of throughput, latency, and processing capability over Apache Storm as use cases in Twitter started increasing, they felt of having new stream processing engine because of the following Storm bottleneck:

- **Debugging**: Twitter faced challenges in debugging due to code errors, hardware failures, and so on. The root cause was very difficult to detect because of no clear mapping of logical unit of computation to physical processing.
- **Scale on Demand**: Storm requires dedicated cluster resources, which needs separate hardware resources to run Storm topology. This restricts Storm from using cluster resources efficiently and limits it to scale on demand. This also limits its ability to share cluster resources across different processing engines but not just Storm.
- **Cluster Manageability**: Running a new Storm topology requires manual isolation of machines. Also killing the topology requires decommissioning of machines allocated to that topology. Think about doing this in production environment. It will cost you more in terms of infrastructure cost, manageability cost, and productivity for users.

 Apache Heron is the successor of Apache Storm, with backward compatibility. Apache Heron provides more power in terms of throughput, latency, and processing capability over Apache Storm.

Keeping all these limitations as an preference, Twitter decided to build a new Stream processing engine, which could overcome these limitations and also run an old Storm production topology efficiently.

Heron architecture

The development of Heron started with Storm's compatibility. Heron also runs topology and all topologies is submitted to the scheduler known as **Aurora scheduler**. Aurora scheduler runs each topology as an Aurora job on multiple containers. Each job consists of multiple topology processes discussed in *Topology architecture* section.

Here is an illustration to help you understand better:

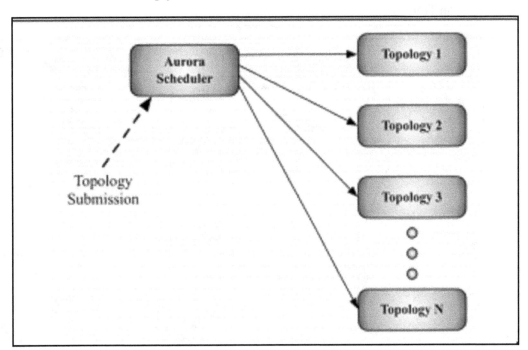

Heron architecture

Heron topology architecture

The Heron topology is similar to Storm topology, which consist of spout and bolt, where spout is responsible for reading the input from source and bolt is responsible for doing the actual processing.

The following core components of Heron topology are discussed in depth in the sections as follows:

- Topology Master
- Container
- Stream Manager
- Heron Instance

- Metrics Manager
- Heron Tracker

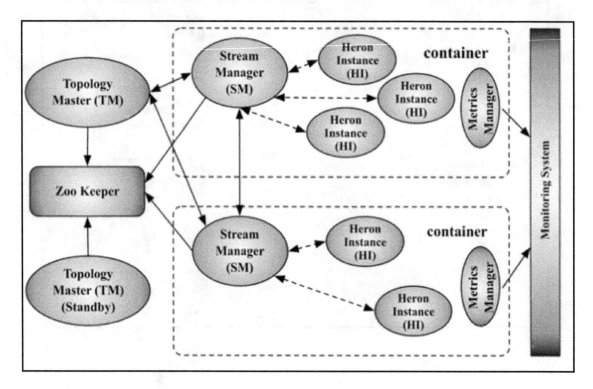

Heron topology architecture

The concepts are explained as follows:

- **Topology Master**: Similar to Application Master in YARN, Heron also creates multiple containers and creates a **Topology Master** (**TM**) on first container which manages end to end life cycle of topology. Topology Master also creates an entry in Zookeeper so that it's easily discoverable and no other Topology Master exists for the same topology.
- **Containers**: The concept of container is similar to that of YARN where one machine can have multiple containers running on their own JVM. Each container has single **Stream Manager** (**SM**), single Metric Manager, and multiple **Heron Instance** (**HI**). Each container communicates with TM to ensure correctness of topology.

- **Stream Manager**: The name itself indicates its functionality; it manages the routing of streams within the topology. All the Stream Managers are connected with each other to ensure back-pressure is handled efficiently. If it finds that any bolt is processing streams very slowly, it manages spout serving data to that bolt and cuts off input to bolt.
- **Heron Instance**: Each Heron Instance in a container is connected to Stream Manager, and they are responsible for running the actual spout and bolt of topology. It helps in making the debugging process very easy, as each Heron instance is a JVM process.
- **Metric Manager**: As discussed previously, each container contains one Metric Manager. Stream Manager and all Heron instances report their metrics to Metric Manager, which then sends these metrics to monitoring system. This makes monitoring of topology simple and saves lots of effort and development time.

Integrating Apache Kafka with Apache Storm - Java

As discussed previously, we are now familiar with the Storm topology concept and will now look into how we can integrate Apache Storm with Apache Kafka. Apache Kafka is most widely used with Apache Storm in production applications. Let us look into different APIs available for integration:

- **KafkaSpout**: Spout in Storm is responsible for consuming data from the source system and passing it to bolts for further processing. KafkaSpout is specially designed for consuming data from Kafka as a stream and then passing it to bolts for further processing. KafkaSpout accepts `SpoutConfig`, which contains information about Zookeeper, Kafka brokers, and topics to connect with.

  Look at the following code:

```
SpoutConfig spoutConfig = new SpoutConfig(hosts, inputTopic, "/" +
zkRootDir, consumerGroup);
spoutConfig.scheme = new SchemeAsMultiScheme(new StringScheme());
spoutConfig.forceFromStart = false;
spoutConfig.startOffsetTime = kafka.api.OffsetRequest.LatestTime();
```

- Spout acts as a Kafka consumer and therefore it needs to manage the offset of records somewhere. Spout uses Zookeeper to store the offset, and the last two parameters in `SpoutConfig` denote the Zookeeper root directory path and `ID` for this particular spout. The offset will be stored as shown next, where 0, 1 are the partition numbers:

```
zkRootDir/consumerID/0
zkRootDir/consumerID/1
zkRootDir/consumerID/2
```

- **SchemeAsMultiScheme**: It indicates how the ByteBuffer consumed from Kafka gets transformed into a Storm tuple. We have used the `StringScheme` implementation which will convert bytebuffer into string.

  Now the configuration is passed to `KafkaSpout` and the spout is set to topology:

```
KafkaSpout kafkaSpout = new KafkaSpout(spoutConfig);
```

We will now take a famous wordcount example and will run our Storm topology.

Example

We will be taking the famous wordcount example for Storm Kafka integration, where `KafkaSpout` will read input from kafka topic and it will be processed by split bolt and count bolt. Let's start with topology class.

Topology Class: The flow connection of spouts and bolts together forms a topology. In the following code, we have the `TopologyBuilder` class which allows us to set the connection flow:

```
TopologyBuilder topologyBuilder = new TopologyBuilder();
 topologyBuilder.setSpout("kafkaspout", new KafkaSpout(kafkaSpoutConfig));
 topologyBuilder.setBolt("stringsplit", new
StringToWordsSpliterBolt()).shuffleGrouping("kafkaspout");
 topologyBuilder.setBolt("counter", new
WordCountCalculatorBolt()).shuffleGrouping("stringsplit");
```

In the preceding code, we can see that spout is set to `KafkaSpout` and then `kafkaspout` is passed an input to string split bolt and splitbolt is passed to wordcount bolt. In this way, end to end topology pipeline gets created.

```
import org.apache.Storm.Config;
import org.apache.Storm.LocalCluster;
```

```
import org.apache.Storm.StormSubmitter;
import org.apache.Storm.kafka.*;
import org.apache.Storm.spout.SchemeAsMultiScheme;
import org.apache.Storm.topology.TopologyBuilder;

public class KafkaStormWordCountTopology {
    public static void main(String[] args) throws Exception {
        String zkConnString = "localhost:2181";
        String topic = "words";
        BrokerHosts hosts = new ZkHosts(zkConnString);

        SpoutConfig kafkaSpoutConfig = new SpoutConfig(hosts, topic, "/" +
topic,
                "wordcountID");
        kafkaSpoutConfig.startOffsetTime =
kafka.api.OffsetRequest.EarliestTime();
        kafkaSpoutConfig.scheme = new SchemeAsMultiScheme(new
StringScheme());

        TopologyBuilder topologyBuilder = new TopologyBuilder();
        topologyBuilder.setSpout("kafkaspout", new
KafkaSpout(kafkaSpoutConfig));
        topologyBuilder.setBolt("stringsplit", new
StringToWordsSpliterBolt()).shuffleGrouping("kafkaspout");
        topologyBuilder.setBolt("counter", new
WordCountCalculatorBolt()).shuffleGrouping("stringsplit");
        Config config = new Config();
        config.setDebug(true);
        if (args != null && args.length > 1) {
            config.setNumWorkers(3);
            StormSubmitter.submitTopology(args[1], config,
topologyBuilder.createTopology());
        } else {
            // Cap the maximum number of executors that can be spawned
            // for a component to 3
            config.setMaxTaskParallelism(3);
            // LocalCluster is used to run locally
            LocalCluster cluster = new LocalCluster();
            cluster.submitTopology("KafkaLocal", config,
topologyBuilder.createTopology());
            // sleep
            try {
                Thread.sleep(10000);
            } catch (InterruptedException e) {
                // TODO Auto-generated catch block
                cluster.killTopology("KafkaToplogy");
                cluster.shutdown();
            }
```

```
                    cluster.shutdown();
            }
        }
    }
```

String Split Bolt: This is responsible for splitting lines into words and then transferring it to the next bolt in the topology pipeline:

```
import org.apache.Storm.task.OutputCollector;
import org.apache.Storm.task.TopologyContext;
import org.apache.Storm.topology.IRichBolt;
import org.apache.Storm.topology.OutputFieldsDeclarer;
import org.apache.Storm.tuple.Fields;
import org.apache.Storm.tuple.Tuple;
import org.apache.Storm.tuple.Values;

import java.util.Map;

public class StringToWordsSpliterBolt implements IRichBolt {
    private OutputCollector collector;

    public void prepare(Map StormConf, TopologyContext context,
                        OutputCollector collector) {
        this.collector = collector;
    }

    public void execute(Tuple input) {
        String line = input.getString(0);
        String[] words = line.split(" ");

        for(String word: words) {
            if(!word.isEmpty()) {
                collector.emit(new Values(word));
            }

        }

        collector.ack(input);
    }

    public void declareOutputFields(OutputFieldsDeclarer declarer) {
        declarer.declare(new Fields("word"));
    }

    @Override
    public void cleanup() {}
```

```
@Override
public Map<String, Object> getComponentConfiguration() {
    return null;
}
```

Wordcount Calculator Bolt: It takes the input emitted by split bolt and then stores its count in Map, which finally gets dumped into console:

```
import org.apache.Storm.task.OutputCollector;
import org.apache.Storm.task.TopologyContext;
import org.apache.Storm.topology.IRichBolt;
import org.apache.Storm.topology.OutputFieldsDeclarer;
import org.apache.Storm.tuple.Tuple;
import java.util.HashMap;
import java.util.Map;

public class WordCountCalculatorBolt implements IRichBolt {
    Map<String, Integer> wordCountMap;
    private OutputCollector collector;


    public void prepare(Map StormConf, TopologyContext context,
                        OutputCollector collector) {
        this.wordCountMap = new HashMap<String, Integer>();
        this.collector = collector;
    }


    public void execute(Tuple input) {
        String str = input.getString(0);
        str = str.toLowerCase().trim();
        if (!wordCountMap.containsKey(str)) {
            wordCountMap.put(str, 1);
        } else {
            Integer c = wordCountMap.get(str) + 1;
            wordCountMap.put(str, c);
        }

        collector.ack(input);
    }


    public void cleanup() {
        for (Map.Entry<String, Integer> entry : wordCountMap.entrySet()) {
            System.out.println(entry.getKey() + " : " + entry.getValue());
        }
    }
}
```

```
    @Override
    public void declareOutputFields(OutputFieldsDeclarer declarer) {

    }

    @Override
    public Map<String, Object> getComponentConfiguration() {
        return null;
    }
}
```

Integrating Apache Kafka with Apache Storm - Scala

This section contains the Scala version of the wordcount program discussed previously.
Topology Class: Let us try the topology class with Scala:

```
import org.apache.Storm.Config
import org.apache.Storm.LocalCluster
import org.apache.Storm.StormSubmitter
import org.apache.Storm.kafka._
import org.apache.Storm.spout.SchemeAsMultiScheme
import org.apache.Storm.topology.TopologyBuilder

object KafkaStormWordCountTopology {

  def main(args: Array[String]): Unit = {
    val zkConnString: String = "localhost:2181"
    val topic: String = "words"
    val hosts: BrokerHosts = new ZkHosts(zkConnString)
    val kafkaSpoutConfig: SpoutConfig =
      new SpoutConfig(hosts, topic, "/" + topic, "wordcountID")
    kafkaSpoutConfig.startOffsetTime =
kafka.api.OffsetRequest.EarliestTime()
    kafkaSpoutConfig.scheme = new SchemeAsMultiScheme(new StringScheme())
    val topologyBuilder: TopologyBuilder = new TopologyBuilder()
    topologyBuilder.setSpout("kafkaspout", new
KafkaSpout(kafkaSpoutConfig))
    topologyBuilder
      .setBolt("stringsplit", new StringToWordsSpliterBolt())
      .shuffleGrouping("kafkaspout")
    topologyBuilder
      .setBolt("counter", new WordCountCalculatorBolt())
      .shuffleGrouping("stringsplit")
    val config: Config = new Config()
```

```
    config.setDebug(true)
    if (args != null && args.length > 1) {
      config.setNumWorkers(3)
      StormSubmitter.submitTopology(args(1),
                                config,
                                topologyBuilder.createTopology())
    } else {
// for a component to 3
        config.setMaxTaskParallelism(3)
// LocalCluster is used to run locally
        val cluster: LocalCluster = new LocalCluster()
        cluster.submitTopology("KafkaLocal",
                            config,
                            topologyBuilder.createTopology())
// sleep
        try Thread.sleep(10000)
        catch {
          case e: InterruptedException => {
            cluster.killTopology("KafkaToplogy")
            cluster.shutdown()
          }

        }
        cluster.shutdown()
    }
// Cap the maximum number of executors that can be spawned
// Cap the maximum number of executors that can be spawned
  }

}
```

String Split Bolt: The same String Split Bolt on Scala:

```
import org.apache.Storm.task.OutputCollector
import org.apache.Storm.task.TopologyContext
import org.apache.Storm.topology.IRichBolt
import org.apache.Storm.topology.OutputFieldsDeclarer
import org.apache.Storm.tuple.Fields
import org.apache.Storm.tuple.Tuple
import org.apache.Storm.tuple.Values
import java.util.Map


class StringToWordsSpliterBolt extends IRichBolt {

  private var collector: OutputCollector = _

  def prepare(StormConf: Map[_, _],
```

```
                context: TopologyContext,
                collector: OutputCollector): Unit = {
    this.collector = collector
  }

  def execute(input: Tuple): Unit = {
    val line: String = input.getString(0)
    val words: Array[String] = line.split(" ")
    for (word <- words if !word.isEmpty) {
      collector.emit(new Values(word))
    }
    collector.ack(input)
  }

  def declareOutputFields(declarer: OutputFieldsDeclarer): Unit = {
    declarer.declare(new Fields("fraudIP"))
  }

  override def cleanup(): Unit = {}

  override def getComponentConfiguration(): Map[String, Any] = null

}
```

Wordcount Bolt: Example of Wordcount Bolt is given next:

```
import org.apache.Storm.task.OutputCollector
import org.apache.Storm.task.TopologyContext
import org.apache.Storm.topology.IRichBolt
import org.apache.Storm.topology.OutputFieldsDeclarer
import org.apache.Storm.tuple.Tuple
import java.util.HashMap
import java.util.Map

class WordCountCalculatorBolt extends IRichBolt {

  var wordCountMap: Map[String, Integer] = _

  private var collector: OutputCollector = _

  def prepare(StormConf: Map[_, _],
                context: TopologyContext,
                collector: OutputCollector): Unit = {
    this.wordCountMap = new HashMap[String, Integer]()
    this.collector = collector
  }
```

```scala
def execute(input: Tuple): Unit = {
  var str: String = input.getString(0)
  str = str.toLowerCase().trim()
  if (!wordCountMap.containsKey(str)) {
    wordCountMap.put(str, 1)
  } else {
    val c: java.lang.Integer = wordCountMap.get(str) + 1
    wordCountMap.put(str, c)
  }
  collector.ack(input)
}

def cleanup(): Unit = {
  for ((key, value) <- wordCountMap) {
    println(key + " : " + value)
  }
}

override def declareOutputFields(declarer: OutputFieldsDeclarer): Unit =
{}

override def getComponentConfiguration(): Map[String, Any] = null

}
```

Use case – log processing in Storm, Kafka, Hive

We will use the same use case of IP Fraud Detection which we used in Chapter 5, *Building Spark Streaming Applications with Kafka*. Let us begin with the code and how it works. Copy the following classes from Chapter 5, *Building Spark Streaming Applications with Kafka*, into your Storm Kafka use case:

pom.xml:

```xml
<?xml version="1.0" encoding="UTF-8"?>
<project xmlns="http://maven.apache.org/POM/4.0.0"
        xmlns:xsi="http://www.w3.org/2001/XMLSchema-instance"
        xsi:schemaLocation="http://maven.apache.org/POM/4.0.0
http://maven.apache.org/xsd/maven-4.0.0.xsd">
    <modelVersion>4.0.0</modelVersion>

    <groupId>com.packt</groupId>
    <artifactId>chapter6</artifactId>
```

```xml
        <version>1.0-SNAPSHOT</version>

        <properties>
            <project.build.sourceEncoding>UTF-8</project.build.sourceEncoding>
        </properties>

        <dependencies>

            <!-- https://mvnrepository.com/artifact/org.apache.Storm/Storm-hive
 -->
            <dependency>
                <groupId>org.apache.Storm</groupId>
                <artifactId>Storm-hive</artifactId>
                <version>1.0.0</version>
                <exclusions>
                    <exclusion><!-- possible scala confilict -->
                        <groupId>jline</groupId>
                        <artifactId>jline</artifactId>
                    </exclusion>
                </exclusions>
            </dependency>


            <dependency>
                <groupId>junit</groupId>
                <artifactId>junit</artifactId>
                <version>3.8.1</version>
                <scope>test</scope>
            </dependency>

            <dependency>
                <groupId>org.apache.hadoop</groupId>
                <artifactId>hadoop-hdfs</artifactId>
                <version>2.6.0</version>
                <scope>compile</scope>
            </dependency>

            <!--
https://mvnrepository.com/artifact/org.apache.Storm/Storm-kafka -->
            <dependency>
                <groupId>org.apache.Storm</groupId>
                <artifactId>Storm-kafka</artifactId>
                <version>1.0.0</version>
            </dependency>
            <!-- https://mvnrepository.com/artifact/org.apache.Storm/Storm-core
 -->
            <dependency>
                <groupId>org.apache.Storm</groupId>
```

```
            <artifactId>Storm-core</artifactId>
            <version>1.0.0</version>
            <scope>provided</scope>
        </dependency>
        <dependency>
            <groupId>org.apache.kafka</groupId>
            <artifactId>kafka_2.10</artifactId>
            <version>0.8.1.1</version>
            <exclusions>
                <exclusion>
                    <groupId>org.apache.zookeeper</groupId>
                    <artifactId>zookeeper</artifactId>
                </exclusion>
                <exclusion>
                    <groupId>log4j</groupId>
                    <artifactId>log4j</artifactId>
                </exclusion>
            </exclusions>
        </dependency>

        <dependency>
            <groupId>commons-collections</groupId>
            <artifactId>commons-collections</artifactId>
            <version>3.2.1</version>
        </dependency>
        <dependency>
            <groupId>com.google.guava</groupId>
            <artifactId>guava</artifactId>
            <version>15.0</version>
        </dependency>

    </dependencies>

    <build>
        <plugins>

            <plugin>
                <groupId>org.apache.maven.plugins</groupId>
                <artifactId>maven-shade-plugin</artifactId>
                <version>2.4.2</version>
                <executions>
                    <execution>
                        <phase>package</phase>
                        <goals>
                            <goal>shade</goal>
                        </goals>
                        <configuration>
                            <filters>
```

```xml
                              <filter>
                                  <artifact>junit:junit</artifact>
                                  <includes>
<include>junit/framework/**</include>
                                      <include>org/junit/**</include>
                                  </includes>
                                  <excludes>
<exclude>org/junit/experimental/**</exclude>
<exclude>org/junit/runners/**</exclude>
                                  </excludes>
                              </filter>
                              <filter>
                                  <artifact>*:*</artifact>
                                  <excludes>
                                      <exclude>META-INF/*.SF</exclude>
                                      <exclude>META-INF/*.DSA</exclude>
                                      <exclude>META-INF/*.RSA</exclude>
                                  </excludes>
                              </filter>
                          </filters>
                          <transformers>
                              <transformer
implementation="org.apache.maven.plugins.shade.resource.ServicesResourceTra
nsformer"/>

                              <transformer
implementation="org.apache.maven.plugins.shade.resource.ManifestResourceTra
nsformer">
<mainClass>com.packt.Storm.ipfrauddetection.IPFraudDetectionTopology</mainC
lass>

                              </transformer>
                          </transformers>
                      </configuration>
                  </execution>
              </executions>
          </plugin>
          <plugin>
              <groupId>org.codehaus.mojo</groupId>
              <artifactId>exec-maven-plugin</artifactId>
              <version>1.2.1</version>
              <executions>
                  <execution>
                      <goals>
                          <goal>exec</goal>
                      </goals>
                  </execution>
              </executions>
              <configuration>
```

```
<includeProjectDependencies>true</includeProjectDependencies>
<includePluginDependencies>false</includePluginDependencies>
                    <executable>java</executable>
                    <classpathScope>compile</classpathScope>
<mainClass>com.packt.Storm.ipfrauddetection.IPFraudDetectionTopology</mainC
lass>
                </configuration>
            </plugin>
            <plugin>
                <groupId>org.apache.maven.plugins</groupId>
                <artifactId>maven-compiler-plugin</artifactId>
                <configuration>
                    <source>1.6</source>
                    <target>1.6</target>
                </configuration>
            </plugin>
        </plugins>
    </build>
</project>
```

Producer

We will be reusing the producer code from the previous chapter.

`streaming.properties` file:

```
topic=iprecord
broker.list=10.200.99.197:6667
appname=IpFraud
group.id=Stream
```

Property Reader:

```
import java.io.FileNotFoundException;
import java.io.IOException;
import java.io.InputStream;
import java.util.Properties;

public class PropertyReader {

    private Properties prop = null;

    public PropertyReader() {

        InputStream is = null;
        try {
            this.prop = new Properties();
```

```
        is =
this.getClass().getResourceAsStream("/streaming.properties");
            prop.load(is);
        } catch (FileNotFoundException e) {
            e.printStackTrace();
        } catch (IOException e) {
            e.printStackTrace();
        }
    }
}

    public String getPropertyValue(String key) {
        return this.prop.getProperty(key);
    }
}
```

Producer code

Our producer application is designed like a real-time log producer, where the producer runs every three seconds and produces a new record with random IP addresses. You can add a few records in the IP_LOG.log file and then the producer will take care of producing millions of unique records from those three records.

We have also enabled auto creation of topics, so you need not create a topic before running your producer application. You can change the topic name in the streaming.properties file mentioned previously.

```
import com.packt.reader.PropertyReader;
import org.apache.kafka.clients.producer.KafkaProducer;
import org.apache.kafka.clients.producer.ProducerRecord;
import org.apache.kafka.clients.producer.RecordMetadata;

import java.io.BufferedReader;
import java.io.File;
import java.io.IOException;
import java.io.InputStreamReader;
import java.util.*;
import java.util.concurrent.Future;


public class IPLogProducer extends TimerTask {
    static String path = "";

    public BufferedReader readFile() {
        BufferedReader BufferedReader = new BufferedReader(new
InputStreamReader(
                this.getClass().getResourceAsStream("/IP_LOG.log")));
```

```
            return BufferedReader;

    }

    public static void main(final String[] args) {
        Timer timer = new Timer();
        timer.schedule(new IPLogProducer(), 3000, 3000);
    }

    private String getNewRecordWithRandomIP(String line) {
        Random r = new Random();
        String ip = r.nextInt(256) + "." + r.nextInt(256) + "." +
r.nextInt(256) + "." + r.nextInt(256);
        String[] columns = line.split(" ");
        columns[0] = ip;
        return Arrays.toString(columns);
    }

    @Override
    public void run() {
        PropertyReader propertyReader = new PropertyReader();

        Properties producerProps = new Properties();
        producerProps.put("bootstrap.servers",
propertyReader.getPropertyValue("broker.list"));
        producerProps.put("key.serializer",
"org.apache.kafka.common.serialization.StringSerializer");
        producerProps.put("value.serializer",
"org.apache.kafka.common.serialization.StringSerializer");
        producerProps.put("auto.create.topics.enable", "true");

        KafkaProducer<String, String> ipProducer = new
KafkaProducer<String, String>(producerProps);

        BufferedReader br = readFile();
        String oldLine = "";
        try {
            while ((oldLine = br.readLine()) != null) {
                String line =
getNewRecordWithRandomIP(oldLine).replace("[", "").replace("]", "");
                ProducerRecord ipData = new ProducerRecord<String,
String>(propertyReader.getPropertyValue("topic"), line);
                Future<RecordMetadata> recordMetadata =
ipProducer.send(ipData);
            }
        } catch (IOException e) {
            e.printStackTrace();
        }
```

```
            ipProducer.close();
        }
    }
```

Fraud IP lookup

The following classes will help us to identify if requests are coming from a fraudulent IP. We have used interface before implementing the class so that we can add more NoSQL databases or any fast lookup services. You can implement this service and add a lookup service by using HBase or any other fast key lookup service.

We are using `InMemoryLookup` and have just added the fraud IP range in the cache. Add the following code to your project:

```
public interface IIPScanner {

    boolean isFraudIP(String ipAddresses);

}
```

`CacheIPLookup` is one implementation for the `IIPScanner` interface which does in-memory lookup.

```
import java.io.Serializable;
import java.util.HashSet;
import java.util.Set;


public class CacheIPLookup implements IIPScanner, Serializable {

    private Set<String> fraudIPList = new HashSet<>();

    public CacheIPLookup() {
        fraudIPList.add("212");
        fraudIPList.add("163");
        fraudIPList.add("15");
        fraudIPList.add("224");
        fraudIPList.add("126");
        fraudIPList.add("92");
        fraudIPList.add("91");
        fraudIPList.add("10");
        fraudIPList.add("112");
        fraudIPList.add("194");
        fraudIPList.add("198");
        fraudIPList.add("11");
        fraudIPList.add("12");
        fraudIPList.add("13");
```

```
        fraudIPList.add("14");
        fraudIPList.add("15");
        fraudIPList.add("16");
    }


    @Override
    public boolean isFraudIP(String ipAddresses) {

        return fraudIPList.contains(ipAddresses);
    }
}
```

Storm application

This section will help you create IP Fraud detection application with the help of Apache Kafka and Apache Storm. Storm will read data from Kafka topic, which contains IP log records, and then will do the necessary detection processing and dump the records into hive and Kafka simultaneously.

Our Topology consist of following component:

- **Kafka Spout**: It will read a Stream of records from Kafka and will send it to two bolts
- **Fraud Detector Bolt**: This bolt will process the record emitted by Kafka spout and will emit fraud records to Hive and Kafka bolt
- **Hive Bolt**: This bolt will read the data emitted by fraud detector bolt and will process and push those records to hive table
- **Kafka Bolt**: This bolt will do the same processing as Hive bolt, but will push the resulting data to a different Kafka topic

`iptopology.properties`:

```
zkhost = localhost:2181
inputTopic =iprecord
outputTopic=fraudip
KafkaBroker =localhost:6667
consumerGroup=id7
metaStoreURI = thrift://localhost:9083
dbName = default
tblName = fraud_ip
```

Hive Table: Create the following table in hive; this table will store the records emitted by Hive bolt:

```
DROP TABLE IF EXISTS fraud_ip;
CREATE TABLE fraud_ip(
ip String,
date String,
request_url String,
protocol_type String,
status_code String
)
PARTITIONED BY (col1 STRING)
CLUSTERED BY (col3) into 5 buckets
STORED AS ORC;
```

IPFraudDetectionTopology: This class will build the topology which indicates how spout and bolts are connected together to form Storm topology. This is the main class of our application and we will use it while submitting our topology to Storm cluster.

```
import com.packt.Storm.example.StringToWordsSpliterBolt;
import com.packt.Storm.example.WordCountCalculatorBolt;
import org.apache.log4j.Logger;
import org.apache.Storm.Config;
import org.apache.Storm.LocalCluster;
import org.apache.Storm.StormSubmitter;
import org.apache.Storm.generated.AlreadyAliveException;
import org.apache.Storm.generated.AuthorizationException;
import org.apache.Storm.generated.InvalidTopologyException;
import org.apache.Storm.hive.bolt.HiveBolt;
import org.apache.Storm.hive.bolt.mapper.DelimitedRecordHiveMapper;
import org.apache.Storm.hive.common.HiveOptions;
import org.apache.Storm.kafka.*;
import org.apache.Storm.spout.SchemeAsMultiScheme;
import org.apache.Storm.topology.TopologyBuilder;
import org.apache.Storm.tuple.Fields;

import java.io.FileInputStream;
import java.io.IOException;
import java.io.InputStream;
import java.util.Properties;


public class IPFraudDetectionTopology {

    private static String zkhost, inputTopic, outputTopic, KafkaBroker,
consumerGroup;
    private static String metaStoreURI, dbName, tblName;
    private static final Logger logger =
```

```
Logger.getLogger(IPFraudDetectionTopology.class);

    public static void Intialize(String arg) {
        Properties prop = new Properties();
        InputStream input = null;

        try {
            logger.info("Loading Configuration File for setting up input");
            input = new FileInputStream(arg);
            prop.load(input);
            zkhost = prop.getProperty("zkhost");
            inputTopic = prop.getProperty("inputTopic");
            outputTopic = prop.getProperty("outputTopic");
            KafkaBroker = prop.getProperty("KafkaBroker");
            consumerGroup = prop.getProperty("consumerGroup");
            metaStoreURI = prop.getProperty("metaStoreURI");
            dbName = prop.getProperty("dbName");
            tblName = prop.getProperty("tblName");

        } catch (IOException ex) {
            logger.error("Error While loading configuration file" + ex);

        } finally {
            if (input != null) {
                try {
                    input.close();
                } catch (IOException e) {
                    logger.error("Error Closing input stream");

                }
            }
        }

    }

    public static void main(String[] args) throws AlreadyAliveException,
InvalidTopologyException, AuthorizationException {
        Intialize(args[0]);
        logger.info("Successfully loaded Configuration ");


        BrokerHosts hosts = new ZkHosts(zkhost);
        SpoutConfig spoutConfig = new SpoutConfig(hosts, inputTopic, "/" +
KafkaBroker, consumerGroup);
        spoutConfig.scheme = new SchemeAsMultiScheme(new StringScheme());
        spoutConfig.startOffsetTime =
kafka.api.OffsetRequest.EarliestTime();
        KafkaSpout kafkaSpout = new KafkaSpout(spoutConfig);
```

```
        String[] partNames = {"status_code"};
        String[] colNames = {"date", "request_url", "protocol_type",
"status_code"};

        DelimitedRecordHiveMapper mapper = new
DelimitedRecordHiveMapper().withColumnFields(new Fields(colNames))
            .withPartitionFields(new Fields(partNames));


        HiveOptions hiveOptions;
        //make sure you change batch size and all paramtere according to
requirement
        hiveOptions = new HiveOptions(metaStoreURI, dbName, tblName,
mapper).withTxnsPerBatch(250).withBatchSize(2)
            .withIdleTimeout(10).withCallTimeout(10000000);

        logger.info("Creating Storm Topology");
        TopologyBuilder builder = new TopologyBuilder();

        builder.setSpout("KafkaSpout", kafkaSpout, 1);

        builder.setBolt("frauddetect", new
FraudDetectorBolt()).shuffleGrouping("KafkaSpout");
        builder.setBolt("KafkaOutputBolt",
            new IPFraudKafkaBolt(zkhost,
"kafka.serializer.StringEncoder", KafkaBroker, outputTopic), 1)
            .shuffleGrouping("frauddetect");

        builder.setBolt("HiveOutputBolt", new IPFraudHiveBolt(),
1).shuffleGrouping("frauddetect");
        builder.setBolt("HiveBolt", new
HiveBolt(hiveOptions)).shuffleGrouping("HiveOutputBolt");

        Config conf = new Config();
        if (args != null && args.length > 1) {
            conf.setNumWorkers(3);
            logger.info("Submiting  topology to Storm cluster");

            StormSubmitter.submitTopology(args[1], conf,
builder.createTopology());
        } else {
            // Cap the maximum number of executors that can be spawned
            // for a component to 3
            conf.setMaxTaskParallelism(3);
            // LocalCluster is used to run locally
            LocalCluster cluster = new LocalCluster();
            logger.info("Submitting  topology to local cluster");
            cluster.submitTopology("KafkaLocal", conf,
```

```
builder.createTopology());
            // sleep
            try {
                Thread.sleep(10000);
            } catch (InterruptedException e) {
                // TODO Auto-generated catch block
                logger.error("Exception ocuured" + e);
                cluster.killTopology("KafkaToplogy");
                logger.info("Shutting down cluster");
                cluster.shutdown();
            }
            cluster.shutdown();

        }

    }
}
```

Fraud Detector Bolt: This bolt will read the tuples emitted by Kafka spout and will detect which record is fraud by using an in memory IP lookup service. It will then emit the fraud records to `hivebolt` and `kafkabolt` simultaneously:

```
package com.packt.Storm.ipfrauddetection;

import com.packt.Storm.utils.CacheIPLookup;
import com.packt.Storm.utils.IIPScanner;
import org.apache.Storm.task.OutputCollector;
import org.apache.Storm.task.TopologyContext;
import org.apache.Storm.topology.IRichBolt;
import org.apache.Storm.topology.OutputFieldsDeclarer;
import org.apache.Storm.topology.base.BaseRichBolt;
import org.apache.Storm.tuple.Fields;
import org.apache.Storm.tuple.Tuple;
import org.apache.Storm.tuple.Values;

import java.util.Map;

public class FraudDetectorBolt extends BaseRichBolt {
    private IIPScanner cacheIPLookup = new CacheIPLookup();
    private OutputCollector collector;


    @Override
    public void prepare(Map map, TopologyContext topologyContext,
OutputCollector outputCollector) {
        this.collector = outputCollector;
    }
```

```
        @Override
        public void execute(Tuple input) {
            String ipRecord = (String) input.getValue(0);
            String[] columns = ipRecord.split(",");

            String IP = columns[0];
            String[] ranges = IP.split("\\.");
            String range = null;
            try {
                range = ranges[0];
            } catch (ArrayIndexOutOfBoundsException ex) {

            }
            boolean isFraud = cacheIPLookup.isFraudIP(range);

            if (isFraud) {
                Values value = new Values(ipRecord);
                collector.emit(value);
                collector.ack(input);
            }
        }

        @Override
        public void declareOutputFields(OutputFieldsDeclarer
    outputFieldsDeclarer) {
            outputFieldsDeclarer.declare(new Fields("fraudip"));
        }
    }
```

`IPFraudHiveBolt`: This call will process the records emitted by fraud detector bolt and
will push the data to Hive using a thrift service:

```
package com.packt.Storm.ipfrauddetection;

import com.packt.Storm.utils.CacheIPLookup;
import com.packt.Storm.utils.IIPScanner;
import org.apache.log4j.Logger;
import org.apache.Storm.task.OutputCollector;
import org.apache.Storm.task.TopologyContext;
import org.apache.Storm.topology.OutputFieldsDeclarer;
import org.apache.Storm.topology.base.BaseRichBolt;
import org.apache.Storm.tuple.Fields;
import org.apache.Storm.tuple.Tuple;
import org.apache.Storm.tuple.Values;

import java.util.Map;
```

```
public class IPFraudHiveBolt extends BaseRichBolt {
    private static final long serialVersionUID = 1L;
    private static final Logger logger =
Logger.getLogger(IPFraudHiveBolt.class);
    OutputCollector _collector;
    private IIPScanner cacheIPLookup = new CacheIPLookup();

    public void prepare(Map StormConf, TopologyContext context,
OutputCollector collector) {
        _collector = collector;
    }

    public void execute(Tuple input) {
        String ipRecord = (String) input.getValue(0);
        String[] columns = ipRecord.split(",");
        Values value = new Values(columns[0], columns[3], columns[4],
columns[5], columns[6]);
        _collector.emit(value);
        _collector.ack(input);


    }

    public void declareOutputFields(OutputFieldsDeclarer ofDeclarer) {
        ofDeclarer.declare(new Fields("ip", "date", "request_url",
"protocol_type", "status_code"));
    }
}
```

`IPFraudKafkaBolt`: This uses the Kafka Producer API to push the processed fraud IP to another Kafka topic:

```
package com.packt.Storm.ipfrauddetection;

import com.packt.Storm.utils.CacheIPLookup;
import com.packt.Storm.utils.IIPScanner;
import org.apache.kafka.clients.producer.KafkaProducer;
import org.apache.kafka.clients.producer.Producer;
import org.apache.kafka.clients.producer.ProducerRecord;
import org.apache.kafka.clients.producer.RecordMetadata;
import org.apache.log4j.Logger;
import org.apache.Storm.task.OutputCollector;
import org.apache.Storm.task.TopologyContext;
import org.apache.Storm.topology.OutputFieldsDeclarer;
import org.apache.Storm.topology.base.BaseRichBolt;
import org.apache.Storm.tuple.Fields;
import org.apache.Storm.tuple.Tuple;
```

```java
import java.util.HashMap;
import java.util.Map;
import java.util.Properties;
import java.util.concurrent.Future;


public class IPFraudKafkaBolt extends BaseRichBolt {
    private static final long serialVersionUID = 1L;
    private Producer<String, String> producer;
    private String zkConnect, serializerClass, topic, brokerList;
    private static final Logger logger =
Logger.getLogger(IPFraudKafkaBolt.class);
    private Map<String, String> valueMap = new HashMap<String, String>();
    private String dataToTopic = null;
    OutputCollector _collector;
    private IIPScanner cacheIPLookup = new CacheIPLookup();


    public IPFraudKafkaBolt(String zkConnect, String serializerClass,
String brokerList, String topic) {
        this.zkConnect = zkConnect;
        this.serializerClass = serializerClass;
        this.topic = topic;
        this.brokerList = brokerList;
    }

    public void prepare(Map StormConf, TopologyContext context,
OutputCollector collector) {
        logger.info("Intializing Properties");
        _collector = collector;
        Properties props = new Properties();
        props.put("zookeeper.connect", zkConnect);
        props.put("serializer.class", serializerClass);
        props.put("metadata.broker.list", brokerList);
        KafkaProducer<String, String> producer = new KafkaProducer<String,
String>(props);


    }

    public void execute(Tuple input) {

        dataToTopic = (String) input.getValue(0);
        ProducerRecord data = new ProducerRecord<String, String>(topic,
this.dataToTopic);
        Future<RecordMetadata> recordMetadata = producer.send(data);
        _collector.ack(input);
```

```
    }

    public void declareOutputFields(OutputFieldsDeclarer declarer) {
        declarer.declare(new Fields("null"));
    }
}
```

Running the project

Execute the following permission before running the project:

```
sudo su - hdfs -c "hdfs dfs -chmod 777 /tmp/hive"
 sudo chmod 777 /tmp/hive
```

- To run in cluster mode, we need to execute as:

```
Storm jar /home/ldap/chanchals/kafka-Storm-integration-0.0.1-
SNAPSHOT.jar
com.packt.Storm.ipfrauddetection.IPFraudDetectionTopology
iptopology.properties TopologyName
```

- To run in local mode, we need to execute as:

```
Storm jar kafka-Storm-integration-0.0.1-SNAPSHOT.jar
com.packt.Storm.ipfrauddetection.IPFraudDetectionTopology
iptopology.properties
```

Summary

In this chapter, we learned about Apache Storm architecture in brief and we also went through the limitations of Storm which motivated Twitter to develop Heron. We also discussed Heron architecture and its components. Later, we went through the API and an example of Storm Kafka integration. We also covered IP Fraud detection use cases and learned how to create a topology.

In the next chapter, we will learn about the Confluent Platform for Apache Kafka, which provides lots of advanced tools and features which we can use with Kafka.

7
Using Kafka with Confluent Platform

In the last chapter, we learned about Apache Storm and Apache Heron. We also went through Integrating Kafka with Storm. In this chapter, we will focus on **Confluent Platform**, which is specially designed to make Kafka more efficient to use in production application.

We will walk through the following topics in this chapter:

- Introduction to Confluent Platform
- Confluent architecture
- Kafka Connectors and Kafka Streams
- Schema Registry and REST proxy
- Camus - moving Kafka data to HDFS

Introduction to Confluent Platform

So far, we have walked through learning internal concepts. We also went through a few programs that helped us use Apache Kafka. Confluent Platform is developed by the creator of Kafka in order to improve usability of Kafka in production applications.

The following are a few reasons to introduce Confluent Platform:

- **Integration with Kafka**: We have seen integration of Spark, Storm with Kafka in the previous chapter. However, these frameworks come with additional rich APIs, and having such Stream processing available in a single platform with Kafka will avoid maintaining other distributed execution engines separately.
- **In-built Connectors**: We saw that writing a Kafka producer or consumer application is very easy using API that Kafka provides. We have seen in many application architectures where Kafka is being used, that the type of source of data remains common, which means it may be the database, server logs, any data generator application server, and so on.

  We have also seen that the final consumption layer where data is stored for drawing some analysis is also common. The data can be used in Elasticsearch, it can be put on HDFS and so on.
  What if we can provide a platform where we just provide configuration, data is available in Kafka, we provide another configuration, and the data is pushed to a destination such as Elasticsearch, HDFS and so on.

- **Client**: We can use Java, Scala client to write Kafka producer or consumer application using Kafka API. People may need to write the same in PHP, .NET, Perl, and so on. This is very much necessary to extend the use of Kafka to a variety of application clients so that users who are comfortable in a particular language can easily develop the Kafka application.
- **Accessibility**: What if an application wants to access Kafka using the RESTful web services? We don't have anything which can do this for applications which need data from Kafka topics using REST calls.

  Exposing REST services to Kafka will simplify the usability of Kafka across many REST clients, who can simply call the REST services exposed to Kafka and serve their application purpose without writing any consumer applications.

- **Storage format**: A common challenge that may occur where the producer and consumer of an application are loosely coupled with each other is data format. We may want to have a contract wherein we say any change in the data on the producer side should not affect all downstream consumer applications, or the producer should not accidentally produce data in a format that is not consumable by the consumer application.

  Both producer and consumer should agree on the contract clauses, which ensures that this type of problem should not affect any of them in case there is any change in the type of data.

- **Monitoring and controlling Kafka performance**: We also want to have a mechanism where we can see the performance of the Kafka cluster, which should provide us with all the valuable metadata information with a good interface. we may want to see the performance of the topic, or we may want to see the CPU utilization of the Kafka cluster which may give us information about consumers at a deep level. All this information may help us optimize our application to a great extent.

All these features are integrated into a single platform called **Confluent Platform**. It allows us to integrate different data sources and manage this data with a reliable and high-performance system. The Confluent Platform provides us with a very simple way to connect many data sources to Kafka, building streaming applications with Kafka. It also provides the ability to secure, monitor, and manage our Kafka cluster efficiently.

Deep driving into Confluent architecture

In this section, we will discuss the architecture of Confluent Platform and its components in detail. The Confluent Platform provides you with underlying built-in Connectors and components that help you focus on the business use case and how to get value out of it. It takes care of the integration of data from multiple sources and its consumption by the target system. The Confluent Platform provides a trusted way of securing, monitoring, and managing the entire Kafka cluster infrastructure. Let's talk about its components one-by-one.

The following image will give a concise idea of the Confluent architecture:

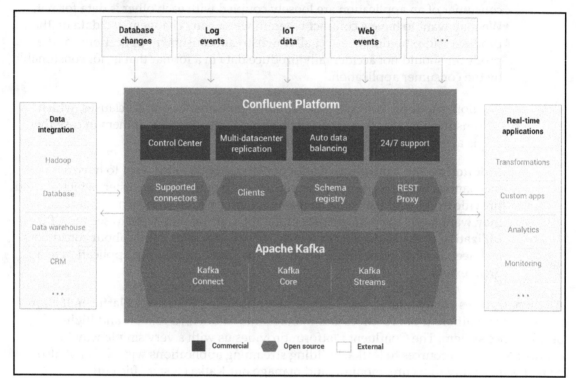

Confluent architecture

In the preceding figure, we can see the three colored components. The dark and light blue represent the enterprise and open source version of the Confluent Platform respectively. Simply put, there are two versions of the Confluent Platform:

- One is an open source version, which they offer for free, and it includes all the components available in light blue color.
- The other is an enterprise version of the Confluent Platform, which contains some advanced components that can be useful in managing and controlling the overall Kafka infrastructure.

Let's look at each component in brief:

- **Supported Connectors**: Connectors are used to move data in and out of Kafka. This is also known as Kafka Connect. Confluent provides the following Connectors:
    - **JDBC Connector**: You may want to bring data from a relational database into Kafka, or you may want to export Kafka data into a relational database or any database supporting JDBC. Confluent provides the JDBC Connector to make life easy for us.
    - **HDFS Connector**: In most cases, you may want to store Kafka data into HDFS for batch analytics processing or to store historical records for later processing.
    - **Elasticsearch Connector:** It helps you move the Kafka data to Elasticsearch. Use cases that require a quick adhoc search on data in Kafka can use this Connector to move data from Kafka to Elasticsearch and do their job.
    - **File Connector**: Confluent also provides you with a Connector that can help you read data from a file and write it into Kafka or export Kafka data into a file. It is also known as a FileSource Connector and FileSink Connector.
    - **S3 Connector**: Similar to HDFS Connector, it helps you export Kafka data into S3 storage.
- **Client**: The Confluent Platform also provides you with an open source Kafka client library that helps you write Kafka producer and consumer applications in different languages such as C, C++, .NET, Python, and many more. It makes Kafka developer-friendly, where developers can build applications in languages they are more comfortable with.
- **Schema Registry**: We discussed the data format issue when both producers and consumers are loosely coupled with each other. Confluent provides a Schema Registry based on Avro Serialization, which maintains all versions of the schema of each Kafka topic that has registered its schema with it. Developers can modify the schema without worrying about their impact on underlying dependent systems.
- **REST Proxy**: It provides a REST-based API to interact with the Kafka cluster. It provides REST services for writing, reading, and metadata access. Application in any language can make a REST-based request to the Kafka cluster. This allows developers to replace their existing components to take advantage of a high-performing messaging system.

All the components discussed in the preceding section are available in the open source Confluent Platform. The following four components are an addition to the enterprise version of the Confluent Platform, which provides a lot of useful functionality:

- **Control Center**: The Confluent platform provides a rich GUI for managing and monitoring the Kafka cluster. It also provides a GUI interface to create your own Kafka pipeline, where you need not write any code, just need to provide some configuration. It also lets you measure the performance of your Kafka producer and consumer at a very deep level by collecting different metrics from the Kafka cluster. All these metrics are very important to effectively monitor and maintain your Kafka cluster and always give high-performance results.

- **Multi-Datacenter replication**: The Confluent Platform provides you with the ability to replicate Kafka data across multiple data centers, or it can allow you to aggregate data from multiple Kafka data centers to another data center without affecting data in the source data center.

  The Kafka data center replicator does this job for us. The control center provides a nice GUI to do this job. However, confluent also provides a command-line-based interface to use data center replication. It provides the ability to replicate the Kafka topic with similar configuration across multiple data centers.

- **Auto Data Balancing**: Kafka is scalable with growing business and application requirements, we need to scale our Kafka cluster. We may create more topics and partitions. We may add more brokers or remove some brokers. This may create a situation wherein one broker will have more workload than other brokers, and this may decrease the performance of the Kafka cluster. The Confluent Auto Data Balancing tool allows you to trigger auto balancing, whenever needed, by reducing the impact of rebalancing on the production workload.

- **24*7 Support**: This feature is auto-enabled in the enterprise confluent version, which collects and reports cluster metrics to the confluent, and then their team helps you by providing regular support on various issues.

Understanding Kafka Connect and Kafka Stream

Kafka Connect is a tool that provides the ability to move data into and out of the Kafka system. Thousands of use cases use the same kind of source and target system while using Kafka. Kafka Connect is comprised of Connectors for those common source or target systems.

Kafka Connect consists of a set of Connectors, and the Connectors are of two types:

- **Import Connectors**: Import Connectors are used to bring data from the source system into Kafka topics. These Connectors accept configuration through property files and bring data into a Kafka topic in any way you wish. You don't need to write your own producer to do such jobs. A few of the popular Connectors are JDBC Connector, file Connector, and so on.

- **Export Connectors**: Unlike Import Connectors, Export Connectors are used to copy data from Kafka topics to the target system. This also works based on the configuration property file, which can vary based on which Connector you are using. Some popular Export Connectors are HDFS, S3, Elasticsearch, and so on.

Kafka Connect does not perform any advanced processing over data available in Kafka, it is just used for ingestion purposes. Kafka Connect can be used in an ETL pipeline wherein it can perform the job of extracting and loading data from and to the source and target system. We will cover Kafka Connect in detail in the next chapter.

Kafka Streams

We have seen Stream processing engines such as Apache Spark and Apache Storm in the previous chapters. These processing engines require separate installation and maintenance efforts. Kafka Streams is a tool to process and analyze data stored in Kafka topics. The Kafka Stream library is built based on popular Stream processing concepts that allow you to run your streaming application on the Kafka cluster itself.

We will look into the terminology used in Kafka Streams; however, a detailed walk-through of Kafka Stream is covered in the upcoming chapter. Kafka Streams has a few concepts similar to what we had in Apache Storm; they are listed as follows:

- **Streams**: Streams is an unbounded set of records that can be used for processing. Stream API consists of a Stream partition, and a Stream partition is a key-value pair of data records. Streams are re-playable and fault tolerant in nature.

- **Stream processing application**: Any application build using Kafka Stream API is said to be a Stream processing application.
- **Topology**: Topology is the logical plan of application computation where Stream processors are connected together to achieve the application objective.
- **Stream processors**: Stream processors are connected together to form a topology, and each processor is responsible for performing some task. Kafka Stream processors also include two special Stream processors:
  - **Source Stream processor**: Source Stream processors are responsible for reading Stream data from Kafka topic and passing this data to the down Stream processor. It is the first processor in streaming topology.
  - **Sink Stream processor**: A Sink processor is the last processor in streaming topology, which receives Stream data from the processor above it and stores it into the target Kafka topic.

Kafka Streams API also provides a client API to perform aggregation, filtering over a Stream of data. It also allows you to save the state of an application and handles fault tolerant in an effective way.

The Kafka Stream application does not require any special framework to be installed other than Kafka. It can be treated as a simple Java application similar to those of producers and consumers. We will look into the details of Kafka streaming in the upcoming chapter.

Playing with Avro using Schema Registry

Schema Registry allows you to store Avro schemas for both producers and consumers. It also provides a RESTful interface for accessing this schema. It stores all the versions of Avro schema, and each schema version is assigned a schema ID.

When the producer sends a record to Kafka topic using Avro Serialization, it does not send an entire schema, instead, it sends the schema ID and record. The Avro serializer keeps all the versions of the schema in cache and stores data with the schemas matching the schema ID.

The consumer also uses the schema ID to read records from Kafka topic, wherein the Avro deserializer uses the schema ID to deserialize the record.

The Schema Registry also supports schema compatibility where we can modify the setting of schema compatibility to support forward and backward compatibility.

Here is an example of Avro schema and producer:

```
kafka-avro-console-producer \
  --broker-list localhost:9092 --topic test \
  --property
value.schema='{"type":"record","name":"testrecord","fields":[{"name":"count
ry","type":"string"}]}'
```

Similarly, an example of Avro schema on consumer:

```
kafka-avro-console-consumer --topic test \
        --Zookeeper localhost:2181 \
        --from-beginning
```

Remember that if the Schema Registry is up and running, the consumer will be able to deserialize the record. Any attempt to push invalid or non-compatible records to Kafka topic will result in an exception.

The schema can also be registered using a REST request as follows:

```
curl -X POST -H "Content-Type: application/vnd.schemaregistry.v1+json" \
  --data '{"schema": "{\"type\": \"string\"}"}' \
  http://localhost:8081/test/Kafka-test/versions
  {"id":1}
```

The ability of the Schema Registry to keep all the versions of the schema and configure their compatibility settings makes Schema Registry more special. Schema registry is very easy to use, and it also removes bottlenecks of the data format issue in a loosely coupled producer and consumer environment.

Moving Kafka data to HDFS

We have discussed the integration of Apache Kafka with various frameworks, which can be used for real-time or near-real-time streaming. Apache Kafka can store data for a configured time of retention period; the default is seven days.

Data will be removed from Kafka when the retention period expires. The organization does not want to lose data, and in many cases, they need data for some batch processing to generate monthly, weekly, or yearly reports. We can store historical records for further processing into a cheap and fault-tolerant storage system such as HDFS.

Kafka data can be moved to HDFS and can be used for different purposes. We will talk about the following four ways of moving data from Kafka to HDFS:

- Using Camus
- Using Gobblin
- Using Kafka Connect
- Using Flume

Camus

LinkedIn first created Kafka for its own log processing use case. As discussed, Kafka stores data for a configured period of time, and the default is seven days. The LinkedIn team felt the need to store data for any batch-reporting purpose or to use it later. Now, to store data in HDFS, which is a distributed storage file system, they started developing a tool that can use a distributed system capability to fetch data from Kafka. They developed Camus, a tool developed using map reduce API to copy data from Kafka to HDFS.

 Camus is just a map-reduce job that has the capability of performing incremental copying of data. It means it will not copy the data from the last committed offset.

The following image gives a good idea of the Camus architecture:

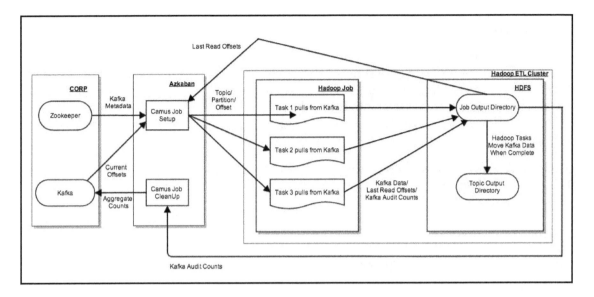

Camus architecture

The preceding figure shows a clear picture of how Camus works. It starts with the Camus setup, which requires Zookeeper to read Kafka metadata. The Camus job is a set of map-reduce jobs that can run on multiple data nodes at a time, resulting in distributed copying of data from Kafka.

Running Camus

Camus mainly consists of two tasks:

- **Reading data from Kafka**: Camus acts as a consumer while reading data from Kafka, and it requires the message decoder class, which can be used to read data from Kafka topics. The `decoder` class must implement `com.linkedin.Camus.coders.MessageDecoder class`. A few default decoders are available, such as `StringMessageDecoder`.
- **Writing data to HDFS**: Camus then writes data read from Kafka into HDFS. To write data into HDFS, it must have a record writer class. The record reader class must implement `com.linkedin.Camus.etl.RecordWriterProvider`.

Running Camus requires the Hadoop cluster. As discussed, Camus is nothing but a map-reduce job, and it can be run using normal Hadoop jobs as in the following case:

```
hadoop jar Camus.jar com.linkedin.Camus.etl.kafka.CamusJob -P
Camus.properties
```

Gobblin

Gobblin is an advanced version of Apache Camus. Apache Camus is only capable of copying data from Kafka to HDFS; however, Gobblin can connect to multiple sources and bring data to HDFS. LinkedIn had more than 10 data sources, and all were using different tools to ingest data for processing. In the shot term, they realized that maintaining all these tools and their metadata was getting complex and required more effort and maintenance resources.

They felt the need to have a single system that can connect to all sources and ingest data to Hadoop. This motivation helped them build Gobblin.

Gobblin architecture

The following image gives a good idea of the Gobblin architecture:

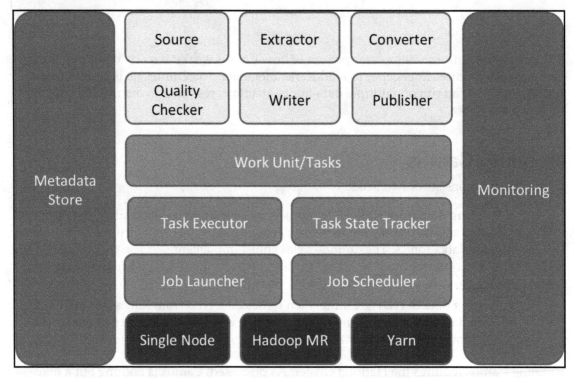

Gobblin architecture

The architecture of Gobblin is built in such a way that a user can easily add new Connectors for new sources, or they can modify existing sources. We can divide the overall architecture into four parts:

- **Gobblin Constructs**: These are responsible for the overall processing of the Gobblin ingestion work. It consists of following:
  - **Source**: This is responsible for acting as a Connector between the data source and Gobblin. It also divides the work into smaller work units, and each work unit is responsible for bringing a few parts of the data.
  - **Extractor**: This is responsible for extracting data from the data source. The source creates an extractor for each work unit, and each extractor fetches a portion of data from the data source. Gobblin also has some prebuilt popular sources and extractors already available for you.
  - **Converters**: These are responsible for converting input records to output records. One or more converter can be connected together to achieve the objective.
  - **Quality checkers**: These are optional constructs, and they are responsible for checking the data quality of each record or all records together.
  - **Writer**: This is associated with the sink, and it is responsible for writing data to the sink it is connected to.
  - **Publisher**: This is responsible for collecting data from each work unit task and storing data in the final directory.
- **Gobblin runtime**: This is responsible for the actual running of Gobblin jobs. It manages job scheduling and resource negotiation to execute these jobs. Gobblin runtime also does error handling and retries the job in case of failure.
- **Supported deployment**: Goblin runtime runs jobs based on the deployment mode. Gobblin can be run on standalone or map reduce mode. It will also support YARN-based deployment soon.
- **Gobblin utility**: Gobblin utility consists of two parts - one is metadata management, and the other is monitoring of Gobblin jobs. This utility allows Gobblin to store metadata in a single place rather than using a third-party tool to do such jobs. It also collects different matrics which can be useful for managing or optimizing Gobblin jobs.

The following configuration file (`kafka_to_hdfs.conf`) contains information about connection URLs, Sink type, output directory, and so on which will be read by Gobblin job to fetch data from Kafka to HDFS:

```
job.name=kafkatohdfs
job.group=Kafka
job.description=Kafka to hdfs using goblin
job.lock.enabled=false

kafka.brokers=localhost:9092
source.class=Gobblin.source.extractor.extract.kafka.KafkaSimpleSource
extract.namespace=Gobblin.extract.kafka
writer.builder.class=Gobblin.writer.SimpleDataWriterBuilder

writer.file.path.type=tablename
writer.destination.type=HDFS
writer.output.format=txt
data.publisher.type=Gobblin.publisher.BaseDataPublisher

mr.job.max.mappers=1
metrics.reporting.file.enabled=true
metrics.log.dir=/Gobblin-kafka/metrics
metrics.reporting.file.suffix=txt

bootstrap.with.offset=earliest
fs.uri=hdfs://localhost:8020
writer.fs.uri=hdfs://localhost:8020
state.store.fs.uri=hdfs://localhost:8020

mr.job.root.dir=/Gobblin-kafka/working
state.store.dir=/Gobblin-kafka/state-store
task.data.root.dir=/jobs/kafkaetl/Gobblin/Gobblin-kafka/task-data
data.publisher.final.dir=/Gobblintest/job-output
```

Run `Gobblin-MapReduce.sh`:

`Gobblin-MapReduce.sh --conf kafka_to_hdfs.conf`

Running a Gobblin job is very easy. They have already done everything you need. We would recommend you visit the Gobblin documentation for more details.

Kafka Connect

We already discussed Kafka Connect in the preceding sections. Kafka Connect refers to the Connectors that can be used to import or export data from Kafka. Kafka HDFS export Connector can be used to copy data from Kafka topic to HDFS.

HDFS Connector polls data from Kafka and writes them to HDFS. We can also specify the partition to be used, and it will divide the data into smaller chunks, where each chunk will represent a file in HDFS. Let's look into how to use this Connector.

Here is an example of Kafka Connect with producer:

```
kafka-avro-console-producer --broker-list localhost:9092 --topic test \
--property
value.schema='{"type":"record","name":"peoplerecord","fields":[{"name":"f1"
,"type":"string"}]}'
```

Run `kafka_to_hdfs.properties`:

```
name=hdfs-sink
Connector.class=io.confluent.connect.hdfs.HdfsSinkConnector
tasks.max=1
topics=test
hdfs.url=hdfs://localhost:8020
flush.size=3
```

Run the following:

```
connect-standalone etc/schema-registry/connect-avro-standalone.properties \
 kafka_to_hdfs.properties
```

You can verify at the HDFS location that if data is available in the Kafka topic, it will be there at the HDFS location.

Flume

Apache Flume is a distributed, reliable, and fault-tolerant system for collecting large volumes of data from different sources to one or more target systems.

It mainly consists of three components:

- Source
- Channel
- Sink

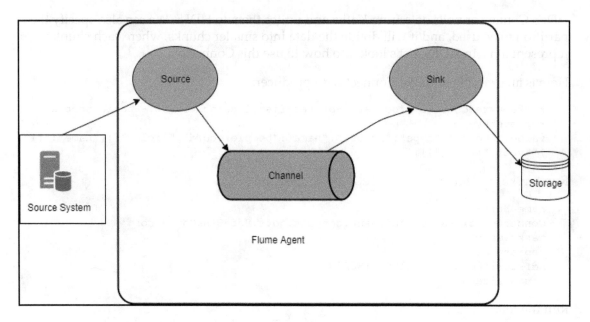

Flume Agent

The three components can be expanded as follows:

- **Source** is responsible for connecting with the source system and bringing data to the channel. Flume can be connected to different sources such as server logs, Twitter, Facebook, and so on. It also provides us the flexibility to connect to Kafka topics and bring data to the Flume channel.
- **Channel** is a temporary storage for data where data is pushed by the source based on the configuration. Source can push data to one or more channel, which can later be consumed by the sink.
- **Sink** is responsible for reading data from the Flume channel and storing it in the permanent storage system or passing it for further processing to some other system. It can be connected to a single channel at a time. Once the data read is acknowledged by sink, Flume removes the data from the channel.

Now you can visualize how to copy Kafka data using Flume and copy data to HDFS. Yes, we need Kafka source, channel, and HDFS sink. Kafka source will read data from Kafka topics, and HDFS sink will read data from the channel and store it to the configured HDFS location. Let's go through the following configuration:

Let us first look into `flumekafka.conf`:

```
pipeline.sources = kafka1
pipeline.channels = channel1
pipeline.sinks = hdfssink

pipeline.sources.kafka1.type = org.apache.flume.source.kafka.KafkaSource
pipeline.sources.kafka1.ZookeeperConnect = zk01.example.com:2181
pipeline.sources.kafka1.topic = test
pipeline.sources.kafka1.groupId = kafkaflume
pipeline.sources.kafka1.channels = channel1
pipeline.sources.kafka1.interceptors = i1
pipeline.sources.kafka1.interceptors.i1.type = timestamp
pipeline.sources.kafka1.kafka.consumer.timeout.ms = 100

pipeline.channels.channel1.type = memory
pipeline.channels.channel1.capacity = 100000
pipeline.channels.channel1.transactionCapacity = 10000

pipeline.sinks.hdfssink.type = hdfs
pipeline.sinks.hdfssink.hdfs.path = /user/hdfspath
pipeline.sinks.hdfssink.hdfs.rollInterval = 10
pipeline.sinks.hdfssink.hdfs.rollSize = 0
pipeline.sinks.hdfssink.hdfs.rollCount = 0
pipeline.sinks.hdfssink.hdfs.fileType = DataStream
pipeline.sinks.hdfssink.channel = channel1
```

If you look at the aforementioned configuration, we have provided configuration for source, channel, and sink. Source will read data from the topic test, and Flume will use it in the memory channel to store data. Sink will connect to the in-memory channel and move data to HDFS.

The following configuration connects the source with the channel:

```
pipeline.sources.kafka1.channels = channel1
```

The following configuration connects the sink with the channel:

```
pipeline.sinks.hdfssink.channel = channel1
```

`pipeline` is an agent name, which you can change according to your wish. Once the agent configuration is ready, we can run Flume using the following command:

```
flume-ng agent -c pathtoflume/etc/flume-ng/conf -f flumekafka.conf -n
pipeline
```

The in-depth overall architecture of Flume is beyond the scope of this chapter. Our intention is to let you know how we can copy Kafka data to HDFS using Flume.

Summary

This chapter has given us a brief understanding of Confluent Platform and it uses. You learned about the architecture of Confluent Platform and how Connectors can make our job of transporting data in and out of Kafka simpler. We also learned about how the Schema Registry solves data format issues and supports schema resolution. We have covered different ways of copying data from Kafka to HDFS and their examples.

In the next chapter, we will cover Kafka Connect in detail and will also look into how we can build a big data pipeline using Kafka and Kafka Connect.

8
Building ETL Pipelines Using Kafka

In the previous chapter, we learned about Confluent Platform. We covered its architecture in detail and discussed its components. You also learned how to export data from Kafka to HDFS using different tools. We went through Camus, Goblin, Flume, and Kafka Connect to cover different ways of bringing data to HDFS. We also recommend you try all the tools discussed in the last chapter to understand how they work. Now we will look into creating an ETL pipeline using these tools and look more closely at Kafka Connect use cases and examples.

In this chapter, we will cover Kafka Connect in detail. The following are the topics we will cover:

- Use of Kafka in the ETL pipeline
- Introduction to Kafka Connect
- Kafka Connect architecture
- Deep dive into Kafka Connect
- Introductory example of Kafka Connect
- Common use cases

Considerations for using Kafka in ETL pipelines

ETL is a process of **Extracting**, **Transforming**, and **Loading** data into the target system, which is explained next. It is followed by a large number of organizations to build their data pipelines.

- **Extraction**: Extraction is the process of ingesting data from the source system and making it available for further processing. Any prebuilt tool can be used to extract data from the source system. For example, to extract server logs or Twitter data, you can use Apache Flume, or to extract data from the database, you can use any JDBC-based application, or you can build your own application. The objective of the application that will be used for extraction is that it should not affect the performance of the source system in any manner.

- **Transformation**: Transformation refers to processing extracted data and converting it into some meaningful form. The application can consume data in two forms: one could be a pull-based approach where data is stored into some intermediate storage by the extractor and the application pulls data from here, the other could be a push-based approach where the extractor directly pushes data to transformers and the application processes it.

- **Loading**: Once data is transformed into a meaningful form, it has to be loaded into a target system for further use. The loading phase generally comprises the loading of meaningful data into the target system. The target system could be any database or file or any system capable of storing data.

Organizations are exploring many analytics opportunities on data. They want to do real-time analysis on some data, and on the same data, they also want to do batch analytics to generate other reports.

There are many frameworks that have been built for real-time stream processing and batch processing and all of them come with some new features, and some of them are similar, but the big challenge lies in the fact that there are no such frameworks that can do all the jobs for you, Ingestion, processing, and exporting it to multiple destinations for further processing have to be run using different frameworks for different phases of ETL, and this requires maintenance, cost, and effort to be put in.

 Kafka is a centralized publish-subscribe messaging system that comes with the support of performing ETL operations without using any other framework or tool.

Let's look into how we can use Kafka in an ETL operation:

- **Working of extracting operation of ETL**: Apache Kafka has introduced the concept of Kafka Connect, which comes with Source and Sink Connectors. Source Connectors can extract data from sources and put them into HDFS. Connectors are easy to use; they can be used by just changing some configuration parameters.
- **Working of transforming operation of ETL**: Apache Kafka has become more powerful with the stream processing feature being added to it. It comes with Kafka Stream, which is capable of handling streams of data and performing operations such as aggregation, filtering, and so on.

  Data from Kafka topic can be exported to HDFS to perform some batch processing. Kafka also provides export tools to do such jobs.

- **Working of loading operation of ETL**: Kafka Connect also comes with Export Connectors, which can be used to load data into the target system. For example, the JDBC Connector can be used to push data into a JDBC-supported database, the Elastic Search Connector can be used to push data into elastic search, the HDFS Connector can be used to push data into HDFS on which you can create a Hive table for further processing or for generating reports.

We will see how we can extract and load data from the source to the target system using Kafka Connect in the next section. Introducing Kafka Connect using Kafka also ensures that we do not need to create a separate serving layer to serve data to the consumer. All consumers maintain an offset of Kafka messages and can read messages from the topic in any manner they want. It simplifies the ETL pipeline problem, where the number of producers and consumers increases over time. With all the capabilities of extracting, transforming, and loading data into the target system, Kafka remains the first choice for lots of organizations today.

Introducing Kafka Connect

Kafka Connect is used to copy data into and out of Kafka. There are already a lot of tools available to move data from one system to another system. You would find many use cases where you want to do real-time analytics and batch analytics on the same data. Data can come from different sources but finally may land into the same category or type.

We may want to bring this data to Kafka topics and then pass it to a real-time processing engine or store it for batch processing. If you closely look at the following figure, there are different processes involved:

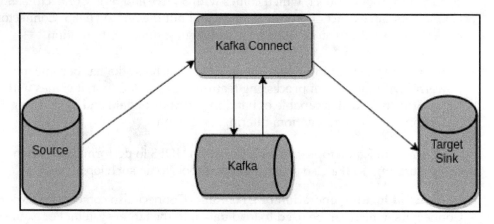

Kafka Connect

Let's look into each component in detail:

- **Ingestion in Kafka**: Data is inserted into Kafka topic from different sources, and most of the time, the type of sources are common. For example you may want to insert server logs into Kafka topics, or insert all records from the database table into topic, or insert records from file to Kafka, and so on. You will use Kafka Producer, which will do this job for you, or you may use some already available tools.

- **Processing**: Data available in Kafka topic needs to be processed to extract business meaning out of it. Data can be consumed by real-time processing engines such as Apache Spark, Apache Storm, and many more. It can be stored to HDFS, Hbase, or some other storage for later processing.

- **Copying Kafka data**: Data available in Kafka can be exported to multiple systems, depending on the use case. It can be exported to Elasticsearch for ad hoc analysis. It can be stored in HDFS for batch processing. Kafka also has a retention period after which data available in Kafka will be removed. You may want to keep a backup of data available in Kafka. The backup can be either HDFS or some other file system.

Kafka Connect is nothing but a prebuilt set of tools that can be used to bring data into Kafka topic and copy data from Kafka topic to different external systems. It provides API to build your own tool for import or export. It also uses parallel processing capability wherein it copies data in parallel. It also uses the offset commit mechanism to ensure it starts from last left point in case of failure.

Deep dive into Kafka Connect

Let's get into the architecture of Kafka Connect. The following figure gives a good idea of Kafka Connect:

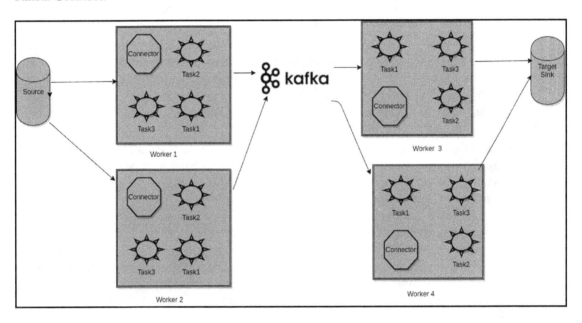

Kafka Connect architecture

Kafka Connect has three major models in its design:

- **Connector**: A Connector is configured by defining the Connector class and configuration. The Connector class is defined based on the source or target of the data, which means that it will be different for the Database source and File source. It is then followed by setting up the configuration for these classes. For example, configuration for the Database source could be the IP of the database, the username and password to connect to the database, and so on. The Connector creates a set of tasks, which is actually responsible for copying data from the source or copying data to the target. Connectors are of two types:
    - **Source Connector**: This is responsible for ingesting data from the source system into Kafka
    - **Sink Connector:** This is responsible for exporting data from Kafka to an external system such as HDFS, Elasticsearch, and so on
- **Worker**: Workers are responsible for the execution of Connector tasks. They acts as a container for the Connector and task. Workers are actual JVM processes that coordinate with each other to distribute the work and guarantee scalability and fault tolerance. The Worker does not manage processes. However, it distributes tasks to any available processes. Processes are managed by resource management tools such as YARN and Mesos.
- **Data**: Connectors are responsible for copying streams of data from one system to another system. We discussed two types of Connectors--source Connector and target Connector. In any case, we may have Kafka as one of the systems to be used with Connectors. This means that Connectors are tightly coupled with Kafka. Kafka Connect also manages the offset of streams. In case of task failure, the offset allows the Connector to resume operation from the last failure point. The offset type can vary based on the type of Connector we use. For example, the offset for the database can be some unique record identifier, the offset for file can be a delimiter, and so on. Kafka Connect also provides data format converters, which allow you to convert data from one format to other. It also supports integration with the Schema Registry.

Introductory examples of using Kafka Connect

Kafka Connect provides us with various Connectors, and we can use the Connectors based on our use case requirement. It also provides an API that can be used to build your own Connector. We will go through a few basic examples in this section. We have tested the code on the Ubuntu machine. Download the Confluent Platform tar file from the Confluent website:

- **Import or Source Connector**: This is used to ingest data from the source system into Kafka. There are already a few inbuilt Connectors available in the Confluent Platform.
- **Export or Sink Connector**: This is used to export data from Kafka topic to external sources. Let's look at a few Connectors available for real-use cases.
- **JDBC Source Connector**: The JDBC Connector can be used to pull data from any JDBC-supported system to Kafka.

Let's see how to use it:

1. Install `sqllite`:

   ```
   sudo apt-get install sqlite3
   ```

2. Start console:

   ```
   sqlite3 packt.db
   ```

3. Create a database table, and insert records:

   ```
   sqlite> CREATE TABLE authors(id INTEGER PRIMARY KEY AUTOINCREMENT
   NOT NULL, name VARCHAR(255));

   sqlite> INSERT INTO authors(name) VALUES('Manish');

   sqlite> INSERT INTO authors(name) VALUES('Chanchal');
   ```

4. Make the following changes in the `source-quickstart-sqlite.properties` file:

   ```
   name=jdbc-test
   Connector.class=io.confluent.connect.jdbc.JdbcSourceConnector
   tasks.max=1
   connection.url=jdbc:sqlite:packt.db
   ```

data:image/png;base64

```
mode=incrementing
incrementing.column.name=id
topic.prefix=test-
```

5. In `connection.url`, the `packt.db` value is the path to your `packt.db` file. Provide the full path to the `.db` file. Once everything is ready, run the following command to execute the Connector script:

```
./bin/connect-standalone etc/schema-registry/connect-avro-
standalone.properties etc/kafka-connect-jdbc/source-quickstart-
sqlite.properties
```

6. Once the script is successfully executed, you can check the output using the following command:

```
bin/kafka-avro-console-consumer --new-consumer --bootstrap-server
localhost:9092 --topic test-authors --from-beginning
```

You will see the following output:

```
SLF4J: Class path contains multiple SLF4J bindings.
SLF4J: Found binding in [jar:file:/home/chanchal/projects/confluent-3.2.2/share/ja
StaticLoggerBinder.class]
SLF4J: Found binding in [jar:file:/home/chanchal/projects/confluent-3.2.2/share/ja
aticLoggerBinder.class]
SLF4J: See http://www.slf4j.org/codes.html#multiple_bindings for an explanation.
SLF4J: Actual binding is of type [org.slf4j.impl.Log4jLoggerFactory]
{"id":1,"name":{"string":"Manish"}}
{"id":2,"name":{"string":"Chanchal"}}
```

 Make sure you have already started Zookeeper, Kafka server, and Schema Registry before running this demo.

JDBC Sink Connector: This Connector is used to export data from Kafka topic to any JDBC-supported external system.

Let's see how to use it:

1. Configure `sink-quickstart-sqlite.properties`:

```
name=test-jdbc-sink
Connector.class=io.confluent.connect.jdbc.JdbcSinkConnector
tasks.max=1
```

```
topics=authors_sink
connection.url=jdbc:sqlite:packt_authors.db
auto.create=true
```

2. Run the producer:

```
bin/kafka-avro-console-producer \
 --broker-list localhost:9092 --topic authors_sink \
 --property
value.schema='{"type":"record","name":"authors","fields":[{"name":"
id","type":"int"},{"name":"author_name", "type": "string"},
{"name":"age", "type": "int"}, {"name":"popularity_percentage",
"type": "float"}]}'
```

3. Run the Kafka Connect Sink:

```
./bin/connect-standalone etc/schema-registry/connect-avro-
standalone.properties etc/kafka-connect-jdbc/sink-quickstart-
sqlite.properties
```

4. Insert the record into the producer:

```
{"id": 1, "author_name": "Chanchal", "age": 26,
"popularity_percentage": 60}

{"id": 2, "author_name": "Manish", "age": 32,
"popularity_percentage": 80}
```

5. Run `sqlite`:

```
sqlite3 packt_authors.db

select * from authors_sink;
```

You will see following output in the table:

```
sqlite> select * from authors_sink;
Chanchal|60.0|1|26
Manish|80.0|2|32
sqlite>
```

Now we know how Kafka Connect can be used to extract and load data from Kafka to the database and from the database to Kafka.

Kafka Connect is not an ETL framework in itself, but it can be part of an ETL pipeline where Kafka is being used. Our intention was to focus on how Kafka Connect can be used in the ETL pipeline and how you can use it to import or export data from Kafka.

Kafka Connect common use cases

You have learned about Kafka Connect in detail. We know Kafka Connect is used for copying data in and out of Kafka.

Let's understand a few common use cases of Kafka Connect:

- **Copying data to HDFS**: User wants to copy data from Kafka topics to HDFS for various reasons. A few want to copy it to HDFS just to take a backup of the history data, others may want to copy it to HDFS for batch processing. However, there are already many open source tools available, such as Camus, Gobblin, Flume, and so on, but maintaining, installing, and running these jobs takes more effort than what Kafka Connect provides. Kafka Connect copies data from topics in parallel and is capable of scaling up more if required.

- **Replication**: Replicating Kafka topics from one cluster to another cluster is also a popular feature offered by Kafka Connect. You may want to replicate topics for various reasons, such as moving from on-premises to cloud or vice versa, changing from one vendor to another, upgrading Kafka cluster, decommissioning the old Kafka cluster, handling disaster management, and so on. One more use case could be you wanting to bring data from many Kafka clusters to a single centralized Kafka cluster for better management and optimal use of data.

- **Importing database records**: Records available in the database can be used for various analytics purposes. We discussed earlier that the same records can be used for real-time analysis and batch analysis. Database records are stored in the topic with the same table name. These records are then passed to the processing engine for further processing.

- **Exporting Kafka records**: In some cases, the data stored in Kafka is already processed, and people want to do some aggregation or sum kind of job on the data. In such cases, they want to store these records in the database for utilizing the powerful features offered by RDBMS. Kafka records can be exported to fast ad hoc search engines such as Elasticsearch for better use cases.

You can also use Kafka Connect to develop your own Connector to import or export data from Kafka. Building Connectors using API is out of the scope of this book.

Summary

In this chapter, we learned about Kafka Connect in detail. We also learned about how we can explore Kafka for an ETL pipeline. We covered examples of JDBC import and export Connector to give you a brief idea of how it works. We expect you to run this program practically to get more insight into what happens when you run Connectors.

In the next chapter, you will learn about Kafka Stream in detail, and we will also see how we can use Kafka stream API to build our own streaming application. We will explore the Kafka Stream API in detail and focus on its advantages.

9
Building Streaming Applications Using Kafka Streams

In the previous chapter, you learned about Kafka Connect and how it makes a user's job simple when it comes to importing and exporting data from Kafka. You also learned how Kafka Connect can be used as an extract and load processor in the ETL pipeline. In this chapter, we will focus on Kafka Stream, which is a lightweight streaming library used to develop a streaming application that works with Kafka. Kafka Stream can act as a transformer in the ETL phase.

We will cover the following topics in this chapter:

- Introduction to Kafka Stream
- Kafka Stream architecture
- Advantages of using Kafka Stream
- Introduction to `KStream` and `KTable`
- Use case example

Introduction to Kafka Streams

The data processing strategy has evolved over time, and it's still being used in different ways. The following are the important terms related to Kafka Streams:

- **Request/response**: In this type of processing, you send a single request. This is sent as request data, and the server processes it and returns the response data as a result. You may take the example of REST servers, where processing is done on request and the response is sent to the client after processing. Processing may involve filtering, cleansing, aggregation, or lookup operations. Scaling such a processing engine requires adding more services in order to handle the increase in traffic.

- **Batch processing**: This is a process where you send a bounded set of input data in batches, and the processing engine sends the response in batches after processing. In batch processing, data is already available in the file or database. Hadoop MapReduce is a good example of a batch processing model. You can increase throughput by adding more processing nodes to the cluster; however, achieving high latency is very challenging in batch processing jobs. The sources of input data and the processing engine are loosely coupled with each other, and hence, the time difference between producing the input data and processing it may be big.

- **Stream processing**: The Stream of data is processed as soon as it is generated from the source system. Data is passed to the Stream processing application in the form of Streams. Streams are ordered sets of unbounded data. Stream processing helps you achieve high latency because you get a processed result for data as soon as it originates from the source.

 You may need to trade off between latency, cost, and correctness when it comes to Stream processing. For example, if you want to develop a fraud analytics application, you will focus more on latency and correctness than on cost. Similarly, if you are just performing an ETL of Stream of data, you may not care about latency in this case, you will look for more correctness.

Using Kafka in Stream processing

Kafka is the persistence queue for data where data is stored in order of time stamp. The following properties of Kafka allow it to occupy its place in most Streaming architecture:

- **Persistence queue and loose coupling**: Kafka stores data in topics, which store data in order. The data producer does not have to wait for a response from the application that processes data. It simply puts data into the Kafka queue, and the processing application consumes data from the Kafka queue to process it.
- **Fault tolerance**: Data stored in Kafka will not be lost even if one or two brokers fail. This is because Kafka replicates topic partition in multiple brokers, so if a broker fails, data will be served from the other broker holding the replica. It has the ability to serve a data Stream without any long delay, which is a critical part of the Stream processing application. Kafka also allows consumers to read messages as per their requirement, meaning you can read from the beginning or you can read from anywhere by providing an offset of the message.
- **Logical ordering**: Data ordering is important for a few critical Streaming applications. Kafka stores data in order of time stamp. Applications such as fraud analytics will not be able to bear the cost of unordered data. The Stream application will be able to read messages in the same order in which they were written in the Kafka topic partition.
- **Scalability**: Kafka has the ability to scale up as per need. All that we need to do is add more broker nodes to the Kafka cluster, and our job is done. You don't need to care about whether your data source will grow exponentially in the future, or whether more applications want to use the same data for multiple use cases. The data is available in Kafka, and any application can read it from here.

Apache Kafka can be easily integrated with any Stream processing application.

Stream processing applications, such as Spark, Storm, or Flink, provide good APIs to integrate Kafka with them. This Stream processing framework provides a nice feature to build the application, but there is some cost and complexity involved. You need to first set up the specific cluster before running the application. You also need to maintain the cluster to identify any problem, to optimize the application, or to check the health of the cluster.

Kafka Stream - lightweight Stream processing library

Kafka Stream is a lightweight Stream processing library that is tightly coupled with Kafka. It does not require any cluster setup or any other operational cost. We will discuss the features that any Stream processing application should persist and how Kafka Stream provides those features.

Before starting this chapter, we recommend you go through the concept of Apache Kafka. You should know about the producer, consumer, topic, parallelism, broker, and other concepts of Apache Kafka to better understand Kafka Stream.

The following are a few important features that Kafka Stream provides you with as an effort to build a robust and reliable Stream processing application:

- **Ordering**: Kafka stores messages/data in topic partitions. Partitions store data in in order of their timestamp. This means that the data in topic partitions is ordered. Kafka Stream utilizes the capability of Kafka and consumes data in order. Order processing can be easily achievable as Kafka also stores the time stamp with messages in topic partition. You can reorder the data in any form using this time stamp property.
- **State management**: Maintaining the state in a Stream processing application is also very important for some state dependent applications. Data processing may require access to recently processed data or derived data, so it is a great idea to maintain the state of the data as close to processing as possible.
  There are two ways to maintain the state:
    - **Remote state**: State is maintained in a third-party storage database, and the application needs to make a connection to the database to retrieve the state of the records. Many large Streaming applications use this practice to maintain the state, but this will cost you high latency as access to the state is remote and depends on network bandwidth and availability.
    - **Local state**: The state is maintained on the same machine where the application instance is running. This allows quick access to the state of records and helps you increase latency.

  Kafka Stream provides a more powerful feature of maintaining the state using the local state management technique. It maintains the local state at each running instance of the application. These local states are shards of the global state. Kafka Stream instance only processes non overlapping subsets of Kafka topic partition.

- **Fault tolerance**: Fault tolerance is a very common and important feature in the Stream processing application. Failure of any instance should not affect the application processing. Kafka Stream maintains change of state in some topic. In case any instance fails, it restarts the process in some other working instance and does the load balancing internally.

- **Time and window**: Time refers to the event time and the processing time of records. Event time is the time when the record is produced or generated, and processing time is the time when the record is actually processed.

  When the record is processed, the data may be processed out of order, irrespective of its event time. Kafka Stream supports the windowing concept, where each record is associated with a time stamp, which helps in the order processing of the event or record. It also helps us deal with late arriving data and to change log efficiently.

- **Partition and scalability**: Kafka Stream utilizes the capability of data parallelism. Multiple instances of the same application work on non overlapping subsets of Kafka topic partitions. Remember that the number of partitions in Kafka is the key to processing parallelism.

  Kafka Stream applications are easily scalable. You just need to ask more instances, and it will do auto load balancing for you.

- **Reprocessing**: This is the ability to reprocess the records from any point. Sometimes you may find that the application logic is missing, or there is a bug that forces you to rewrite the logic or make changes in the existing code and reprocess the data. Kafka Stream can reprocess the records by simply resetting the offset in the Kafka topic.

Kafka Stream architecture

Kafka Streams internally uses the Kafka producer and consumer libraries. It is tightly coupled with Apache Kafka and allows you to leverage the capabilities of Kafka to achieve data parallelism, fault tolerance, and many other powerful features.

In this section, we will discuss how Kafka Stream works internally and what the different components involved in building Stream applications using Kafka Streams are. The following figure is an internal representation of the working of Kafka Stream:

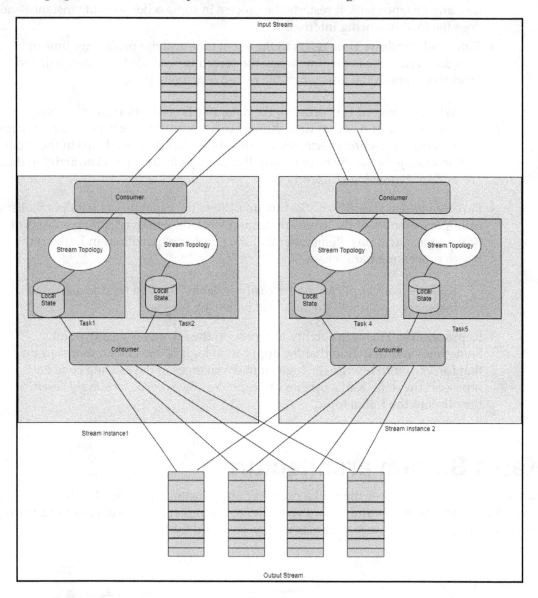

Kafka Stream architecture

Stream instance consists of multiple tasks, where each task processes non overlapping subsets of the record. If you want to increase parallelism, you can simply add more instances, and Kafka Stream will auto distribute work among different instances.

Let's discuss a few important components seen in the previous figure:

- **Stream topology**: Stream topology in Kafka Stream is somewhat similar to the topology of Apache Storm. The topology consists of Stream processor nodes connected with each other to perform the desired computation.
  Stream topology contains three types of processors:
    - **Source processor**: This is responsible for consuming records from the source topic and forwarding records to the downstream processor. It does not have any upstream processor, meaning that it is the first node or processor in Stream topology.
    - **Stream processor**: This is responsible for computing data. The logic of data transformation is handled by the Stream processor. There can be multiple such processors in a single topology.
    - **Sink processor**: This is responsible for consuming data from Stream processors and then writing them to the target topic or system. It is the last processor in the topology, meaning it does not have any downstream processor.

- **Local state**: Kafka Stream maintains a local state for each instance of the application. It provides two types of operators: one is a stateless operator, and the other is a stateful operator. It is similar to the concepts of transformations and actions in Spark; stateless operators are equivalent to transformations, and stateful operators are equivalent to actions.

  When Kafka Stream encounters any stateful operation, it creates and manages the local state store. The data structure used for the state store can be an internal map or a DB.

- **Record cache**: Kafka Stream caches data before storing it to the local state or forwarding it to any downstream. The cache helps in improving read and write performance of the local state store. It can be used as a write-back buffer or as a read buffer. It also allows you to send records in batches to the local state store, which significantly reduces write--request calls to the local state store.

Integrated framework advantages

Kafka Stream is tightly integrated with Apache Kafka. It provides reach sets of API and offers powerful features to build the Stream processing application. If you are using Kafka as a centralized storage layer for your data and want to do Stream processing over the it, then using Kafka Stream should be preferred because of the following reasons:

- **Deployment**: An application built using Kafka Stream does not require any extra setup of the clusters to run. It can be run from a single-node machine or from your laptop. This is a huge advantage over other processing tools, such as Spark, Storm, and so on, which require clusters to be ready before you can run the application. Kafka Stream uses Kafka's producer and consumer library.

  If you want to increase parallelism, you just need to add more instances of the application, and Kafka Stream will do the auto load balancing for you. Just because Kafka Streams is framework free does not mean that Kafka Stream will not need Kafka; Kafka Stream is tightly coupled with Kafka and will not work if you do not have the Kafka cluster running. You need to specify the details of the Kafka cluster when you write your Stream application.

- **Simple and easy features:** Developing the Kafka Stream application is easy compared to other Streaming applications. Kafka Stream simply reads data from the Kafka topic and outputs data to the Kafka topic. Stream partition is similar to Kafka partition Streams, and it works for them too. The Stream application just acts as another consumer that utilizes the capability of Kafka's consumer offset management; it maintains states and other computations in the Kafka topic, and so it does not require an externally dependent system.

- **Coordination and fault tolerance**: Kafka Stream does not depend on any resource manager or third-party application for coordination. It uses the Kafka cluster for the load balancing application when a new instance is added or an old instance fails. In case of failure of load balancing, relievers automatically receive a new partition set to process from the broker.

Understanding tables and Streams together

Before we start discussing tables and Streams, let's understand the following simple code of a word count program written in Java using a Kafka Stream API, and then we will look into the concepts of `KStream` and `KTable`. We have been discussing the concepts of Kafka Stream; in this section, we will discuss `KStream`, `KTable`, and their internals.

Maven dependency

The Kafka Stream application can be run from anywhere. You just need to add library dependency and start developing your program. We are using Maven to build our application. Add the following dependency into your project:

```xml
<dependency>
    <groupId>org.apache.Kafka</groupId>
    <artifactId>Kafka-Streams</artifactId>
    <version>0.10.0.0</version>
</dependency>
```

Kafka Stream word count

The following code is a simple word count program built using a Stream API. We will go through the important APIs used in this program, and will talk about their uses:

```java
package com.packt.Kafka;

import org.apache.Kafka.common.serialization.Serde;
import org.apache.Kafka.common.serialization.Serdes;
import org.apache.Kafka.Streams.KafkaStreams;
import org.apache.Kafka.Streams.KeyValue;
import org.apache.Kafka.Streams.StreamsConfig;
import org.apache.Kafka.Streams.kStream.KStream;
import org.apache.Kafka.Streams.kStream.KStreamBuilder;

import java.util.Arrays;
import java.util.Properties;

public class KafkaStreamWordCount {
    public static void main(String[] args) throws Exception {
        Properties KafkaStreamProperties = new Properties();
// Stream configuration
        KafkaStreamProperties.put(StreamsConfig.APPLICATION_ID_CONFIG,
"Kafka-Stream-wordCount");
        KafkaStreamProperties.put(StreamsConfig.BOOTSTRAP_SERVERS_CONFIG,
"localhost:9092");
        KafkaStreamProperties.put(StreamsConfig.ZOOKEEPER_CONNECT_CONFIG,
"localhost:2181");
        KafkaStreamProperties.put(StreamsConfig.KEY_SERDE_CLASS_CONFIG,
Serdes.String().getClass().getName());
        KafkaStreamProperties.put(StreamsConfig.VALUE_SERDE_CLASS_CONFIG,
Serdes.String().getClass().getName());

        Serde<String> stringSerde = Serdes.String();
```

```
        Serde<Long> longSerde = Serdes.Long();

        KStreamBuilder StreamTopology = new KStreamBuilder();

//Kstream to read input data from input topic
        KStream<String, String> topicRecords =
StreamTopology.Stream(stringSerde, stringSerde, "input");
        KStream<String, Long> wordCounts = topicRecords
            .flatMapValues(value ->
Arrays.asList(value.toLowerCase().split("\\W+")))
            .map((key, word) -> new KeyValue<>(word, word))
            .countByKey("Count")
            .toStream();

//Store wordcount result in wordcount topic
        wordCounts.to(stringSerde, longSerde, "wordCount");

        KafkaStreams StreamManager = new KafkaStreams(StreamTopology,
KafkaStreamProperties);
//Running Stream job
        StreamManager.start();

        Runtime.getRuntime().addShutdownHook(new
Thread(StreamManager::close));
    }


}
```

The application starts with a configuration where we define the set, Kafka Stream provides two important abstractions: one is KStream, and the other is KTable.

KStream is an abstraction of a key-value pair record Stream of Kafka's topic record. In KStream, each record is independent, meaning that a record with a key does not replace an old record with the same key. KStream can be created in two ways:

- **Using the Kafka topic**: Any Kafka Stream application starts with KStream, which consumes data from the Kafka topic. If you look into the earlier program, the following lines create KStream topicRecords, which will consume data from the topic input:

```
        KStream<String, String> topicRecords =
        StreamTopology.Stream(stringSerde, stringSerde, "input");
```

- **Using transformation**: KStream can be created by doing transformation on the existing KStream. If you look at the previous program, you will see that there are transformations such as flatMapValues and map that are used on KStream topicRecords. KStream can also be created by converting KTable into KStream. In the same example, countByKey will create KTable Count, and then we convert it to KStream using toStream():

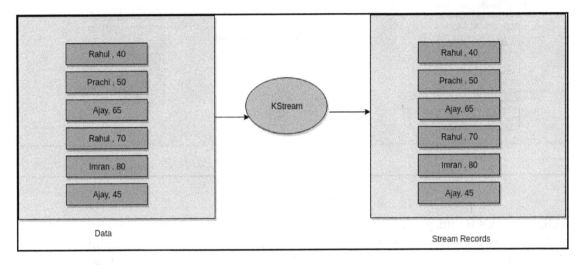

KStream record representation

KTable

KTable is a representation of Changelog, which does not contain a record with the same key twice. This means that if KTable encounters a record with the same key in the table, it will simply replace the old record with the current record.

If the same record represented in the previous diagram for KStream is converted to KTable, it will look like this:

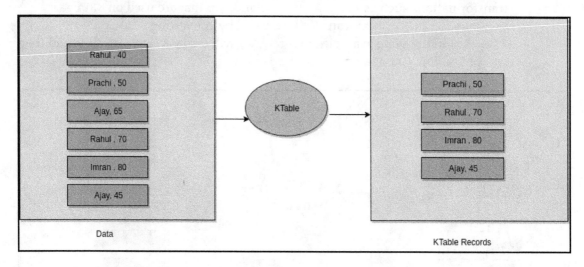

KTable record representation

In the previous figure, you can see that the records of Rahul and Ajay have been updated and the old entries have been removed. KTable is similar to the update operation in Map. Whenever a duplicate key is inserted, the old value gets replaced by a new value. We can perform various operations on KTable and join it to other KStream or KTable instances.

Use case example of Kafka Streams

We will take the same example of IP fraud detection that we used in Chapter 5, *Building Spark Streaming Applications with Kafka,* and Chapter 6, *Building Storm Application with Kafka.* Let's start with how we can build the same application using Kafka Stream. We will start with the code, take the producer, and look up the code from Chapter 6, *Building Storm Application with Kafka,* which can be utilized here as well.

Maven dependency of Kafka Streams

The best part of Kafka Stream is that it does not require any extra dependency apart from Stream libraries. Add the dependency to your pom.xml:

```
<?xml version="1.0" encoding="UTF-8"?>
<project xmlns="http://Maven.apache.org/POM/4.0.0"
```

```
        xmlns:xsi="http://www.w3.org/2001/XMLSchema-instance"
        xsi:schemaLocation="http://Maven.apache.org/POM/4.0.0
http://Maven.apache.org/xsd/Maven-4.0.0.xsd">
    <modelVersion>4.0.0</modelVersion>

    <groupId>com.packt</groupId>
    <artifactId>KafkaStream</artifactId>
    <version>1.0-SNAPSHOT</version>
    <build>
        <plugins>
            <plugin>
                <groupId>org.apache.Maven.plugins</groupId>
                <artifactId>Maven-compiler-plugin</artifactId>
                <configuration>
                    <source>1.8</source>
                    <target>1.8</target>
                </configuration>
            </plugin>
        </plugins>
    </build>
    <dependencies>
        <!--
https://mvnrepository.com/artifact/org.apache.Kafka/Kafka-Streams -->
        <dependency>
            <groupId>org.apache.Kafka</groupId>
            <artifactId>Kafka-Streams</artifactId>
            <version>0.10.0.1</version>
        </dependency>

    </dependencies>

</project>
```

Property reader

We are going to use the same property file and property reader that we used in Chapter 6, *Building Storm Application with Kafka,* with a few changes. Kafka Stream will read the record from the `iprecord` topic and will produce the output to the `fraudIp` topic:

```
topic=iprecord
broker.list=localhost:9092
output_topic=fraudIp
```

Here is the property reader class:

```
package com.packt.Kafka.utils;
```

```
import java.io.FileNotFoundException;
import java.io.IOException;
import java.io.InputStream;
import java.util.Properties;

public class PropertyReader {

    private Properties prop = null;

    public PropertyReader() {

        InputStream is = null;
        try {
            this.prop = new Properties();
            is =
this.getClass().getResourceAsStream("/Streaming.properties");
            prop.load(is);
        } catch (FileNotFoundException e) {
            e.printStackTrace();
        } catch (IOException e) {
            e.printStackTrace();
        }
    }

    public String getPropertyValue(String key) {
        return this.prop.getProperty(key);
    }
}
```

IP record producer

Again, the producer is the same as we used in Chapter 5, *Building Spark Streaming Applications with Kafka*, and Chapter 6, *Building Storm Application with Kafka*, which generates records with random IPs. The producer will auto-create the topic if it does not exist. Here is how the code goes:

```
package com.packt.Kafka.producer;

import com.packt.Kafka.utils.PropertyReader;
import org.apache.Kafka.clients.producer.KafkaProducer;
import org.apache.Kafka.clients.producer.ProducerRecord;
import org.apache.Kafka.clients.producer.RecordMetadata;

import java.io.BufferedReader;
import java.io.IOException;
import java.io.InputStreamReader;
```

```
import java.util.*;
import java.util.concurrent.Future;


public class IPLogProducer extends TimerTask {

    public BufferedReader readFile() {
        BufferedReader BufferedReader = new BufferedReader(new
InputStreamReader(
                this.getClass().getResourceAsStream("/IP_LOG.log")));
        return BufferedReader;

    }

    public static void main(final String[] args) {
        Timer timer = new Timer();
        timer.schedule(new IPLogProducer(), 3000, 3000);
    }

    private String getNewRecordWithRandomIP(String line) {
        Random r = new Random();
        String ip = r.nextInt(256) + "." + r.nextInt(256) + "." +
r.nextInt(256) + "." + r.nextInt(256);
        String[] columns = line.split(" ");
        columns[0] = ip;
        return Arrays.toString(columns);
    }

    @Override
    public void run() {
        PropertyReader propertyReader = new PropertyReader();

        Properties producerProps = new Properties();
        producerProps.put("bootstrap.servers",
propertyReader.getPropertyValue("broker.list"));
        producerProps.put("key.serializer",
"org.apache.Kafka.common.serialization.StringSerializer");
        producerProps.put("value.serializer",
"org.apache.Kafka.common.serialization.StringSerializer");
        producerProps.put("auto.create.topics.enable", "true");

        KafkaProducer<String, String> ipProducer = new
KafkaProducer<String, String>(producerProps);

        BufferedReader br = readFile();
        String oldLine = "";
        try {
            while ((oldLine = br.readLine()) != null) {
```

```
                       String line =
getNewRecordWithRandomIP(oldLine).replace("[", "").replace("]", "");
                   ProducerRecord ipData = new ProducerRecord<String,
String>(propertyReader.getPropertyValue("topic"), line);
                   Future<RecordMetadata> recordMetadata =
ipProducer.send(ipData);
           }
       } catch (IOException e) {
           e.printStackTrace();
       }
       ipProducer.close();
   }
}
```

Verify the producer record using the console producer. Run the following command on the Kafka cluster:

```
Kafka-console-consumer --zookeeper localhost:2181 --topic iprecord --from-
beginning
```

Remember that we are producing multiple records by changing the IP address randomly. You'll be able to see the records as shown in the following figure:

```
Using the ConsoleConsumer with old consumer is deprecated and will be removed in a future major release. Consider using the new consumer
sing [bootstrap-server] instead of [zookeeper].
49.10.237.128, -, -, 07/Mar/2004:16:05:49, -0800, "GET, /twiki/bin/edit/Main/Double_bounce_sender?topicparent=Main.ConfigurationVariables
/1.1", 401, 12846
169.100.71.241, -, -, 07/Mar/2004:16:06:51, -0800, "GET, /twiki/bin/rdiff/TWiki/NewUserTemplate?rev1=1.3&rev2=1.2, HTTP/1.1", 200, 4523
90.131.75.45, -, -, 07/Mar/2004:16:10:02, -0800, "GET, /mailman/listinfo/hsdivision, HTTP/1.1", 200, 6291
58.202.218.174, -, -, 07/Mar/2004:16:11:58, -0800, "GET, /twiki/bin/view/TWiki/WikiSyntax, HTTP/1.1", 200, 7352
202.63.36.26, -, -, 07/Mar/2004:16:20:55, -0800, "GET, /twiki/bin/view/Main/DCCAndPostFix, HTTP/1.1", 200, 5253
18.250.52.72, -, -, 07/Mar/2004:16:23:12, -0800, "GET, /twiki/bin/oops/TWiki/AppendixFileSystem?template=oopsmore&param1=1.12&param2=1.12
/1.1", 200, 11382
59.90.177.88, -, -, 07/Mar/2004:16:24:16, -0800, "GET, /twiki/bin/view/Main/PeterThoeny, HTTP/1.1", 200, 4924
0.64.150.25, -, -, 07/Mar/2004:16:29:16, -0800, "GET, /twiki/bin/edit/Main/Header_checks?topicparent=Main.ConfigurationVariables, HTTP/1.
1, 12851
76.148.132.191, -, -, 07/Mar/2004:16:30:29, -0800, "GET, /twiki/bin/attach/Main/OfficeLocations, HTTP/1.1", 401, 12851
139.133.221.180, -, -, 07/Mar/2004:16:31:48, -0800, "GET, /twiki/bin/view/TWiki/WebTopicEditTemplate, HTTP/1.1", 200, 3732
67.44.110.109, -, -, 07/Mar/2004:16:32:50, -0800, "GET, /twiki/bin/view/Main/WebChanges, HTTP/1.1", 200, 40520
55.24.117.232, -, -, 07/Mar/2004:16:33:53, -0800, "GET, /twiki/bin/edit/Main/Smtpd_etrn_restrictions?topicparent=Main.ConfigurationVariab
TTP/1.1", 401, 12851
122.232.93.84, -, -, 07/Mar/2004:16:35:19, -0800, "GET, /mailman/listinfo/business, HTTP/1.1", 200, 6379
139.232.241.115, -, -, 07/Mar/2004:16:36:22, -0800, "GET, /twiki/bin/rdiff/Main/WebIndex?rev1=1.2&rev2=1.1, HTTP/1.1", 200, 46373
98.74.200.147, -, -, 07/Mar/2004:16:37:27, -0800, "GET, /twiki/bin/view/TWiki/DontNotify, HTTP/1.1", 200, 4140
48.220.6.25, -, -, 07/Mar/2004:16:39:24, -0800, "GET, /twiki/bin/view/Main/TokyoOffice, HTTP/1.1", 200, 3853
220.105.174.45, -, -, 07/Mar/2004:16:43:54, -0800, "GET, /twiki/bin/view/Main/MikeMannix, HTTP/1.1", 200, 3686
```

IP lookup service

As mentioned earlier, the lookup service is reused from Chapter 5, *Building Spark Streaming Applications with Kafka,* and Chapter 6, *Building Storm Application with Kafka*. Note that this is in the memory lookup created over the interface, so you can add your own lookup service by simply providing implementation for isFraud(), and you are done.

The **IP scanner interface** looks like this:

```
package com.packt.Kafka.lookup;

public interface IIPScanner {

    boolean isFraudIP(String ipAddresses);

}
```

We have kept the in-memory IP lookup very simple for an interactive execution of the application. The lookup service will scan the IP address and detect whether the record is a fraud or not by comparing the first 8 bits of the IP address:

```
package com.packt.Kafka.lookup;

import java.io.Serializable;
import java.util.HashSet;
import java.util.Set;


public class CacheIPLookup implements IIPScanner, Serializable {

    private Set<String> fraudIPList = new HashSet<>();

    public CacheIPLookup() {
        fraudIPList.add("212");
        fraudIPList.add("163");
        fraudIPList.add("15");
        fraudIPList.add("224");
        fraudIPList.add("126");
        fraudIPList.add("92");
        fraudIPList.add("91");
        fraudIPList.add("10");
        fraudIPList.add("112");
        fraudIPList.add("194");
        fraudIPList.add("198");
        fraudIPList.add("11");
        fraudIPList.add("12");
        fraudIPList.add("13");
        fraudIPList.add("14");
        fraudIPList.add("15");
        fraudIPList.add("16");
    }


    @Override
    public boolean isFraudIP(String ipAddresses) {
```

```
            return fraudIPList.contains(ipAddresses);
    }
}
```

Fraud detection application

The fraud detection application will be running continuously, and you can run as many instances as you want; Kafka will do the load balancing for you. Let's look at the following code that reads the input from the iprecord topic and then filters out records that are fraud using the lookup service:

```java
package com.packt.Kafka;


import com.packt.Kafka.lookup.CacheIPLookup;
import com.packt.Kafka.utils.PropertyReader;
import org.apache.Kafka.common.serialization.Serde;
import org.apache.Kafka.common.serialization.Serdes;
import org.apache.Kafka.Streams.KafkaStreams;
import org.apache.Kafka.Streams.StreamsConfig;
import org.apache.Kafka.Streams.kStream.KStream;
import org.apache.Kafka.Streams.kStream.KStreamBuilder;

import java.util.Properties;

public class IPFraudKafkaStreamApp {
    private static CacheIPLookup cacheIPLookup = new CacheIPLookup();
    private static PropertyReader propertyReader = new PropertyReader();

    public static void main(String[] args) throws Exception {
        Properties KafkaStreamProperties = new Properties();
        KafkaStreamProperties.put(StreamsConfig.APPLICATION_ID_CONFIG, "IP-
Fraud-Detection");
        KafkaStreamProperties.put(StreamsConfig.BOOTSTRAP_SERVERS_CONFIG,
"localhost:9092");
        KafkaStreamProperties.put(StreamsConfig.ZOOKEEPER_CONNECT_CONFIG,
"localhost:2181");
        KafkaStreamProperties.put(StreamsConfig.KEY_SERDE_CLASS_CONFIG,
Serdes.String().getClass().getName());
        KafkaStreamProperties.put(StreamsConfig.VALUE_SERDE_CLASS_CONFIG,
Serdes.String().getClass().getName());

        Serde<String> stringSerde = Serdes.String();

        KStreamBuilder fraudDetectionTopology = new KStreamBuilder();
//Reading fraud record from topic configured in configuration file
```

```
        KStream<String, String> ipRecords =
fraudDetectionTopology.Stream(stringSerde, stringSerde,
propertyReader.getPropertyValue("topic"));
//Checking if record is fraud using in memory lookup service

        KStream<String, String> fraudIpRecords = ipRecords
                .filter((k, v) -> isFraud(v));
//Storing fraud IP's to topic
        fraudIpRecords.to(propertyReader.getPropertyValue("output_topic"));

        KafkaStreams StreamManager = new
KafkaStreams(fraudDetectionTopology, KafkaStreamProperties);
        StreamManager.start();

        Runtime.getRuntime().addShutdownHook(new
Thread(StreamManager::close));
    }

//Fraud ip lookup method
    private static boolean isFraud(String record) {
        String IP = record.split(" ")[0];
        String[] ranges = IP.split("\\.");
        String range = null;
        try {
            range = ranges[0] + "." + ranges[1];
        } catch (ArrayIndexOutOfBoundsException ex) {
                //handling here
        }
        return cacheIPLookup.isFraudIP(range);
    }
}
```

Summary

In this chapter, you learned about Kafka Stream and how it makes sense to use Kafka Stream to do transformation when we have Kafka in our pipeline. We also went through the architecture, internal working, and integrated framework advantages of Kafka Streams. We covered KStream and KTable in brief and understood how they are different from each other. A detailed explanation of the Kafka Stream API is out of the scope of this book.

In the next chapter, we will cover the internals of Kafka clusters, capacity planning, single-cluster and multi-cluster deployment, and adding and removing brokers.

10
Kafka Cluster Deployment

In the previous chapters, we talked about the different use cases associated with Apache Kafka. We shed light on different technologies and frameworks associated with the Kafka messaging system. However, putting Kafka to production use requires additional tasks and knowledge. Firstly, you must have a very thorough understanding of how the Kafka cluster works. Later on, you must determine the hardware required for the Kafka cluster by performing adequate capacity planning. You need to understand Kafka deployment patterns and how to perform day-to-day Kafka administrating activities. In this chapter, we will cover the following topics:

- Kafka cluster internals
- Capacity planning
- Single-cluster deployment
- Multi-cluster deployment
- Decommissioning brokers
- Data migration

In a nutshell, this chapter focuses on Kafka cluster deployment on enterprise grade production systems. It covers deep topics of Kafka clusters such as how to do capacity planning, how to manage single/multi cluster deployments, and so on. It also covers how to manage Kafka in a multitenant environment. It further walks through the different steps involved in Kafka data migrations.

Kafka cluster internals

Well, this topic has been covered in bits and pieces in the introductory chapters of this book. However, in this section, we are covering this topic with respect to components or processes that play an important role in Kafka cluster. We will not only talk about different Kafka cluster components but will also cover how these components communicate with each other via Kafka protocols.

Role of Zookeeper

Kafka clusters cannot run without Zookeeper servers, which are tightly coupled with Kafka cluster installations. Therefore, you should first start this section by understanding the role of Zookeeper in Kafka clusters.

If we must define the role of Zookeeper in a few words, we can say that Zookeeper acts a Kafka cluster coordinator that manages cluster membership of brokers, producers, and consumers participating in message transfers via Kafka. It also helps in leader election for a Kafka topic. It is like a centralized service that manages cluster memberships, relevant configurations, and cluster registry services.

Zookeeper also keeps track of brokers that are alive and nodes that have joined or left the cluster. It can be configured to work in quorum or replicated mode, where the same data and configurations are replicated across multiple nodes to support high availability and load balancing of incoming requests. Standalone modes are good for development or testing purposes. In a production environment where high availability and performance matters, you should always deploy Zookeeper in the replicated mode.

If you are looking for detailed documentation on Zookeeper, you can always consider Apache docs for the same at `https://zookeeper.apache.org/`, but we believe in the context of Kafka, there are two important aspects you should learn. The first is how Kafka cluster data is maintained on Zookeeper nodes, and the second is how Zookeeper is used in the leader election process. Let's look at those aspects in the following paragraphs.

Let's discuss how the Kafka topic leader election process works. Each Kafka cluster has a designated broker, which has more responsibilities than the other brokers. These additional responsibilities are related to partition management. This broker is called **controller**. One of the prime responsibilities of the controller is to elect partition leaders. Generally, it is the first broker that starts in the cluster. After it starts, it creates an ephemeral znode (`/controller`) in Zookeeper. In that `/controller` location, it maintains metadata about brokers that are alive and about topic partitions along with their data replication status.

To monitor broker live status controller, keep a watch on the ephemeral znodes (`/brokers`) created by other brokers. In case the broker leaves the cluster or dies down, the ephemeral znode created by the broker is deleted. The controller is now aware that the partitions for which that broker was the leader needs to have a new leader.

After collecting all the information about the partitions that need a new leader, it finds out the next replica broker for those partitions and sends them leader requests. The same information is passed to all the followers so that they can start syncing data from the newly elected leader. After receiving the leader requests, the new leader brokers know that they must serve the producer and consumer requests for that topic partition.

 To summarize, the Zookeeper ephemeral znode feature is used by Kafka to elect a controller and to notify the controller when other broker nodes join and leave the cluster. This notification triggers the leader election process by the controller.

Now that we are aware of the leader election process in Kafka, let's consider the different znodes maintained by Kafka cluster. Kafka uses Zookeeper for storing a variety of configurations and metadata in key-value format in the ZK data tree and uses them across the cluster. The following nodes are maintained by Kafka:

- `/controller`: This is the Kafka znode for controller leader election
- `/brokers`: This is the Kafka znode for broker metadata
- `/kafka-acl`: This is the Kafka znode for `SimpleACLAuthorizer` ACL storage
- `/admin`: This is the Kafka admin tool metadata
- `/isr_change_notification`: This denotes the track changes to in sync replication
- `/controller_epoch`: This denotes the track movement of the controller
- `/consumers`: This is the Kafka consumer list
- `/config`: This denotes the entity configuration

Replication

One of the important aspects of Kafka is that it is highly available, and this is guaranteed through data replication. Replication is the core principle of Kafka design. Any type of client (producer or consumer) interacting with Kafka cluster is aware of the replication mechanism implemented by Kafka.

You should understand that in Kafka, replications are driven by topic partitions. All these replicas are stored in different brokers participating in Kafka cluster.

You should always see replications in terms of leaders and followers. To further elaborate on this, you always set the replication factor of the topic. Based on this replication number, the data in every partition of the topic is copied over to that many different brokers. In the context of fail over, if the replication factor is set to n, then Kafka cluster can accommodate n-1 failures to ensure guaranteed message delivery.

The diagram following represents how replication works in Kafka:

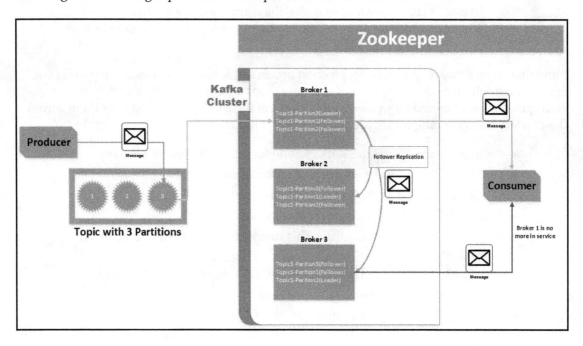

Partition leaders receive messages from producer applications. Followers send the fetch requests to the leaders to keep replicas in sync. You can think of followers as another consumer application trying to read data from the leaders of the partition.

Once all the replicas are in sync, the consumer can consume messages from the partition leader. Controllers with the help of Zookeeper keep track of the leader of the partition, and in case of leader failure, they choose another leader. Once a new leader is chosen, consumers start consuming from the new leader of the partition.

There are two types of replication supported by Kafka--synchronous and asynchronous:

- **Synchronous replication**: In synchronous replication, a producer finds out a leader of topic partition from Zookeeper and publishes the message. Once the message is published, it is written to the leader's log. The followers of the leader then start reading the messages. The order of the messages is always ensured. Once a follower successfully writes the message to its own log, it sends an acknowledgement to the leader. When the leader knows that the replication is done and the acknowledgment is received, it sends the acknowledgment to the producer about successful publishing of the message.
- **Asynchronous replication**: In asynchronous replication, the acknowledgement to the producer is sent immediately after the leader writes the message to its own log. The leader does not wait for any acknowledgement from its follower, and this practice does not ensure guaranteed message delivery in case of broker failure.

Metadata request processing

Before we jump into producer or consumer request processing, we should understand some of the common activities that any Kafka client or broker would perform irrespective of whether it is a write request or fetch request. One such request is to understand how metadata is requested or fetched by Kafka clients.

Following are the steps involved in metadata requests for producing a message:

1. Based on the configuration files, the client prepares a list of topics they are interested in along with the first broker they would send the metadata request to.
2. It sends the requests to the broker with an array of topics prepared from step 1. If the array of topics is null, the metadata for all the topics is fetched. Along with the list of topics, it also sends a Boolean flag `allow_auto_topic_creation` to the broker for creating topics that don't exist.
3. If the response is received from the broker, then send the write request to the leader of the partition. If no valid response is received or the request times out, the other broker from the configuration list is picked for the metadata fetch request.
4. Finally, the client would receive the acknowledgement from the broker for successful or unsuccessful message writes.

Both the broker and the client cache the metadata information and refresh them at some specific time interval. In general, if the client receives a *Not a leader* response from a broker, it realizes that the cached metadata is old. It then requests fresh metadata from the broker as an error indicates that the client metadata has expired.

Producer request processing

Client requests that are intended to write messages to Kafka queues are called producer requests. Based on the information received from the metadata request, the client issues a write request to the leader broker. All the write requests contain a parameter called **ack**, which determines when brokers should respond with a successful write to the client. Following are the possible values of the ack configuration:

- **1**: This means the message is accepted only by the leader
- **all**: This means all in-sync replicas along with the leader have accepted the message
- **0**: This means do not wait for acceptance from any of the brokers

On the other hand, the broker first checks whether all the relevant information is in the request. It checks whether the user issuing the request has all the relevant privileges or not and whether the ack variable has relevant values (1, 0, or all).

For all acks, it checks whether there are enough in sync replicas for writing the messages. If all relevant parameters and checks are in place, the broker will write messages to the local disk. The broker uses the OS page cache to write the messages and does not wait for it to be written to the disk. Once the messages are written to the cache, the relevant response is sent back to the client.

So, if the ack value is set to *0*, the broker sends the response back to the client as soon as it receives it. If it is set to *1*, the broker sends a response back to the client once it has written the messages to the file cache. If the acks configuration is set to all, the request will be stored in a **purgatory buffer**. In this case, the response will be sent to the client when the leader receives an acknowledgement from all the followers.

Consumer request processing

Same as the producer requests, consumer fetch requests start with metadata requests. Once the consumer is aware of the leader information, it forms a fetch request containing an offset from which it wants to read the data. It also provides the minimum and maximum number of messages it wants to read from the leader broker.

The consumer can pre-allocate memory for the response from the broker, and therefore, we should specify the maximum limit of memory allocation. If the minimum limit is not specified, there could be inefficient utilization of resources when the broker sends a small portion of the data for which very little memory is required. Instead of processing a small amount of data, the consumer can wait for more data to come and then run a batch job to process the data.

The brokers upon receiving the fetch requests, checks whether an offset exists or not. If the offset exists, the broker will read messages till the batch size reaches the limit set by the client and then eventually send the response back to the client. It is important to note that all the fetch requests are handled using the **zero copy** approach. This kind of approach is very common in a Java-based system for efficiently transferring data over the network. Using this approach, the broker does not copy intermediate data to memory buffers, instead, it is sent to network channels immediately. This saves a lot of CPU cycles and, hence, increases performance.

In addition to the preceding information, it is important for you to remember two other important aspects of consumer request processing. One is about the minimum number of messages required by the fetch request. The other is that consumers can only read messages that are written to all followers of the leader of the partition.

In other words, consumers can only fetch those messages that all in-sync replicas have received and registered to their local files' system cache.

Capacity planning

Capacity planning is mostly required when you want to deploy Kafka in your production environment. Capacity planning helps you achieve the desired performance from Kafka systems along with the required hardware. In this section, we will talk about some of the important aspects to consider while performing capacity planning of Kafka cluster.

Note that there is no one definite way to perform Kafka capacity planning. There are multiple factors that come into the picture, and they vary depending upon your organizational use cases.

Our goal here is to give you a good starting point for Kafka cluster capacity planning with some pointers that you should always keep in mind. Let's consider these one by one.

Capacity planning goals

This is the most important thing while performing capacity planning of your Kafka cluster. You should be very clear with your capacity planning goals. You should understand that without having clear goals in mind, it is very difficult to perform appropriate capacity planning.

Generally, capacity planning goals are driven by **latency** and **throughput**. Some of the additional goals could be fault tolerance and high availability.

 We suggest you derive quantifiable goals so that you can always come up with logical mathematical conclusions to capacity planning numbers. Moreover, your goals should also consider future data growth or increase in the number of requests.

Replication factor

Replication factor is one of the main factors in capacity planning. As a rule of thumb, one single broker can only host only one partition replica. If that had not been the case, one broker failure could have caused Kafka to become unavailable.

Hence, the number of brokers must be greater than, or equal to, the number of replicas. As you can clearly observe, the number of replicas not only decides the number of failures Kafka can handle, but also helps in deciding the minimum number of broker servers required for your Kafka cluster.

Memory

Kafka is highly dependent on the file system for storing and caching messages. All the data is written to the page cache in the form of log files, which are flushed to disk later. Generally, most of the modern Linux OS use free memory for disk cache. Kafka ends up utilizing 25-30 GB of page cache for 32 GB memory.

Moreover, as Kafka utilizes heap memory very efficiently, 4-5 GB of heap size is enough for it. While calculating memory, one aspect you need to remember is that Kafka buffers messages for active producers and consumers. The disk buffer cache lives in your RAM. This means that you need sufficient RAM to store a certain time of messages in cache. While calculating buffer requirements, there are two things you should keep in mind: one is the amount of time you want to buffer messages (this can vary from 30 seconds to 1 minute), the second is the read or write throughput goal you have in mind.

Based on that, you can calculate your memory needs using this formula:

*Throughput * buffer time*

Generally, a 64 GB machine is decent for a high performance Kafka cluster. 32 GB would also meet those needs. However, you should avoid using anything less than 32 GB as you may end up having smaller machines to load balance your read and write requests.

Hard drives

You should try to estimate the amount of hard drive space required per broker along with the number of disk drives per broker. Multiple drives help in achieving good throughput. You should also not share Kafka data drives with Kafka logs, Zookeeper data, or other OS file system data. This ensures good latency.

Let's first talk about how to determine disk space requirements per broker. You should first estimate your average message size. You should also estimate your average message throughput and for how many days you would like to keep the messages in the Kafka cluster.

Based on these estimates, you can calculate the space per broker using the following formula:

*(Message Size * Write Throughput * Message Retention Period * Replication Factor) / Number of Brokers*

SSDs provide significant performance improvements for Kafka. There are two reasons for it, and they are explained as follows:

- Write to disk from Kafka is asynchronous and no operations of Kafka wait for disk sync to complete. However, the disk sync happens in the background. If we use a single replica for topic partition, we may lose data completely because the disk may crash before it syncs data to disk.

- Each message in Kafka is stored in a particular partition, which stores data sequentially in the write ahead log. We may say reads and writes in Kafka happen in a sequence. Sequential reads and writes are heavily optimized by SSD.

You should avoid **network attached storage (NAS)**. NAS is slower with a higher latency and bottleneck as a single point of failure. RAID 10 is also recommended, but at times, due to additional cost, people do not opt for it. In that case, you should configure your Kafka server with multiple log directories, each directory mounted on a separate drive.

Network

Kafka is a distributed messaging system. The network plays a very important role in a distributed environment. A bad network design may affect the performance of the overall cluster. A fast and reliable network ensures that nodes can communicate with each other easily.

A cluster should not span multiple data centers, even if data centers are close to each other. High latency will complicate the problem in any distributed system and will make debugging and resolution look difficult.

CPU

Kafka does not have very high CPU requirement. Although more CPU cores are recommended. Choose a next-generation processor with more cores. Common clusters consist of 24 core machines. CPU cores help you add extra concurrency, and more cores will always improve your performance.

If you want to use SSL with Kafka, it may increase your CPU core requirement as SSL occupies a few cores for its operation.

Single cluster deployment

This section will give you an overview of what Kafka cluster would look like in a single data center. In a single cluster deployment, all your clients would connect to one data center, and read/write would happen from the same cluster. You would have multiple brokers and Zookeeper servers deployed to serve the requests. All those brokers and Zookeepers would be in the same data center within the same network subnet.

The following diagram represents what single cluster deployments would look like:

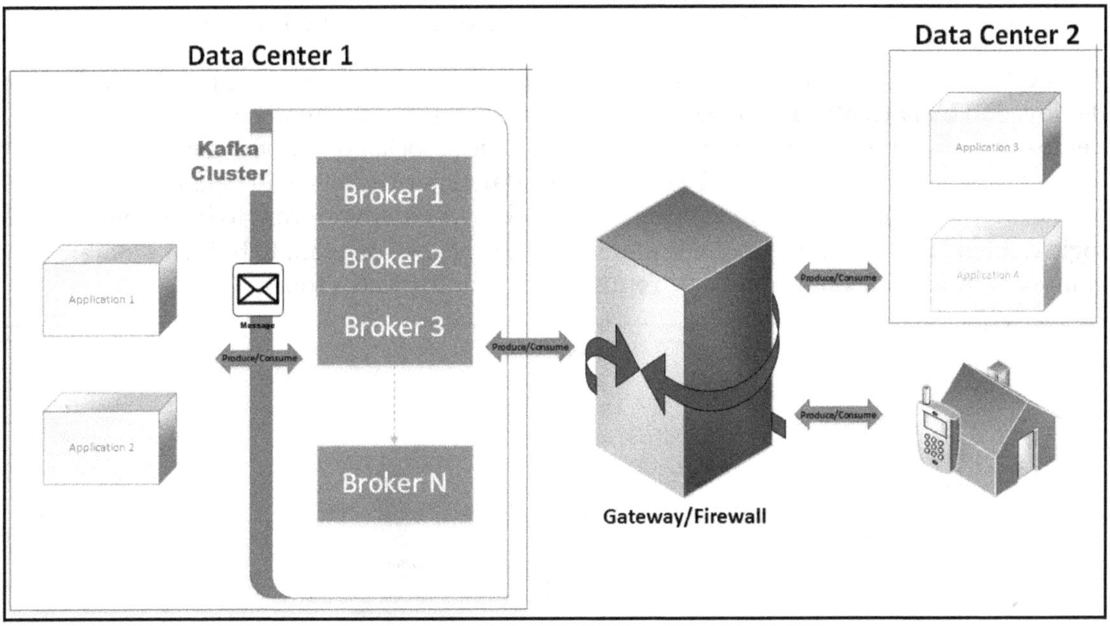

In the preceding diagram, Kafka is deployed in **Data Center 1**. Just like any other single Kafka cluster deployment, there are internal clients (**Application 1** and **Application 2**), remote clients in different Data Centers (**Application 3** and **Application 4**), and direct remote clients in the form of mobile applications.

As you can clearly see, this kind of setup has dependency on a single data center. This can cause stoppage of your critical functionalities in case of data center outage. Moreover, due to cross-region data travel, sometimes the response time is also delayed. Sometimes, due to a very high request load, single data center resources are not enough to ensure latency and throughput SLAs. To avoid such problems, you can adopt multicluster Kafka deployment. We will discuss that in the following section.

Multicluster deployment

Generally, multicluster deployment is used to mitigate some of the risks associated with single cluster deployment. We have mentioned to you, some of those risks in the preceding section. Multicluster deployment can come in two flavors - distributive models and aggregate models.

The distributive model diagram is shown in the following figure. In this model, based on the topics, messages are sent to different Kafka clusters deployed in different data centers. Here, we have chosen to deploy Kafka cluster on Data Center 1 and Data Center 3.

Applications deployed in **Data Center 2** can choose to send data to any of the Kafka clusters deployed in **Data Center 1** and **Data Center 3**. They will use different a data center-deployed Kafka cluster depending on the Kafka topic associated with the messages. This kind of message routing can also be done using some intermediate load balancer application as well. It's a choice that you must make; whether you want to have routing logic written in your producer or consumer application, or you want to build a separate component to decide on the message routing-based on the Kafka topic.

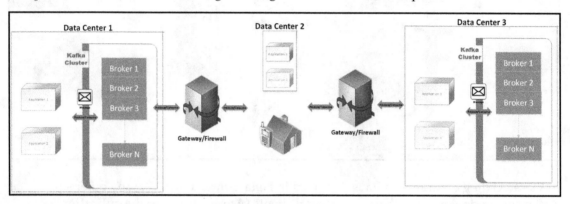

The aggregate model is another example of multicluster deployment. In this model, data is synced between clusters in Data Center 1 and Data Center 3 using a tool called **Mirror Maker**. Mirror maker uses a Kafka consumer to consume messages from the source cluster and republishes those messages to the local (target) cluster using an embedded Kafka producer. A detailed document on it can be found at `https://kafka.apache.org/documentation.html#basic_ops_mirror_maker`. Clients can use any of the clusters for reading and writing to any of the clusters. Aggregate models support more availability and scalability as requests are load balanced equally between the two data centers. Moreover, it has more tolerance for failure as in case of one data center outage, the other data center can serve all requests.

Following is a representation of the aggregate model:

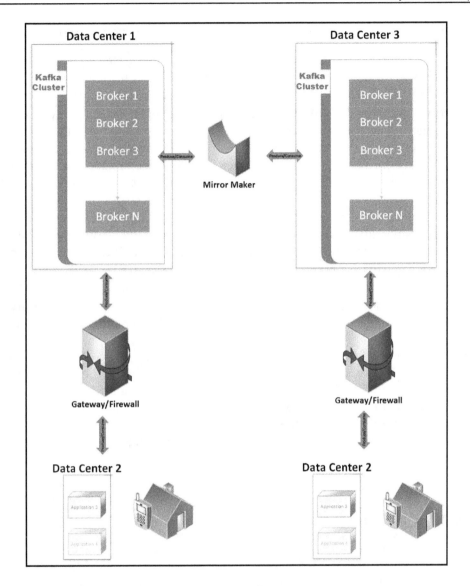

Decommissioning brokers

Kafka is a distributed and replicated messaging system. Decommissioning brokers can become a tedious task sometimes. In lieu of that, we thought of introducing this section to keep you informed about some of the steps you should perform for decommissioning the broker.

You can automate this using any scripting language. In general, you should perform the following steps:

1. Log in to the Zookeeper shell, and from there, collect the relevant broker information based on the broker IP or hostname.

2. Next, based on the broker information collected from Zookeeper, you should gather information about which topics and partition data need to be reassigned to different brokers. You can use Kafka topic shell-based utilities to gather such information. Basically, topic partitions that require reassignment are identified with leader and replicas values that are equal to the broker ID of the node that is to be decommissioned.

3. You then should prepare a reassignment partition JSON file, which will contain information about topic partitions and newly assigned broker IDs. Remember these broker IDs should be different from the one that is decommissioned. Details of JSON can be found at `https://cwiki.apache.org/confluence/display/KAFKA/Replication+tools#Replicationtools-6.ReassignPartitionsTool`.

4. Then you should run the `kafka-reassign-partitions.sh` shell utility to reassign the partitions. Details of the utility can be found at `https://cwiki.apache.org/confluence/display/KAFKA/Replication+tools#Replicationtools-6.ReassignPartitionsTool`.

5. Finally, check whether partitions are reassigned to different brokers using Kafka topic shell utilities. You can use the same reassignment utility to verify the re-assignment as well. Run test produce and consume request for those topic partitions as well. Sometimes, re-assignment does take some time, so it is always advisable to run the re-assignment script in the background and keep on checking its state periodically.

Data migration

Data migration in Kafka cluster can be viewed in different aspects. You may want to migrate data to newly-added disk drives in the same cluster and then decommission old disks. You may want to move data to a secure cluster or to newly-added brokers and then decommission old brokers. You may want to move data to a different new cluster altogether or to the Cloud. Sometimes, you also end up migrating Zookeeper servers. In this section, we will, in general, discuss one of the scenarios mentioned earlier.

Let's consider the scenario where we want to add new hard drives/disks and decommission old ones on broker servers. Kafka data directories contain topic and partition data. You can always configure more than one data directory, and Kafka will balance the partition or topic data across these directory locations.

One important thing to note here is that Kafka does not have a feature to balance partition data across multiple directories. It does not automatically move existing data to new data directories. If this needs to be achieved, it must be done manually.

However, in scenarios where you must decommission old disks, there are multiple approaches that can be taken. One such approach is to just delete the old directories' content after taking relevant backups and then configure the new directory location. After the broker restarts, Kafka would replicate all partition or topic data to the new directories. This approach is sometimes time consuming if the data that needs to be replicated is huge. Moreover, while the data is migrated, this broker would not be serving any requests. This will bring load on other brokers. Network utilization is also high during the migration period.

Data migration is a huge topic. We cannot cover all aspects of it in this book. However, we want to touch base with it to give you a sense of how data migration can be done in Kafka. In any data migration, we believe there are two important things that you should always do: the first is to ensure you have all the relevant backups done along with recovery plans in case of migration failure, the second is to avoid a lot of manual work and let Kafka's replication framework do the bulk of work. This will be much safer and would avoid errors.

Summary

In this chapter, we dove deep into Kafka cluster. You learned how replication works in Kafka. This chapter walked you through how the Zookeeper maintains its znodes and how Kafka uses Zookeeper servers to ensure high availability. In this chapter, we wanted you to understand how different processes work in Kafka and how they are coordinated with different Kafka components. Sections such as *Metadata request processing*, *Producer request processing*, and *Consumer request processing*, were written keeping that goal in mind.

You also learned about the different types of Kafka deployment models along with the different aspects of Capacity Planning Kafka cluster. Capacity Planning is important from the perspective of deploying Kafka cluster in the production environment. This chapter also touched base with complex Kafka administration operations such as broker decommissioning and data migration. Overall, this chapter helped you improve your skills regarding the internal working of Kafka cluster, cluster deployment model, planning and managing production grade Kafka cluster.

11
Using Kafka in Big Data Applications

In the earlier chapters, we covered how Kafka works, what kind of different components Kafka has, and what some of the Kafka tools that we can utilize for some specific use cases are. In this chapter, our focus is on understanding the importance of Kafka in big data applications. Our intention is for you to understand how Kafka can be used in any big data use cases and what are different types of design aspects you should keep in mind while using Kafka in this manner.

Kafka is becoming the standard tool for messaging in big data applications. There are some specific reasons for it. One of the reasons for it is that we can not use databases as the one-stop destination for all. Earlier, due to lack of elegant storage systems, databases tend to be the only solution for any type of data store. If you use a database, over a period of time, the system will become highly complex to handle and expensive. Databases expects all data to be present in certain data formats. To fit all types of data in the expected data formats tends to make things more complex.

Gone are the days when you would need databases to store every type of data. The last decade has seen changes in that paradigm, and specialized systems have been built to cater to different types of use cases. Moreover, we have improved the process of collecting data from different systems or devices. Each of those systems has different data formats and data types. The same data is also utilized to feed in different data pipelines such as real-time alerting, batch reports, and so on.

Kafka is `apt` for situations like these because of the following reasons:

- It has the support to store data of any types and formats
- It uses commodity hardware for storing high volumes of data
- It is a high-performance and scalable system

- It stores data on disk and can be used to serve different data pipelines; it can be used in real-time event processing and batch processing
- Due to data and system redundancy, it is highly reliable, which is an important requirement in enterprise grade production-deployed big data application

The following topics will be covered in the chapter:

- Managing high volumes in Kafka
- Kafka message delivery semantics
- Failure handling and retry-ability
- Big data and Kafka common usage patterns
- Kafka and data governance
- Alerting and monitoring
- Useful Kafka matrices

Managing high volumes in Kafka

You must be wondering why we need to talk about high volumes in this chapter, considering how aspects such as high volumes, performance, and scalability are in the genes of Kafka architecture. Well, you are thinking in the right direction, but certain parameters need to be tuned to manage Kafka latency and throughput requirements.

Moreover, you have to choose the right set of hardware and perform appropriate capacity planning. Therefore, we thought that it is better to discuss it. In a nutshell, when we talk about high volumes in Kafka, you have to think of following aspects:

- High volume of writes or high message writing throughput
- High volumes of reads or high message reading throughput
- High volume of replication rate
- High disk flush or I/O

Let's look at some of the components that you should consider for high volumes in Kafka.

Appropriate hardware choices

Kafka is a commodity hardware run tool. In cases where volumes are very high, you should first have a clear understanding of which Kafka components are affected and which one of them would need more hardware.

The following diagram will help you understand some of the hardware aspects in case of high volumes:

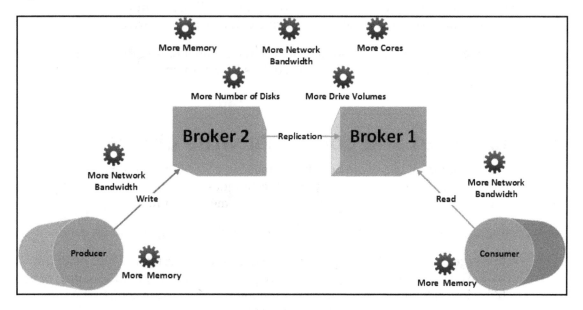

High volume impact on Kafka hardwares

In the case of a high volume of writes, producers should have more capacity to buffer records. That means it should have more memory available to it.

Since batching is always suggested for a high volume of writes, you would require more network bandwidth for a connection between the producer component and the broker. One batch would have more number of messages and, hence, more bandwidth. Similar is the case with high volume reads where you would need more memory for consumer application. Just like producer application, you would need more network bandwidth for a connection between the consumer component and the broker.

For brokers, you need to give more thought to the hardware as with high volumes, brokers do majority of the work. Brokers are multi-threaded applications. They run parallel threads for both receiving requests and reading/writing data. High volumes in Kafka result in more read/write requests and more disk I/O threads. Therefore, broker servers need more cores to support high number of threads. The case with replication threads is similar.

The higher the number of the replication factor, the higher the number of threads spawned by brokers to copy data. Accordingly, more cores would be required. Since Kafka stores everything on disks, to support high volumes, you would need more drive volumes or hard drive space.

Lastly, to manage high throughput and low latency, the number of disk drives play an important role. As you increase number of disk drives for Kafka, more parallel threads can efficiently perform I/O on disks.

Producer read and consumer write choices

We talked about choices of hardware one should make in case of high volumes. In this section, we will talk about some of the important techniques to manage high throughput and low latency in case of reading and writing high volume data in Kafka.

We are listing some of the techniques that you can use while writing or reading data:

- **Message compression:** The producer generates the compression type of all the data. The value for the compression type property are none, GZIP, Snappy, or lZ4. More batching leads to better compression ratio because compression happens on the entire batch. You may need to compromise with more CPU cycles to complete the compression process, but it will definitely save the network bandwidth later.

  The reason is simple--compression reduces the data size, and exchanging less data over the network saves time. If you wish to disable the compression, make `compression.type=none`. Sometimes, good compression codec also helps in achieving low latency.

- **Message batches:** This property is specific to producers in the asynchronous mode. A small-sized batch may reduce throughput, and setting batch size to zero will disable the batch size. Setting a large batch size is also not recommended, as it will force us to allocate more memory to the producer side, which sometime results in wastage of memory. The messages going to the same partition are batched together, and then they are sent to Kafka brokers in a single request for persisting it to topic partitions.

Remember that a large-sized batch results in fewer requests to Kafka brokers, which results in less producer overhead and less brokers CPU overhead to process each request. You can set the `batch.size` property along with the `linger.ms` property, which allows producer to send a batch in case it is taking longer to fill batch.

- **Asynchronous send**: If you set the `producer.type` flag to `async`, the producer will internally use `AsyncProducer`. It offers the capability to do sends on a separate thread that isolates the network I/O from the thread doing computation and allows multiple messages to be sent in a single batch. Both isolation and batching are desirable for good performance on the producer side.

- **Linger time**: The producer sends buffer once it is available and does not wait for any other trigger. Linger time allows us to set the maximum time in which data can be buffered before the producer sends it for storage.
  Sending messages in batches will always reduce the number of requests, but we cannot wait for the batch reach the configured size as it may cost us in throughput and latency. The `linger.ms` property allows us to configure the maximum time our producer should wait before sending the batch of data.

- **Fetch size:** The `fetch.message.max.bytes` consumer application property sets the maximum message size a consumer can read. It must be at least as large as `message.max.bytes`. This should be appropriately set to manage high volumes. The number of partitions defines the maximum number of consumers from the same consumer group who can read messages from it.
  The partitions are split between consumers in the same consumer group, but if the consumer count in the same consumer group is greater than the number of partitions, a few consumers will be idle. However, this does not affect the performance.

  You can mark the last read message offset, and this allows you to locate the missing data in case the consumer fails, but enabling this checkpoint for every message will impact the performance. However, if you enable checkpoint for every 100 messages, the impact on throughput will be reduced with a good margin of safety.

Kafka message delivery semantics

Semantic guarantees in Kafka need to be understood from the perspective of producers and consumers.

At a very high level, message flows in Kafka comprise the producer writing messages that are read by consumers to deliver it to the message processing component. In other words, producer message delivery semantics impact the way messages are received by the consumer.

For example, suppose the producer component does not receive successful `acks` from brokers because of network connectivity. In that case, the producer re-sends those messages even if the broker has received them. This results in duplicate messages sent to the consumer application. Therefore, it is important to understand that the way messages are delivered by the producer effects the manner in which the consumer would receive the messages. This would ultimately have impact on applications processing those consumer received messages.

In general, there are three types of message delivery semantics. They are as follows:

- **At most once**: In this case, messages are only read or written once. The messages are not redelivered or sent again even if they are lost in between due to component unavailability or loss of network connectivity. This semantic can result in message loss.
- **At least once**: In this case, messages are read or written at least once, and they are never lost. There is a possibility to duplicate messages, because the same message might be delivered again.
- **Exactly Once**: This is the most favorable delivery semantics as it ensures messages are delivered once and only once. This ensures no message loss and no duplication.

Now that we are clear about message delivery semantics, let's see how those works in the producer and consumer context.

At least once delivery

In the producer context, at least once delivery can happen if `acks` are lost in network translation. Suppose the producer has configuration of `acks=all`. This means the producers will wait for success or failure acknowledgement from the brokers after messages are written and replicated to relevant brokers.

In case of timeout or some other kind of error, the producer re-sends those messages assuming that they are not written to topic partitions. But what if the failure happens right after the messages are written to Kafka topic but `ack` can not be sent? In that case, the producer will retry sending that message, resulting in messages being written more than once.

In this kind of scenario, generally, message de-duplication techniques are applied on data processing components after consumers have read the messages.

The following diagram, and the step numbers therein, depicts how at least once delivery semantics works in the producer context:

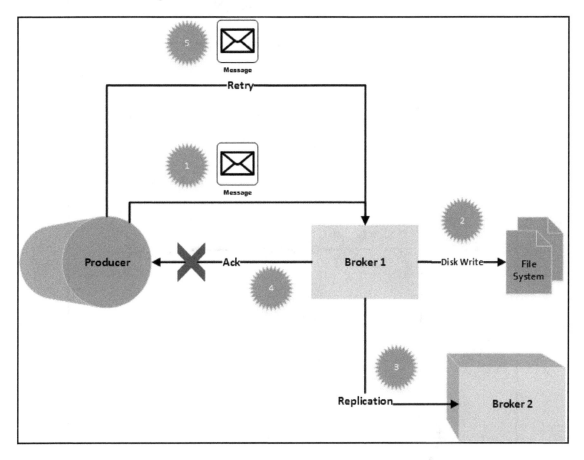

At least once delivery semantics of producers

In the consumer context, at least once processing corresponds to the fact that the consumer has received the messages and has saved it for further processing. However, the consumer process fails before committing its offset.

Once we restart the consumer processes or some other consumer processes started reading messages from same partition, then it will read the same message as its offset is not committed, although the message has already been saved once for further processing. This is called at least once semantics in case of consumer component failure.

The following diagram depicts how at least once delivery semantics works in the consumer context. Follow the step numbers to understand it in sequence:

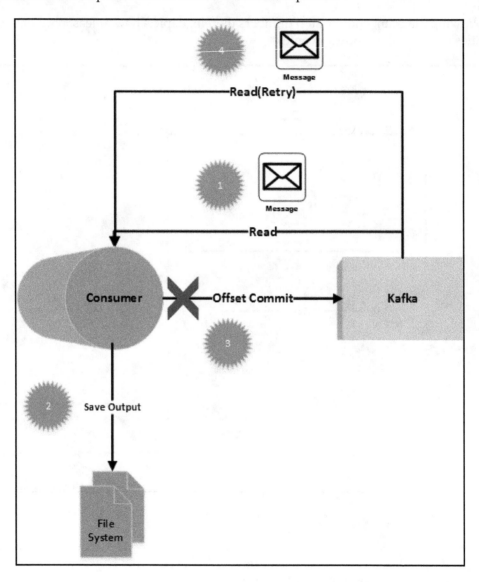

At least once delivery semantics of consumers

Consumers first read the records from Kafka topics and save them to the file systems for processing applications as depicted in step 2. File systems are just taken as an example here. A consumer can directly send data to data processing applications or store it in databases. Step 3 is about committing the offset. In the case that offset commits failed, consumers will retry reading those messages again (after restart or some new consumer processes in the consumer group). It will then eventually save the duplicate message as earlier offset commit has failed.

At most once delivery

In the producer context, at most delivery can happen if the broker has failed before receiving messages or `acks` are not received and the producer does not try sending the message again. In that case, messages are not written to Kafka topic and, hence, are not delivered to the consumer processes. This will result in message loss.

The following diagram depicts how at most once delivery semantics works in the producer context. Follow the step numbers to understand it in sequence:

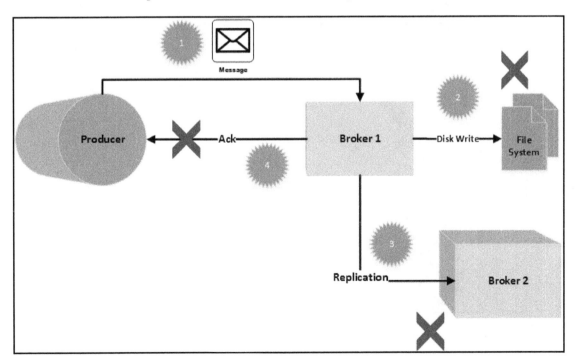

At Most Once Delivery Semantics of Producers

The producers in step 1 attempt to write topic messages to Broker 1. Broker 1 fails immediately after receiving the messages. In case of at most once delivery semantics, Broker 1 after failure, would not be able to save the records on the local file system, or able to replicate it to Broker 2. It will not even send any Ack to the the producer application. Since producer application is not configured to wait for acknowledgement, it will not resend the messages. This will result in message loss.

The following diagram depicts how at most once delivery semantics works in the consumer context. Follow the step numbers to understand it in sequence:

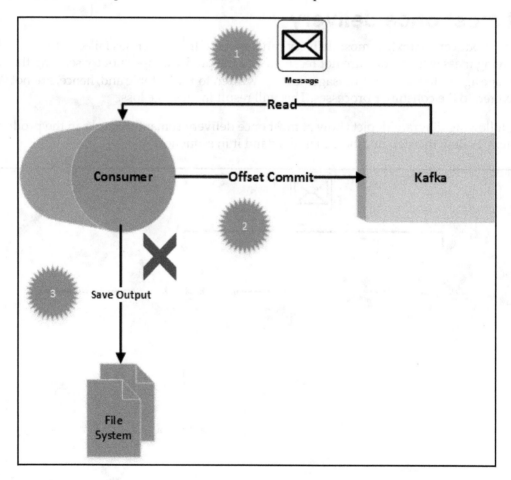

At Most Once Delivery Semantics of Consumers

In the consumer context, as shown in previous figure, at most processing corresponds to the fact that the consumer has read the messages (step 1) and committed message offset (step 2). However, it crashes after committing message offset and before saving the message to output files (step 3) for further message processing. In case the consumer restarts, it will start reading from the next offset as the previous offset has been committed. This will result in message loss.

Exactly once delivery

Exactly once delivery needs to be understood in the complete messaging system and not only in the producer or consumer context.

 Exactly once delivery refers to the semantics that ensures that the broker or consumer receives only one message, irrespective of how many times the producer sends the message. In case of failure, the partially completed steps should either be reverted or the system should store or process messages in a way that duplicates are ignored.

To ensure exactly once delivery, Kafka has provisions for idempotent producers. These kinds of producers ensure that one, and only one, message is written to a Kafka log. This will be irrespective of how many retries happen from producer side.

Idempotent producers generate a unique key identifier for each batch of messages. This unique identifier remains unchanged in case of message retries. When the message batches are stored by the broker in Kafka logs, they also have a unique number. So, the next time the brokers receive a message batch with an already received unique identifier, they do not write those messages again.

The other option that is provided with new versions of Kafka is support for transactions. New versions of Kafka have support for transactions APIs, which ensure automatic message writes to multiple partitions at a time. Producers can send a batch of messages to write to multiple partitions using transaction APIs. Ultimately, either all messages of a batch will be available for consumers to read or none of them will be visible to consumers. With both the producer features, one can ensure exactly once delivery semantics with producer applications.

On the consumer side, you have two options for reading transactional messages, expressed through the `isolation.level` consumer config:

- `read_committed`: In addition to reading messages that are not part of a transaction, this allows reading the ones that are, after the transaction is committed.
- `read_uncommitted`: This allows reading all messages in the offset order without waiting for transactions to be committed. This option is similar to the current semantics of a Kafka consumer.

To use transactions, you need to configure the consumer to use the right `isolation.level`, use the new producer APIs, and set a producer config `transactional.id` to some unique ID. This unique ID is needed to provide continuity of the transactional state across application restarts.

Big data and Kafka common usage patterns

In the big data world, Kafka can be used in multiple ways. One of the common usage patterns of Kafka is to use it as a streaming data platform. It supports storing streaming data from varied sources, and that data can later be processed in real time or in batch.

The following diagram shows a typical pattern for using Kafka as a streaming data platform:

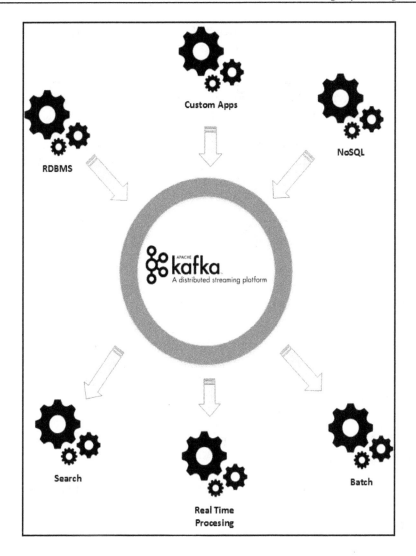

Kafka as streaming data platform

The previous diagram depicts how Kafka can be used for storing events from a variety of data sources. Of course, the data ingestion mechanism would differ depending upon the type of data sources. However, once data is stored in Kafka topics, it can be used in data search engines, real-time processing, or alerting and even for batch processing.

Batch processing engines, such as Gobblin, read data from Kafka and use Hadoop MapReduce to store data in Hadoop. Real-time processing engines such as Storm can read data, micro batch processing engines, such as Spark can read data from Kafka topics and use their distributed engines to process records. Similarly, components such as Kafka Connect can be used to index Kafka data into search engines such as Elasticsearch.

Nowadays, Kafka is used in micro-services or IOT-based architecture. These kinds of architecture are driven by request responses and event-based approaches with Kafka as a central piece of it. Services or IOT devices raise events that are received by Kafka brokers. The messages can then be used for further processing.

Overall, Kafka, due to its high scalability and performance-driven design, is used as an event store for many different types of applications, including big data applications.

Kafka and data governance

In any enterprise grade Kafka deployment, you need to build a solid governance framework to ensure security of confidential data along with who is dealing with data and what kind of operations are performed on data. Moreover, governance framework ensures who can access what data and who can perform operations on data elements. There are tools available such as Apache Atlas and Apache Ranger, which will help you define a proper governance framework around Kafka.

The fundamental data element in Kafka is **Topic**. You should define all your governance processes around Topic data element.

The following diagram represents how data governance can be applied in Kafka using Apache Atlas and Ranger:

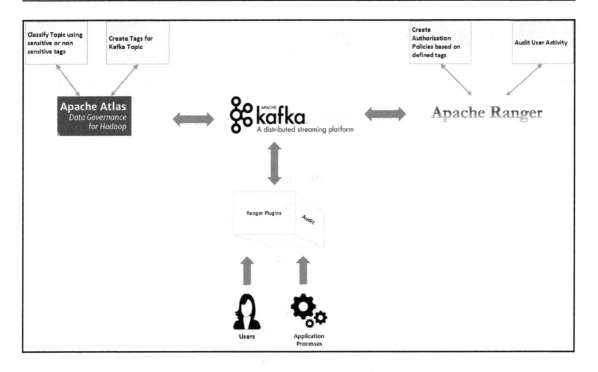

Atlas Data Governance in Kafka

To give an overview of the diagram, we can sum up all the steps as follows:

1. Create tags in Apache Atlas. Each tag corresponds to a Topic data element in Kafka. You can utilize the topic tags to classify data into sensitive or non-sensitive.
2. Using Atlas and Ranger integration, sync the tags created in Atlas into Ranger.
3. After the sync is complete, use those tags to define authorization policies for users or application processes that will be accessing Kafka topics.
4. Ranger can be used for audit purposes as well.

The preceding steps are just directional in nature to give you a brief overview of how we can apply data governance to Kafka topics. If you want to explore more and go in to more detail, you can look into Hortonworks and Apache documents about Apache Atlas and Apache Ranger.

Alerting and monitoring

If you have properly configured the Kafka cluster and it is functioning well, it can handle a significant amount of data. If you have Kafka as a centralized messaging system in your data pipeline and many applications are dependent on it, any cluster disaster or bottleneck in the Kafka cluster may affect the performance of all application dependent on Kafka. Hence, it is important to have a proper alerting and monitor system in place that gives us important information about the health of the Kafka cluster.

Let's discuss some advantages of monitoring and alerting:

- **Avoid data loss**: Sometimes it may happen that topic partitions are under replicated, meaning they have fewer number of replicas available in the cluster. If there are more such partitions, the risk of losing data for partition increases. A proper triggering system may help us avoid such problems so that we can take necessary action before any partition becomes completely unavailable.
- **Producer performance**: The alerting and monitoring system will also help us improve the producer performance by observing its metrics. We may find that the producer is producing more data than it can send, or we may find that the producer memory is insufficient for buffering partition data. Getting alerts for such scenario will help us tune the producer application.
- **Consumer performance**: We may also observe that the consumer is not able to process data as fast as the producer is producing it, or that the consumer is not able to consume data due to some network bandwidth issue. If we monitor consumer metrics for such scenarios, we may find scope for improvement of the consumer application.
- **Data availability**: Sometimes, the leaders for partitions are not assigned, or it takes time for the assignment to happen. In such cases, these partitions will not be available for any read and write operation. If we find such information beforehand, we may avoid application trying and retrying read and write to partition whose leader is not available.

There are a lot more benefits of having an alerting and monitoring system in place for Kafka; covering all those is out of the scope of this book.

Useful Kafka matrices

For useful monitoring and performance measures, we need to have certain matrices, and we will talk about those matrices in this section.

We will look into the matrices of Kafka cluster component in detail. The matrices are as follows:

- Kafka producer matrices
- Kafka broker matrices
- Kafka consumer matrices

Producer matrices

Producers are responsible for producing data to Kafka topics. If the producer fails, the consumer will not have any new messages to consume and it will be left idle. The performance of the producer also plays an important role in achieving high throughput and latency. Let's look into a few important matrices of Kafka producer:

- **Response rate**: The producer sends records to the Kafka broker, and the broker acknowledges when a message is written to a replica in case of a request. Required `.acks` is set to -1. The response rate depends on the value assigned to this property. If set to, -0, the broker will immediately return a response when it receives a request from the producer before it writes data to disk. If set to 1, the producer first writes data to its disk and then returns a response. Obviously, less fewer write operations will lead to high performance, but there will be chances of losing data in such cases.
- **Request rate**: The request rate is the number of records the producer produces within a given time.
- **I/O wait time**: The producer sends data and then waits for data. It may wait for network resources when the producing rate is more than the sending rate. The reason for a low producing rate could be slow disk access, and checking the I/O wait time can help us identify the performance of reading the data. More waiting time means producers are not receiving data quickly. In such cases, we may want to use fast access storage such as SSD.
- **Failed send rate**: This gives the number of message requests failed per second. If more messages are failing, it triggers an alarm to find out the root cause of the problem and then fix it.
- **Buffer total bytes**: This represents the maximum memory the producer can use to buffer data before it sends it to brokers. The maximum buffer size will result in high throughput.
- **Compression rate**: This represents the average compression rate for batch records for topic. A higher compression rate triggers us to change the compression type or look for some way to reduce it.

Broker matrices

Brokers are responsible for serving producer and consumer requests. They also contain important matrices that can help you avoid some critical issues. There are a lot of metrics available, but we will only look into a few important ones.

For more metrics, you may visit `https://kafka.apache.org/documentation/#monitoring`.

Metrics	Description
`kafka.server:type=ReplicaManager, name=UnderReplicatedPartitions`	This represents the number of under-replicated partitions. A higher number of under-replication partition may result in losing more data in case the broker fails.
`kafka.controller:type=KafkaController, name=OfflinePartitionsCount`	This represents the total number of partitions that are not available for read or write because of no active leader for those partitions.
`kafka.controller:type=KafkaController, name=ActiveControllerCount`	This defines the number of active controllers per cluster. There should not be more than one active controller per cluster.
`kafka.server:type=ReplicaManager, name=PartitionCount`	This represents the number of partitions on the broker. The value should be even across all brokers.
`kafka.server:type=ReplicaManager, name=LeaderCount`	This represents the number of leaders on the broker. This should also be even across all brokers; if not, we should enable auto rebalancer for the leader.

Consumer metrics

Consumers are responsible for consuming data from topic and doing some processing on it, if needed. Sometimes, your consumer may be slow, or it may behave unacceptably. The following are some important metrics that will help you identify some parameters that indicate optimization on the consumer side:

- `records-lag-max`: The calculated difference between the producer's current offset and the consumer's current offset is known as record lag. If the difference is very big, it's fairly indicative of the consumer processing data much slower than the producer. It sends alerts for suitable action to fix up this issue, either by adding more consumer instance or by increasing partitions and increasing consumers simultaneously.

- `bytes-consumed-rate`: This represents the number of bytes consumed per second by the consumer. It helps in identifying the network bandwidth of your consumer.

- `records-consumed-rate`: This defines the number of messages consumed per second. This value should be constant and generally helps when compared with `byte-consumed-rate`.

- `fetch-rate`: This represents the number of records fetched per second by the consumer.
- `fetch-latency-max`: This represents the maximum time taken for the fetch request. If it's high, it triggers to optimize the consumer application.

There are more parameters available in Kafka documentation. We recommend you go through them.

Summary

We walked you through some of the aspects of using Kafka in big data applications. By the end of this chapter, you should have clear understanding of how to use Kafka in big data Applications. Volume is one of the important aspects of any big data application. Therefore, we have a dedicated section for it in this chapter, because you are required to pay attention to granular details while managing high volumes in Kafka. Delivery semantics is another aspect you should keep in mind. Based on your choice of delivery semantics, your processing logic would differ. Additionally, we covered some of the best ways of handling failures without any data loss and some of the governance principles that can be applied while using Kafka in big data pipeline. We gave you an understanding of how to monitor Kafka and what some of the useful Kafka matrices are. You learned a good detail of advanced use of Kafka consumers for high volumes, important aspects of message delivery semantics, data governance in Kafka, and Kafka monitoring and alerting.

In the next chapter, we will be covering Kafka security in detail.

12
Securing Kafka

In all the earlier chapters, you learned how to use Kafka. In this chapter, our focus is more towards securing Kafka. Securing Kafka is one of the important aspect in enterprise adoption of Kafka. Organizations have lot of sensitive information that needs to be stored in secure environment to ensure security compliance. In this chapter, we focus on ways of securing sensitive information in Kafka. We will focus on the different security aspects of Apache Kafka and will cover the following topics:

- An overview of securing Kafka
- Wire encryption using SSL
- Kerberos SASL for authentication
- Understanding ACL and authorization
- Understanding Zookeeper authentication
- Apache Ranger for authorization
- Best practices for Kafka security

An overview of securing Kafka

Kafka is used as a centralized event data store, receiving data from various sources, such as micro services and databases.

In any enterprise deployment of Kafka, security should be looked at from five paradigms. They are as follows:

- **Authentication**: This establishes *who* the client(producer or consumer) is that trying to use Kafka services. Kafka has support for the Kerberos authentication mechanism.

- **Authorization**: This establishes *what kind of permission* the client (producer or consumer) has on topics. Kafka has support for ACLs for authorization. Apache tools, such as Ranger, can also be used for Kafka authorization.
- **Wire encryption**: This ensures that any sensitive data traveling over the network is encrypted and not in plain text. Kafka has support for SSL communication between the client (producer or consumer) and the broker. Even inter-broker communication can be encrypted.
- **Encryption at rest**: This ensures that any sensitive data that is stored on the disk is encrypted. Kafka does not have any direct support for encrypting data on the disk. However, you can utilize OS level disk encryption techniques for the same. There are lot of third party paid services for the same.
- **Auditing**: This is to ensure that every user activity is logged and analyzed for security compliance. Kafka logs form a very useful tool for auditing. Apart from that, Apache Ranger also provides auditing capabilities.

The following diagram summarizes the different Kafka security paradigms:

Wire encryption using SSL

In Kafka, you can enable support for **Secure Sockets Layer** (**SSL**) wire encryption. Any data communication over the network in Kafka can be SSL-wire encrypted. Therefore, you can encrypt any communication between Kafka brokers (replication) or between client and broker (read or write).

The following diagram represents how SSL encryption works in Kafka:

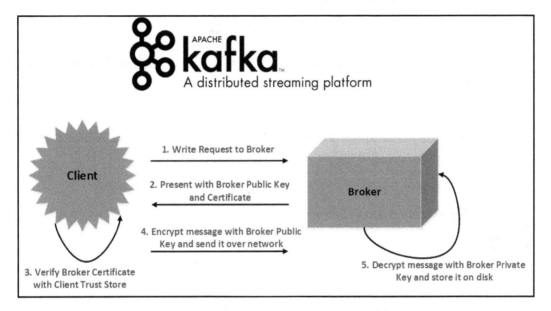

The preceding diagram depicts how communication between broker and client is encrypted. This is valid for both producer and consumer communications. Every broker or client maintains their keys and certificates. They also maintain **truststores** containing certificates for authentication. Whenever certificates are presented for authentication, they are verified against certificates stored in truststores of respective components.

Steps to enable SSL in Kafka

Let's now look into the steps to enable SSL in Kafka. Before you begin, you should generate the key, SSL certificate, keystore, and truststore that will be used by Kafka clients and brokers. You can follow the link `https://kafka.apache.org/documentation/#security_ssl_key` to create broker keys and certificate, the link `https://kafka.apache.org/documentation/#security_ssl_ca` to create your own certificate authority, and the link `https://kafka.apache.org/documentation/#security_ssl_signing` to sign the certificates. You should perform the same activity for clients (producer and consumer) applications) as well. Once you are done creating certificates, you can enable Kafka SSL using the following steps.

Configuring SSL for Kafka Broker

The following changes are required in each broker server:

1. To enable SSL for communications between brokers, make the following changes in the broker properties:

   ```
   security.inter.broker.protocol = SSL
   ```

2. To configure communication protocols and set SSL ports, make the following changes in server properties:

   ```
   listeners=SSL://host.name1:port,SSL://host.name2:port
   ```

    If you have not set SSL for inter-broker communication, you will need to set listeners properties such as this: `listeners=PLAINTEXT://host.name:port,SSL://host.name:port`

3. To give SSL keystore and truststores path for each broker, you should make the following changes in the server properties of each broker:

   ```
   ssl.keystore.location = /path/to/kafka.broker.server.keystore.jks
   ssl.keystore.password = keystore_password
   ssl.key.password = key_password
   ssl.truststore.location =
   /path/to/kafka.broker.server.truststore.jks
   ssl.truststore.password = truststore_password
   ```

    Some other additional properties like security.inter.broker.protocol can also be used. Use the link `https://kafka.apache.org/documentation/#security_configbroker` for additional properties.

Configuring SSL for Kafka clients

The configuration properties for Kafka producer and consumer are the same. The following are the configuration properties you need to set for enabling SSL. If client authentication is not required (`ssl.client.auth = none`), you need to set the following properties:

```
security.protocol = SSL
ssl.truststore.location = /path/to/kafka.client.truststore.jks
ssl.truststore.password = trustore_password
```

Technically, you can use truststore without a password, but we strongly recommend using a truststore password, as it helps in integrity checks.

If client authentication is required (`ssl.client.auth = required`), you need to set the following properties:

```
security.protocol = SSL
ssl.truststore.location = /path/to/kafka.client.truststore.jks
ssl.truststore.password = trustore_password
ssl.keystore.location = /path/to/kafka.client.keystore.jks
ssl.keystore.password = keystore_password
ssl.key.password = key_password
```

Kerberos SASL for authentication

Kerberos is an authentication mechanism of clients or servers over secured network. It provides authentication without transferring the password over the network. It works by using time-sensitive tickets that are generated using symmetric key cryptography.

It was chosen over the most-widely-used SSL-based authentication. Kerberos has the following advantages:

- **Better performance**: Kerberos uses symmetric key operations. This helps in faster authentication, which is different from SSL key-based authentication.
- **Easy integration with Enterprise Identity Server**: Kerberos is one of the established authentication mechanisms. Identity servers such as Active Directory have support for Kerberos. In this way, services such as Kafka can be easily integrated with centralized authentication servers.
- **Simpler user management**: Creating, deleting, and updating users in Kerberos is very simple. For example, removing a user can be done by simply deleting the user from the centrally managed Kerberos servers. For SSL authentication, certificates have to be removed from all server truststores.
- **No passwords over the network**: Kerberos is a secured network authentication protocol that provides strong authentication for client/server applications without transferring the password over the network. Kerberos works by using time-sensitive tickets that are generated using the symmetric key cryptography.

- **Scalable**: It is KDC that maintains the passwords or secret keys. This makes the system scalable for authenticating a large number of entities as the entities only need to know their own secret keys and set the appropriate key in KDC.

Let's also understand how Kerberos authentication flows work in Kafka. They need to be looked at from different perspectives. There is a need to understand how services and clients are authenticated and how communication happens between authenticated clients and authenticated services. We also need to understand in detail how symmetric key cryptography works in Kerberos authentication and how passwords are not communicated over the network.

Services authenticate themselves with Kerberos during startup. During startup, Kafka services will authenticate with KDC directly using the service principal and key tab using configuration files. Similarly, it is essential for the end user to authenticate to Kerberos when it accesses Kafka service via client tool or other mechanism, using his/her own user principals.

The following diagram represents how Kerberos authentication works:

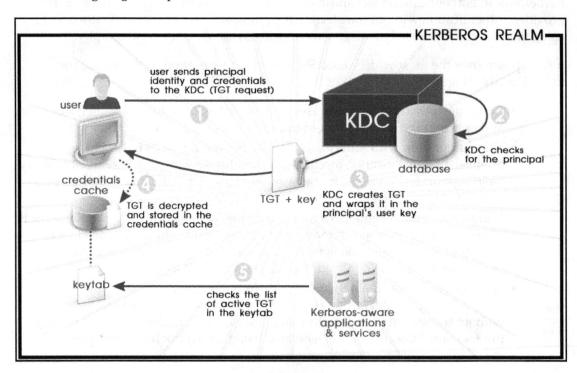

Kerberos User Authentication(Ref: access.redhat.com)

To further explore this, let's now look into how Kafka SASL authentication works. The following diagram represents the steps involved in Kafka Kerberos authentication:

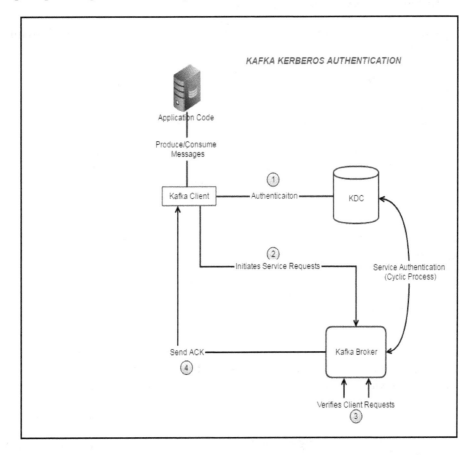

Kafka Kerberos User Authentication Steps

Steps to enable SASL/GSSAPI - in Kafka

In the following paragraphs, we will walk you through configurations that are required for enabling Kerberos authentication in Kafka. We will divide our conversation into two parts--one is about broker **SASL (Simple Authentication and Secure Layer)** configurations, and the other is about client SASL configurations.

Configuring SASL for Kafka broker

Here is how to configure SASL for Kafka broker:

1. Create JAAS configuration files for each broker server, using the following for the content of JAAS files:

```
KafkaServer {
 com.sun.security.auth.module.Krb5LoginModule required
 useKeyTab=true
 keyTab="/path/to/kafka.service.keytab"
 storeKey=true
 useTicketCache=false
 serviceName="kafka"
 principal="kafka/brokerhost.fqdn@REALM";
 };

Client { // used for zookeeper connection
 com.sun.security.auth.module.Krb5LoginModule required
 useKeyTab=true
 keyTab="/path/to/kafka.service.keytab"
 storeKey=true
 useTicketCache=false
 serviceName="zookeeper"
 principal="kafka/brokerhost.fqdn@EXAMPLE.COM";
 };
```

2. Once you have saved JAAS configuration to a specific location, you can pass the JAAS file location to each broker's JAVA OPTS as shown in the following code:

```
-Djava.security.auth.login.config=/path/to/kafka_broker_jaas.conf
```

3. Make the following changes into the broker `server.properties` files. If you have SSL enabled in Kafka, make the following property file changes:

```
listeners=SASL_SSL://broker.host.name:port
advertised.listeners=SASL_SSL://broker.host.name:port
security.inter.broker.protocol=SASL_SSL
sasl.mechanism.inter.broker.protocol=GSSAPI
sasl.enabled.mechanisms=GSSAPI
sasl.kerberos.service.name=kafka
```

4. If you do not have SSL enabled in Kafka, make following property file changes:

```
listeners=SASL_PLAINTEXT://broker.host.name:port
advertised.listeners=SASL_PLAINTEXT://broker.host.name:port
security.inter.broker.protocol=SASL_PLAINTEXT
```

```
sasl.mechanism.inter.broker.protocol=GSSAPI
sasl.enabled.mechanisms=GSSAPI
sasl.kerberos.service.name=kafka
```

Configuring SASL for Kafka client - producer and consumer

To configure the SASL for Kafka client, follow the following instructions:

1. The first step you should perform is to create JAAS configuration files for each producer and consumer application. Use the following for the content of the JAAS files:

```
sasl.jaas.config=com.sun.security.auth.module.Krb5LoginModule
required
useKeyTab=true
storeKey=true
keyTab="/path/to/kafka_client.keytab"
principal="kafka-client@REALM";
```

2. The aforementioned JAAS configuration is for Java processes or for applications acting as producer or consumer. If you want to use SASL authentication for command line tools, use the following configurations:

```
KafkaClient {
    com.sun.security.auth.module.Krb5LoginModule required
    useTicketCache=true;
};
```

3. Once you have saved JAAS configuration to specific location, you can pass the JAAS file location to each client's JAVA OPTS as shown here:

```
-Djava.security.auth.login.config=/path/to/kafka_client_jaas.conf
```

4. Make the following changes to the `producer.properties` or `consumer.properties` files. If you have SSL enabled in Kafka, make the following property file changes:

```
security.protocol=SASL_SSL
sasl.mechanism=GSSAPI
sasl.kerberos.service.name=kafka
```

5. If you do not have SSL enabled in Kafka, make the following property file changes:

```
security.protocol=SASL_PLAINTEXT
sasl.mechanism=GSSAPI
sasl.kerberos.service.name=kafka
```

Kafka has support for other types of SASL mechanisms such as the following:

- Plain (https://kafka.apache.org/documentation/#security_sasl_plain)
- SCRAM-SHA-256 (https://kafka.apache.org/documentation/#security_sasl_scram)
- SCRAM-SHA-512 (https://kafka.apache.org/documentation/#security_sasl_scram)

You can use them as well. However, GSSAPI (Kerberos) is the most frequently adopted as it easily integrates with Kerberos-enabled Hadoop services.

Understanding ACL and authorization

Apache Kafka comes with a pluggable authorizer known as Kafka **Authorization Command Line** (ACL) Interface, which is used for defining users and allowing or denying them to access its various APIs. The default behavior is that only a superuser is allowed to access all the resources of the Kafka cluster, and no other user can access those resources if no proper ACL is defined for those users. The general format in which Kafka ACL is defined is as follows:

Principal P is Allowed OR Denied Operation O From Host H On Resource R.

The terms used in this definition are as follows:

- Principal is the user who can access Kafka
- Operation is read, write, describe, delete, and so on
- Host is an IP of the Kafka client that is trying to connect to the broker
- Resource refers to Kafka resources such as topic, group, cluster

Let's discuss a few common ACL types:

- **Broker or server ACL**: The operation between brokers, such as updating broker and partition metadata, changing the leader of partition, and so on, needs to be authorized. Brokers also need to have access to topic because a broker has to perform replication and some internal operation on topic and it requires read and describe operation access on topic.
- **Topic**: The principle using Kafka client to connect to brokers for topic creation will require `Read` and `Describe` permissions to be able to create topic. Sometimes clients are not allowed to create topics on cluster due to security policies, and in such cases, they need to connect to the Admin to create the topic.
- **Producer**: The producer is responsible for producing data for topic and storing it in the topic partition. It requires `Read` and `Write` access on topic resources to do so.
- **Consumer**: The consumer reads data from topic, and hence, `Read` operation access is required on the topic's resources.

Common ACL operations

Let's now look into the basic operations of the ACL:

1. Kafka provides a simple authorizer; to enable this authorizer, add the following line to server properties of Kafka:

    ```
    authorizer.class.name=kafka.security.auth.SimpleAclAuthorizer
    ```

2. As discussed in previous paragraphs, by default, only a superuser will have access to resources if no ACL is found. However, this behavior can be changed if we want to allow everyone to access resources if no ACL is set. Add the following line to server properties:

    ```
    allow.everyone.if.no.acl.found=true
    ```

3. You can also add more superusers to your Kafka cluster by adding users to the following property in the server property file:

    ```
    super.users=User:Bob;User:Alice
    ```

4. **Adding an ACL**: An ACL can be added using the command line interface. For example, if you want to add an ACL where `principals User: Chanchal` and `User: Manish` are allowed to perform `Read` and `Write` operations on `topic Packt` from `10.200.99.104` and `10.200.99.105`, it can be done using the following command:

```
kafka-acls.sh --authorizer kafka.security.auth.SimpleAclAuthorizer
--authorizer-properties zookeeper.connect=localhost:2181 --add --
allow-principal User:Chanchal --allow-principal User:Manish --
allow-hosts 10.200.99.104,10.200.99.105 --operations Read,Write --
topic Packt
```

`--deny-principal` and `--deny-host` options can be used if you want to restrict the user or host from accessing topic.

5. **Removing ACL**: The ACL added in the preceding part can be removed using the following command:

```
kafka-acls.sh --authorizer kafka.security.auth.SimpleAclAuthorizer
--authorizer-properties zookeeper.connect=localhost:2181 --remove -
-allow-principal User:Chanchal --allow-principal User:Manish --
allow-hosts 10.200.99.104,10.200.99.105--operations Read,Write --
topic Packt
```

List ACLs

You can also list all the ACLs applied on following resources:

1. For example, if you want to see all ACLs applied in the topic Packt, you can do it using the following command:

```
kafka-acls.sh --authorizer kafka.security.auth.SimpleAclAuthorizer
--authorizer-properties zookeeper.connect=localhost:2181 --list --
topic Packt
```

2. **Producer and consumer ACL**: Adding a user as the producer or consumer is a very common ACL used in Kafka. If you want to add user `Chanchal` as a producer for `topic Packt`, it can be done using the following simple command:

```
kafka-acls --authorizer-properties
zookeeper.connect=localhost:2181\
    --add --allow-principal User:Chanchal \
    --producer --topic Packt
```

3. To add a consumer ACL where `Manish` will act as the consumer for `topic` `Packt` with consumer `group` `G1`, the following command will be used:

```
kafka-acls --authorizer-properties
zookeeper.connect=localhost:2181\
    --add --allow-principal User:Manish \
    --consumer --topic Packt --group G1
```

4. There are lots of resources for which you can create an ACL list for allowing or not allowing access on particular resources for particular users. Covering all ACLs is out of the scope of this book.

Understanding Zookeeper authentication

Zookeeper is the metadata service for Kafka. SASL-enabled Zookeeper services first authenticate access to metadata stored in Zookeeper. Kafka brokers need to authenticate themselves using Kerberos to use Zookeeper services. If valid, the Kerberos ticket is presented to Zookeeper, it then provides access to the metadata stored in it. After valid authentication, Zookeeper establishes connecting user or service identity. This identity is then used to authorize access to metadata Znodes guarded by ACLs.

One important thing for you to understand is that Zookeeper ACLs restrict modifications to Znodes. Znodes can be read by any client. The philosophy behind this behavior is that sensitive data is not stored in Zookeeper. However, modifications by an unauthorized user can disrupt your cluster's behavior. Hence, Znodes are world readable, but not world modifiable. Although authentication must be established irrespective of what kind of access you have on Znodes, without a valid Kerberos ticket, you cannot access Zookeeper services at all.

In a highly-secured cluster, to mitigate this risk, you can always use network IP filtering via firewalls to restrict Zookeeper service access for selective servers. Zookeeper authentications use **Java Authentication and Authorization Service (JAAS)** to establish the login context for connecting clients. JAAS establishes the login context using a standard configuration file and it directs the code to use the login context to drive authentication. JAAS login context can be defined in two ways:

1. One is using Kerberos key tabs. An example of such login context can be seen as follows:

```
Client {
    com.sun.security.auth.module.Krb5LoginModule required
    useKeyTab=true
    keyTab="/path/to/client/keytab(Kafka keytab)"
    storeKey=true
    useTicketCache=false
    principal="yourzookeeperclient(Kafka)";
};
```

2. The second one is by user login credential cache. An example of such login context can be seen as follows:

```
Client {
    com.sun.security.auth.module.Krb5LoginModule required
    useKeyTab=false
    useTicketCache=true
    principal="client@REALM.COM";
    doNotPrompt=true
};
```

Apache Ranger for authorization

Ranger is a used to monitor and manage security across the Hadoop ecosystem. It provides a centralized platform from which to create and manage security policies across the cluster. We will look at how we can use Ranger to create policies for the Kafka cluster.

Adding Kafka Service to Ranger

The following screenshot shows the user interface in Ranger which is used to add services. We will add Kafka service here to configure policies for it later:

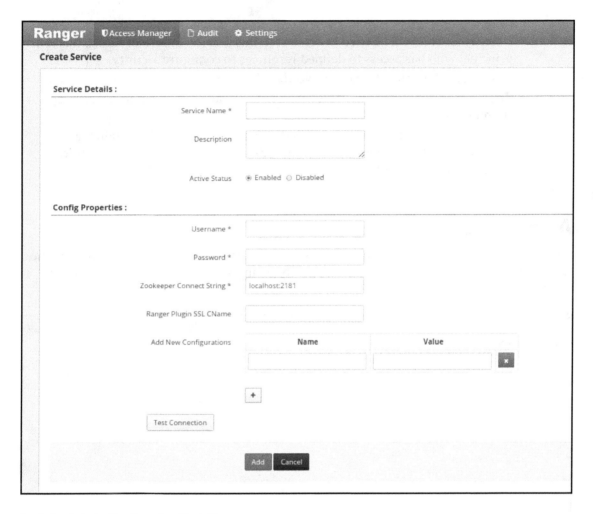

Let's look into the **Service Details** :

- **Service name**: The service name needs to be set up in agent config. For example, in this case, it can be Kafka
- **Description**: This represents what this service will do
- **Active Status**: This refers to enabling or disabling this service

Config properties :

- **Username**: This will be used to connect to this service. In case of Kafka, this is a principal who has access to defined resources to configure security.
- **Password**: This refers to the password of the user for authentication.
- **Zookeeper Connect String**: This refers to the IP address and port of Zookeeper running on cluster. The default value is `localhost:2181`.
- **Ranger Plugin SSL CName**: You need to install Ranger Kafka plugin for integrating Kafka with Ranger and provide a common name for the certificate, which is then registered.

Adding policies

Once the service is configured and enabled, you can start adding policies by going into the Kafka policy listing page, which looks like the following screenshot. On the left side, you can see the **Add New Policy** tab:

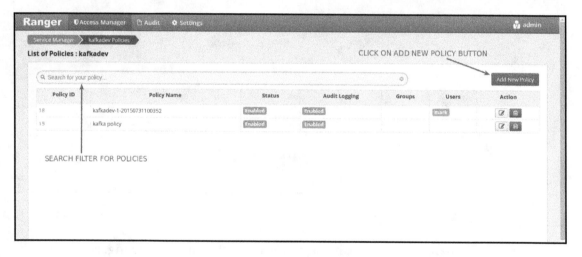

Kafka policy listing page

Once you click on the **Add New Policy** tab, you will be redirected to the following page, where you need to specify permission and policy detail:

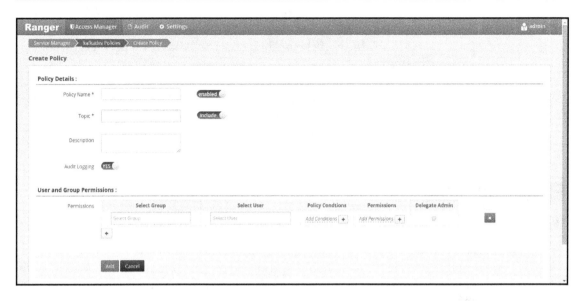

Kafka add policy page

Let's discuss the parameters available in the preceding screenshot and see their meaning:

Policy Detail:

- **Policy Name:** This defines what this policy is meant for. The policy name should match the objective of the policy.
- **Enable Policy:** You can enable or disable this policy.
- **Topic:** This refers to the Kafka Topic name for which the policy is being created.
- **Description:** This refers to a detailed description of why you are creating this policy.
- **Audit Logging:** This needs to be enabled or disabled for auditing this policy.

User and Group Permission :

- **Select Group:** This refers to the user group name from the list of user groups configured in the cluster. You can assign permissions to the group as well.
- **Select User:** This refers to the username (Principal) from the group for which permission has to be given.
- **Permission:** This defines the type of permission you want to grant to this user:
    - **Publish**: If a given user can produce data to Kafka topic
    - **Consume**: If a given user can consume data from topic partitions
    - **Configure**: If a given user can configure brokers/clusters

- **Describe**: Permission to fetch metadata on the topic
- **Kafka Admin**: If checked, the user will have the permissions of an admin

Ranger is easy to configure and provides a nice user interface. You can install Ranger and try using this policy creation. All the diagram reference for Ranger is taken from `https://cwiki.apache.org/confluence/display/RANGER`.

Best practices

Here is a list of best practices to optimize your experience with Kafka:

- **Enable detailed logs for Kerberos**: Troubleshooting Kerberos issues can be a nightmare for technical stakeholders. Sometimes it is difficult to understand why Kerberos authentication is not working. It also happens that errors are not that very informative and you get the root cause by looking at the actual authentication flows. Hence, you need to have a proper debugging set for Kerberos. In Kafka or, as a matter of fact, in any JAVA Kerberos-enabled application, you can set the Kerberos debug level using the following property:

  ```
  sun.security.krb5.debug=true
  ```

- **Integrate with Enterprise Identity Server**: You should always integrate your Kerberos authentication with Enterprise Identity Servers. It has many benefits. You do not have to manage more than one version of users. Any user deletion activity is simplified. Enterprise security policy can be easily enforced.
- **OS-level Kerberos Integration**: One important thing you should always remember is that OS users and groups get propagated to Kerberos authentication, especially when you are logging into a server and using Kafka through console. It is always beneficial to integrate OS to your Enterprise Identity Servers such as Active Directory. This way, you will have Kerberos tickets issued to you as soon as you login to servers via SSH. Users do not have to perform separate authentication with Kerberos.
- **SSL Certificates Rotation**: You should always have processes in place to rotate SSL certificates for brokers and clients. SSL Certification Rotation has the advantage that, in case of certificate breaches, the compromised certificates will work for a very short and limited period of time until we replace the old certificates with new certificates in truststores.

- **Automating SSL certificate management**: This is an extension of the previous point. You must have automation scripts for managing certificates. On a typical production cluster, you will be managing a large number of servers and processes. Manually performing SSL management on a large number of servers is cumbersome and error prone. Therefore, you must start creating scripts for managing certificates in a large-node Kafka cluster.
- **Security log aggregation**: You should understand the fact that one log is not going to give you a complete big picture of user activity in the Kafka cluster. Therefore, you should have the mechanism or scripts in place to aggregate logs from all servers in a cluster to a single location or file. You can index it with tools such as Solr, Elasticsearch, or Splunk for further security analysis on top of it. You should ideally aggregate producer application logs, consumer application logs, Kerberos Logs, Zookeeper logs, and broker logs.
- **Centralized security auditing**: Every enterprise has a security and auditing team. They have a mechanism of collecting system logs to one place and then monitoring it for malicious activities. When you are designing your Kafka cluster, you should always have provisions to route your logs to Enterprise Security Monitoring systems. One way to do this is to first aggregate all your cluster logs and then route them to syslogs processes to feed data to **SIEM** (**Security Information and Event Management**) systems for real-time monitoring. Another way is to collect all logs to some SFTP servers and then send them to SIEM systems.
- **Security breach alerting**: Well, you can think of this as part of the Centralized Auditing System. You should have provisions for security breach alerting based on organization's policies and rules. If your SIEM systems are not in position to perform such alerting, you can use tools such as NAGIOS and Ganglia.

Summary

In this chapter, we covered different Kafka security paradigms. Our goal with this chapter is to ensure that you understand different paradigms of securing Kafka. We wanted you to first understand what are different areas you should evaluate while securing Kafka. After that, we wanted to address how parts of securing Kafka. One thing to note here is that Authentication and Authorization is something you have to always implement in a secure Kafka cluster. Without these two, your Kafka cluster is not secure. SSL can be optional but is strongly recommended for highly sensitive data. Please keep not of best practices of securing Kafka as these are more gathered from practical industry implementation experiences of securing Kafka.

13
Streaming Application Design Considerations

Streaming is becoming an important pillar for organizations dealing with big data nowadays. More and more organizations are leaning toward faster actionable insights from the massive data pool that they have. They understand that timely data and appropriate actions based on those timely data insights has a long-lasting impact on profitability. Apart from in-time actions, streaming opens channels to capture unbound, massive amounts of data from different business units across an organization.

Keeping these important benefits in mind, this chapter focuses on factors that one should keep in mind while designing any streaming application. The end results of any such design are driven by organization business goals. Controlling these factors in any streaming application design helps achieving those defined goals appropriately. In lieu of that, let's look at these factors one by one.

The following topics will be covered in this chapter:

- Latency and throughput
- Data persistence
- Data sources
- Data lookups
- Data formats
- Data serialization
- Level of parallelism
- Data skews
- Out-of-order events
- Memory tuning

Latency and throughput

One of the fundamental features of any streaming application is to process inbound data from different sources and produce an outcome instantaneously. Latency and throughput are the important initial considerations for that desired feature. In other words, performance of any streaming application is measured in terms of latency and throughput.

The expectation from any streaming application is to produce outcomes as soon as possible and to handle a high rate of incoming streams. Both factors have an impact on the choice of technology and hardware capacity to be used in streaming solutions. Before we understand their impact in detail, let's first understand the meanings of both terms.

 Latency is defined as the unit of time (in milliseconds) taken by the streaming application in processing an event or group of events and producing an output after the events have been received by it. Latency can be expressed in terms of average latency, best case latency, or worst case latency. Sometimes, it is also represented as the percentage of total events received in each time window.

For example, it can be defined as 2 ms for 85% of messages that are received in the last 24 hours.

 Throughput is defined as the number of outcomes produced by streaming applications at each unit of time. Basically, throughput derives the number of events that can be processed by a streaming application at each unit of time.

In a streaming application design, you usually consider the maximum throughput that the system can handle, keeping end-to-end latency within the agreed upon SLAs. When the system is in a state of maximum throughput, all system resources are fully utilized and beyond this, events will be in the wait state till resources are freed.

Now that we are clear with the definitions of both latency and throughput, it can be easily understood that both are not independent of each other.

 High latency means more time to process an event and produce an output. This also means that for an event, system resources are occupied for a longer duration of time and hence, at a time, lesser number of parallel events can be processed. Hence, if system capacity is limited, high latency will result in less throughput.

There are multiple factors that should be kept in mind while striking a balance between the throughput and latency of your streaming application. One such factor is the load distribution across multiple nodes. Load distribution helps in utilizing each system resource optimally and ensuring end-to-end low latency per node.

Most of the stream processing engines have such a mechanism built-in by default. However, at times, you must ensure that it avoid too much data shuffling at runtime and data partitions are defined appropriately. To achieve the desired throughput and frequency, you must perform capacity planning of your cluster accordingly.

The number of CPUs, RAM, page cache, and so on are some of the important factors that affect your streaming application performance. To keep your streaming application performance at the desired level, it is imperative that you program your streaming application appropriately. Choice of program constructs and algorithms affect garbage collection, data shuffling, and so on. Lastly, factors such as network bandwidth also affect your latency and throughput.

Data and state persistence

Data integrity, safety, and availability are some of the key requirements of any successful streaming application solution. If you give these factors a thought, you will understand that to ensure integrity, safety, and availability, persistence plays an important role. For example, it is absolutely essential for any streaming solution to persists its state. We often call it checkpointing. Checkpointing enables streaming applications to persist their states over a period of time and ensures recovery in case of failures. State persistence also ensures strong consistency, which is essential for data correctness and exactly-once message delivery semantics.

Now you must have understood why persisting state is important. Another aspect of persistence is the outcomes of data processing or raw unprocessed events. This serves a two-fold purpose. It gives us an opportunity to replay messages and to compare the current data with historical data. It also gives us the ability to retry messages in case of failures. It also helps us handle back-pressure on the source system in case of peak throughput time periods.

Careful thought must be given to the storage medium used to persist the data. Some factors that really drive a storage medium for streaming applications are low latency read/write, hardware fault tolerance, horizontal scalability, and optimized data transfer protocols with support for both synchronous and asynchronous operations.

Data sources

One of the fundamental requirements for any streaming application is that the sources of data should have the ability to produce unbound data in terms of streams. Streaming systems are built for unbound data streams. If source systems have the support for such kinds of data streams, then streaming solutions are the way to go, but if they do not have support for data streams, then either you must build or use prebuilt custom components that build data streams out of those data sources or go for batch-oriented non-streaming-based solutions.

Either way, the key takeaway is that streaming solutions should have data stream producing data sources. This is one of the key design decisions in any streaming application. Any streaming solution or design should ensure that continuous unbound data streams are input to your stream processing engines.

External data lookups

The first question that must be in your mind is why we need external data lookups in the stream processing pipeline. The answer is that sometimes you need to perform operations such as enrichment, data validation, or data filtering on incoming events based on some frequently changing external system data. However, in the streaming design context, these data lookups pose certain challenges. These data lookups may result in increased end-to-end latency as there will be frequent calls to external systems. You cannot hold all the external reference data in-memory as these external datasets are too big to fit in-memory. They also change too frequently, which makes refreshing memory difficult. If these external systems are down, then they will become a bottleneck for streaming solutions.

Keeping these challenges in mind, there are three important factors while designing solutions involving external data lookups. They are performance, scalability, and fault tolerance. Of course, you can achieve all of these and there are always trade-offs between the three.

One criterion of data lookups is that they should have minimized impact on event processing time. Even a response time in seconds is not acceptable, keeping in mind the millisecond response time of stream processing solutions. To comply with such requirements, some solutions use caching systems such as Redis to cache all the external data. Streaming systems use Redis for data lookups. You also need to keep network latency in mind. Hence, the Redis cluster is generally co-deployed with your streaming solutions. By caching everything, you have chosen performance over fault tolerance and scalability.

Data formats

One of the important characteristics of any streaming solution is that it serves as an integration platform as well. It collects events from varied sources and performs processing on these different events to produce the desired outcomes. One of the pertinent problems with such integration platforms is different data formats. Each type of source has its own format. Some support XML formats and some support JSON or Avro formats. It is difficult for you to design a solution catering to all formats. Moreover, as more and more data sources get added, you need to add support for data formats supported by the newly added source. This is obviously a maintenance nightmare and buggy.

Ideally, your streaming solution should support one data format. Events should be in the key/value model. The data format for these key/value events should be one agreed-on format. You should pick one single data format for your application. Choosing a single data format and ensuring that all data sources and integration points comply to it is important while designing and implementing streaming solutions.

One of the common solutions that is employed for one common data format is to build a message format conversion layer before data is ingested for stream processing. This message conversion layer will have REST APIs exposed to different data sources. These data sources push events in their respective formats to this conversion layer using REST APIs and later, it gets converted to a single common data format. The converted events will be pushed to stream processing. Sometimes, this layer is also utilized to perform some basic data validation on incoming events. In a nutshell, you should have data format conversion separate from stream processing logic.

Data serialization

Almost all the streaming technology of your choice supports serialization. However, key for any streaming application performance is the serialization technique used. If the serialization is slow, then it will affect your streaming application latency.

Moreover, if you are integrating with an old legacy system, it might be that the serialization of your choice is not supported. Key factors in choosing any serialization technique for your streaming application should be the amount of CPU cycles required, time for serialization/deserialization, and support from all integrated systems.

Level of parallelism

Any stream processing engine of your choice has ways to tune stream processing parallelism. You should always give a thought to the level of parallelism required for your application. A key point here is that you should utilize your existing cluster to its maximum potential to achieve low latency and high throughput. The default parameters may not be appropriate as per your current cluster capacity. Hence, while designing your cluster, you should always come up with the desired level of parallelism to achieve your latency and throughput SLAs. Moreover, most of the engines are limited by their automatic ability to determine the optimal number of parallelism.

Let's take Spark's processing engine as an example and see how parallelism can be tuned on that. In very simple terms, to increase parallelism, you must increase the number of parallel executing tasks. In Spark, each task runs on one data partition.

So if you want to increase the number of parallel tasks, you should increase the number of data partitions. To achieve this, you can repartition the data with the desired number of partitions or we can increase the number of input splits from the source. Level of parallelism also depends on the number of cores available in your cluster. Ideally, you should plan your level of parallelism with two or three tasks per CPU core.

Out-of-order events

This is one of the key problems with any unbound data stream. Sometimes an event arrives so late that events that should have been processed after that out of order event are processed first. Events from varied remote discrete sources may be produced at the same time and, due to network latency or some other problem, some of them are delayed. The challenge with out-of-order events is that as they come very late, processing them involves data lookups on relevant datasets.

Moreover, it is very difficult to determine the conditions that help you decide if an event is an out-of-order event. In other words, it is difficult to determine if all events in each window have been received or not. Moreover, processing these out-of-order events poses risks of resource contentions. Other impacts could be increase in latency and overall system performance degradation.

Keeping these challenges in mind, factors such as latency, easy maintenance, and accurate results play an important role in processing out-of-order events. Depending on enterprise requirements, you can drop these events. In case of event drops, your latency is not affected and you do not have to manage additional processing components. However, it does affect the accuracy of processing outcomes.

Another option is to wait and process it when all events in each window are received. In this case, your latency will take a hit and you must maintain additional software components. Another one of the commonly applied techniques is to process such data events at the end of the day using batch processing. In this way, factors such as latency are moot. However, there will be a delay in getting accurate results.

Message processing semantics

Exactly-once delivery is the holy grail of streaming analytics. Having duplicates of events processed in a streaming job is inconvenient and often undesirable, depending on the nature of the application. For example, if billing applications miss an event or process an event twice, they could lose revenue or overcharge customers. Guaranteeing that such scenarios never happen is difficult; any project seeking such a property will need to make some choices with respect to availability and consistency. One main difficulty stems from the fact that a streaming pipeline might have multiple stages, and exactly-once delivery needs to happen at each stage. Another difficulty is that intermediate computations could potentially affect the final computation. Once results are exposed, retracting them causes problems.

It is useful to provide exactly-once guarantees because many situations require them. For example, in financial examples such as credit card transactions, unintentionally processing an event twice is bad. Spark Streaming, Flink, and Apex all guarantee exactly-once processing. Storm works with at least-once delivery. With the use of an extension called **Trident**, it is possible to reach exactly-once behavior with Storm, but this may cause some reduction in performance.

De-duplication is one way of preventing multiple execution of an operation and achieving exactly-once processing semantics. De-duplication is achievable if the application action is a database update. We can consider some other action such as a web services call.

Summary

At the end of this chapter, you should have a clear understanding of various design considerations for streaming applications. Our goal with this chapter was to ensure that you have understood various complex aspects of a streaming application design.

Although the aspects may vary from project to project, based on our industry experience, we feel that these are some of the common aspects that you will end up considering in any streaming application design. For example, you cannot design any streaming application without defining SLAs around latency and throughput.

You can use these principals irrespective of your choice of technology for stream processing--be it micro-batch Spark streaming applications or real-time Storm/Heron stream processing applications. They are technology agnostic. However, the way they can be achieved varies from technology to technology. With this, we conclude this chapter and hopefully, you will be able to apply these principles to your enterprise applications.

Index

A

Access Control Lists (ACLs) 39
ack parameter 198
ACL types
  broker ACL 239
  consumer 239
  producer 239
  sever ACL 239
  topic 239
altering
  advantages 224
AMQP (Advance Message Queuing Protocol)
  about 11, 18
  components 19
  message exchanges methods 19
Apache Flume
  about 157
  components 158
Apache Heron 114
Apache Kafka
  integrating, with Apache Storm-Java 117, 118
  integrating, with Apache Storm-Scala 122
Apache Storm 110
Apache Storm application
  bolt 112
  spout 112
  topology 112
application integration system design
  common interface definitions 8
  latency 9
  loose coupling 8
  reliability 9
array 27
Aurora scheduler 114
Authorization Command Line (ACL) 238
  adding 240
  listing 240, 241
  operations 239
Avro
  about 8, 45
  working with 150

B

batch processing 174
batching 43, 57
big data streaming applications
  layers 19
  messaging systems, using in 19, 20, 21, 22
bolt 112
broker matrices, Kafka 226
brokers
  about 45
  decommissioning 205, 206
ByteArrays 42

C

Camus
  running 153
  used, for moving Kafka data to HDFS 152
capacity planning
  about 199
  CPU 202
  goals 200
  hard drives 201, 202
  memory 200, 201
  network 202
  replication factor 200
channels 11
checkpoint 90
commit, Kafka consumer
  asynchronous commit 69
  auto commit 68
  current offset commit 68

committed offset 38
components, Apache Flume
  channel 158
  sink 158
  source 158
components, Confluent architecture
  24*7 support 148
  Auto Data Balancing 148
  client 147
  Control Center 148
  Multi-Datacenter replication 148
  REST Proxy 147
  schema registry 147
  supported connectors 147
components, Kafka Stream
  local state 179
  record cache 179
  Stream topology 179
concepts, messaging
  data transmission protocols 11
  message queues 11
  messages (data packets) 11
  receiver (consumer) 11
  sender (producer) 11
  transfer mode 12
configuration properties, Kafka producer
  acks 52
  batch.size 53
  buffer.memory 52
  compression.type 53
  linger.ms 53
  max.in.flight.requests.per.connection 54
  partitioner.class 54
  retires 53
Confluent architecture
  about 146
  components 147
Confluent Platform
  about 144
  features 144, 145
Connector
  about 166
  Sink Connector 166
  Source Connector 166
connectors, Confluent architecture

Elasticsearch Connector 147
  File Connector 147
  HDFS Connector 147
  JDBC Connector 147
  S3 Connector 147
constructs, Gobblin
  converters 155
  extractor 155
  publisher 155
  quality checkers 155
  source 155
  writer 155
consumer 11, 27
consumer group
  continuous data processing 75
  discrete data processing 76, 77
consumer metrics, Kafka
  bytes-consumed-rate 226
  fetch-latency-max 227
  fetch-rate 227
  records-consumed-rate 226
  records-lag-max 226
controller 194
controllers 33
custom partition 51

D

data migration, Kafka cluster 206, 207
data transmission protocol 11
directed acyclic graph (DAG) 83, 86

E

exactly one processing, WAL 90
executors 82
Extract Transform Load (ETL) tools 26

F

features, Kafka Stream
  fault tolerance 177
  reprocessing 177
  state management 176
  time 177
  window 177
file share 9
fire-and-forget pattern 56

fire-and-forget processing 14
functionalities, Kafka consumer
   consumer offset position 63
   deserialization 63
   heartbeats 63
   messages, replaying 63
   messages, rewinding 63
   messages, skipping 63
   offset commits 63
   subscribing, to topic 62

G

Gobblin 154
Gobblin architecture
   about 154
   constructs 155
   run-time 155
   supported deployment 155
   utility 155

H

Heron architecture 115
Heron Instance (HI) 117
Heron topology architecture
   about 115
   containers 116
   Heron Instance 117
   Metric Manager 117
   Stream Manager 117
   Topology Master 116
high volumes, Kafka
   appropriate hardware choices 210, 211, 212
   managing 210
   message batches 212
   read choices 212
   write choices 212
HTTP (Hypertext Transfer Protocol) 11

I

in sync replica (ISR) 35
Input/Output (IO) 30
IP Fraud detection application
   creating 133, 134

J

Java Authentication and Authorization Service
   (JAAS) 242
Java example
   for direct approach 95
   for receiver-based integration 91
Java Kafka consumer 71
Java Kafka producer
   example 54
JSON
   reference 206

K

Kafka architecture 27, 28
Kafka broker
   SASL, configuring for 236
Kafka Broker
   SSL, configuring for 232
Kafka client
   SASL, configuring for 237
Kafka clients
   SSL, configuring for 232
Kafka cluster
   conceptual layout 27
   internals 194
   replication 195, 196
   Zookeeper 195
Kafka Connect
   about 149, 157, 163, 165
   component 164
   examples 167
   Export Connectors 149
   Import Connectors 149
   models 166
   use cases 170
Kafka consumer APIs 65
Kafka consumer
   additional configuration 70, 71
   best practices 78
   commit 68
   configuration 65, 66
   data, fetching from 64
   functionalities 62, 63
   internals 62

polling 68
properties 65
subscription 67
Kafka data, moving to HDFS
about 151
Camus used 152
Gobblin 154
Kafka integration, with Spark
direct approach 93, 94, 95
receiver-based integration 88, 89
Kafka matrices
about 224
broker matrices 226
consumer matrices 226
producer matrices 225
Kafka Producer APIs 46, 47
Kafka producer
asynchronous messaging 49, 50
configuration properties 52
internals 42, 43, 44, 45
synchronous messaging 49
Kafka queues 27
Kafka service
adding, to Ranger 242, 244
Kafka Stream, with Apache Kafka
advantages 180
Kafka Stream
about 149, 175
architecture 177, 178
batch processing 174
components 179
features 176, 177
IP lookup service 188
IP record producer 186
Maven dependency 181, 184
property reader 185
request/response 174
simple word count program 181, 183
Stream processing 174
stream processing application 150
stream processors 150
streams 149
topology 150
use case example 184
Kafka topic ACLs 39

Kafka topics 27
Kafka, in ETL operations
working 163
Kafka, in ETL pipelines
considerations 162
Kafka, in Stream processing
fault tolerance 175
logic ordering 175
loose coupling 175
persistence queue 174, 175
scalability 175
Kafka
about 25
asynchronous replication 197
consumer request processing 198, 199
data governance 222, 223
message delivery semantics 214
optimization, best practices 246, 247
origins 26
producer request processing 198
securing 229
SSL, enabling in 231
using, as streaming data platform 220, 221
KafkaSpout 117, 118
Kerberos SASL
for authentication 233, 234
Kerberos
advantages 233
KTable 183, 184

L

layers, in big data streaming applications
consumption layer 20
ingestion layers 19
processing layer 20
leader 28
Lineage 83
LinkedIn portal 26
local state 179

M

MapReduce 82
matrices, Kafka producer
buffer total bytes 225
compression rate 225

failed send rate 225
I/O wait time 225
request rate 225
response rate 225
Maven 97
message 11
message consumers 37, 38
message consuming patterns
  continuous data processing 75
  discrete data processing 76, 77
message delivery semantics, Kafka
  at least once 214, 215, 216
  at most once 214, 217, 218, 219
  exactly once 214, 219, 220
message exchange methods, AMQP (Advance
    Message Queuing Protocol)
  direct exchange 19
  fan-out exchange 19
  topic exchange 19
message partitions
  about 31
  large number of partitions, cons 31, 32, 33
  large number of partitions, pros 31, 32, 33
message producers 37
message queue 11
message topics
  about 29
  buffering 30
  compaction 30
  leader 30
  offset 30
  partitions 30
  retention period 30
  space retention policy 30
messaging publishing patterns
  batching 57
  fire-and-forget 56
  one message transfers 57
messaging systems
  about 9, 10
  principles 8, 9
  using, in big data streaming applications 19, 20,
    21, 22
messaging
  concepts 11

Metric Manager 117
Mirror Maker 204
models, Kafka Connect
  Connector 166
  workers 166
monitoring
  advantages 224
MQTT (Message Queue Telemetry Protocol) 11
multicluster deployment 203, 204
multiple brokers 28

N
network attached storage (NAS) 202

O
one message transfers 57

P
partitions 27
point-to-point (PTP) messaging model 13
  about 12
  fire-and-forget processing 14
  request/reply model 14
poll loop 64
primary backup approach
  about 34
  read 35
  write 35
processor, Stream topology
  sink processor 179
  source processor 179
  Stream processor 179
producer application
  best practices, for designing 58, 59
producer code
  about 102, 130
  fraud IP lookup 132
producer object 48
producer
  about 11, 41, 101
  property reader 101
ProducerRecord object 48
producers 27
properties, Kafka consumer
  bootstrap.servers 65

    group.id 66
    key.deserializer 65
    value.deserializer 66
property reader
    fraud IP lookup 104
    hive table, exposing 105
    producer code 102
    Streaming code 106
publish/subscribe (Pub/Sub) messaging model 15,
    16, 17

Q

queue 12
quorum-based approach 34

R

Ranger
    for authorization 242
    Kafka policy, adding 244
    Kafka service, adding to 242, 244
RDD partitions
    action operation 86
    transformation operation 85
receiver 11
receiver-based approach
    disadvantages 91
record cache 179
reliable spout 112
remote procedure calls (RPC) 9
replication 34
request/reply model 14
Resilient Distributed Dataset (RDD) 84

S

SASL mechanism, Kafka 238
SASL/GSSAPI
    enabling 235
SASL
    configuring, for Kafka broker 236
    configuring, for Kafka client 237
Scala example
    for direct approach 96
    for receiver-based integration 93
Scala Kafka consumer
    about 73

listeners, rebalancing 74
Schema Registry
    used, for working with Avro 150
SchemeAsMultiScheme 118
Secure Sockets Layer (SSL) 230
security, Kafka
    auditing 230
    authentication 229
    authorization 230
    encryption at rest 230
    wire encryption 230
sender 11
serialization 45
shared databases 9
SIEM (Security Information and Event
    Management) 247
single cluster deployment 202, 203
Sink Connector 166
Sink Stream processor 150
Source Connector 166
Source Stream processor 150
Spark architecture 82, 83
Spark core 87
Spark driver
    about 82
    tasks 83
Spark ecosystem 86
Spark GraphX 88
Spark MLlib 88
Spark SQL 88
Spark Streaming 87, 88
Spark workers
    about 84
    backend process 84
    executors 84
Spark
    about 82
    Directed acyclic graph (DAG) 86
    Resilient Distributed Dataset (RDD) 84
spout
    about 112
    reliable spout 112
    unreliable spout 112
SSL
    configuring, for Kafka Broker 232

configuring, for Kafka clients 232
  enabling, in Kafka 231
state management
  local state 176
  remote state 176
stateless 28
STOMP (Streaming Text Oriented Message
    Protocol) 11
Storm cluster architecture
  about 110
  supervisor 110
Storm Kafka
  wordcount example 118
Stream processing 174
Stream topology
  processors 179
streaming application
  data and state persistence 251
  data formats 253
  data serialization 254
  data sources 252
  external data lookups 252, 253
  latency and throughput 250, 251
  level of parallelism 254
  message processing semantics 255, 256
  out-of-order events 255
streaming applications
  key points 22
Streams 180

T

tables 180
tasks, Spark driver
  DAG creation 83
  RDD metadata 84
  Spark Context 83
  stage creation 84
  task execution 84
  task schedule 84

techniques, for reading/writing data
  message compression 212
topic 17, 222
topology 112
Topology Master (TM) 116
transfer mode 12
Trident 256

U

unit of parallelism 31
unreliable spout 112
use case example, Kafka Stream
  about 184
  fraud detection application 190
use case log processing
  about 125
  fraud IPs list 97
  producer 97, 129
  Spark Streaming 97

W

web service invocation 9
wire encryption
  with SSL 230, 231
workers 166
Write-ahead Log (WAL) 90

Z

zero copy approach 199
Zookeeper authentication 241, 242
Zookeeper
  about 29, 194
  broker metadata 39
  client quota information 39
  controller, selecting 38
  reference 194
  role 38
  topic metadata 39

www.ingramcontent.com/pod-product-compliance
Lightning Source LLC
Chambersburg PA
CBHW060111090326
40690CB00064B/4899